# Sartre and Magic

Also available from Bloomsbury:

*Jean-Paul Sartre's Anarchist Philosophy*, William L. Remley
*Sartre and Theology*, Kate Kirkpatrick
*Existentialism and Excess: The Life and Times of Jean-Paul Sartre*, Gary Cox

# Sartre and Magic

## Being, Emotion and Philosophy

by Daniel O'Shiel

BLOOMSBURY ACADEMIC
LONDON • NEW YORK • OXFORD • NEW DELHI • SYDNEY

BLOOMSBURY ACADEMIC
Bloomsbury Publishing Plc
50 Bedford Square, London, WC1B 3DP, UK
1385 Broadway, New York, NY 10018, USA

BLOOMSBURY, BLOOMSBURY ACADEMIC and the Diana logo are trademarks of
Bloomsbury Publishing Plc

First published in Great Britain 2019
Paperback edition published 2021

Cover design by Maria Rajka
Cover image © Alex/ Getty Images

A catalogue record for this book is available from the British Library.

A catalog record for this book is available from the Library of Congress.

ISBN: HB: 978-1-3500-7766-9
PB: 978-1-3502-3094-1
ePDF: 978-1-3500-7767-6
eBook: 978-1-3500-7768-3

Typeset by Deanta Global Publishing Services, Chennai, India

To find out more about our authors and books visit www.bloomsbury.com
and sign up for our newsletters.

# Contents

# Acknowledgements

I have received permission from *Continental Philosophy Review* to reuse an article (O'Shiel 2015a) published there, here modified for this context. Additionally, some small parts of section 'Experiencing and evoking absence: Perception, imagination and the analogon' in Chapter 3 are modified versions from an earlier article (O'Shiel 2011). Finally, certain passages from Chapter 2 were drawn from another article (O'Shiel [2016] 2017) on a related but different issue.

I also need to make a number of other formal and personal acknowledgements. First of all, I need to sincerely thank both of my PhD supervisors, Professors R. Breeur and R. Visker, for all of their critiques, support and encouragement for my thesis, 'Magical Being: A Sartrean Account of Emotion, Using the Case of Disgust', from which a significant amount of material has been drawn. This work would not be what it is today were it not for their continued interest and help. I sincerely hope I have produced a work worthy of their guidance and influence.

Second of all, I would like to thank the Research Foundation – Flanders (FWO), whose funding provided me with the perfect opportunity to concentrate and produce my doctoral thesis.

Third of all, Professor J. Slaby was very helpful for a number of important aspects during my research time in Berlin. Also, more recently Professor J. Webber was very helpful during and after my PhD defence, including a stay at Cardiff, from which time some significant material has been added.

Fourth of all, I would like to thank numerous current and former members of the Institute of Philosophy at KU Leuven, namely Professors A. De Block, N. de Warren, J. Jansen, U. Melle and P. Moyaert, for remarks and input that, although more marginal, were nevertheless extremely helpful in certain developments of this work. Additionally, the Institute of Philosophy itself, its world-class library, and all of the people that make it possible, is a significant influence.

Fifth of all, I would like to sincerely thank Frankie Mace, formerly of Bloomsbury, for all her help, guidance and recommendations through the writing and editing process. I would also like to thank the various anonymous reviewers and the production team, who have all certainly improved this work throughout this process as well.

Sixth of all, I would like to thank my friends who, throughout the years and various discussions, both formal and informal, both directly related and not, have all helped show me that no work is an island: Arnis, Can, Cody, Dani, Daniel Luis, Elise, Ian R., Joel, Kaspar, Nuno, Patrick, Philipp, Seb, Sunael, Tomas, Viestarts and Viktoras. Also thanks to all at The Hand (you know who you are!) for providing much-needed and welcome breaks during the writing and editing process.

Seventh of all, I would like to thank my parents, Kevin and Olivia, whose unconditional support, trust and love still defy my comprehension.

Finally, to Julie, who brought a level of brightness to my life, both intellectual and otherwise, that I did not think possible.

# List of Abbreviations

ASJ/RQJ    Sartre, J.-P. [1946] (1995/2013), *Anti-Semite and Jew*, trans.
G. J. Becker, New York: Schocken Books/*Réflexions sur la question juive*, Paris: Éditions Gallimard.

BN/EN    Sartre, J.-P. [1943] (2005/2012), *Being and Nothingness. An Essay on Phenomenological Ontology*, trans. H. E. Barnes, London: Routledge/*L'être et le néant. Essai d'ontologie phénoménologique*, Paris: Éditions Gallimard.

IM    Sartre, J.-P. [1940] (2004/2005), *The Imaginary. A phenomenological psychology of the imagination*, trans. J. Webber, London and New York: Routledge/*L'imaginaire. Psychologie phénoménologique de l'imagination*, Paris: Éditions Gallimard.

N    Sartre, J.-P. [1938] (2000/2014), *Nausea*, Penguin Books/ *La nausée*, Éditions Gallimard.

STE/ETE    Sartre, J.-P. [1938] (2002/2009), *Sketch for a Theory of the Emotions*, trans. P. Mairet, London and New York: Routledge/*Esquisse d'une théorie des émotions*, Hermann.

TE    Sartre, J.-P. [1936] (2004/2003), *The Transcendence of the Ego*, trans. S. Richmond, London and New York: Routledge/ 'La transcendance de l'Ego', in V. de Coorebyter (ed.), *La Transcendance de l'Ego et autres textes phénoménologiques*, 93–131, Librairie Philosophique J. VRIN.

Emphasis is always in the originals.

# Introduction: Magic, Sartre and His Melting Pot

What does a magician do when he pulls a rabbit out of a hat? He flouts the laws of nature. Our childlike wonder is present because we always ask, 'How he managed to do that!'; the hat looks too small for such a rabbit, I did not see him put it in and so on. Here, magic involves a suspension or corruption of the normal, causal chain of events. This magician is a magician because he plays with the causal reality of the world.

With Jean-Paul Sartre I will show that, in a sense, we are all magicians. His highly technical and multifaceted concept of magic will show us a human nature that cannot be fully grasped by simple causal explanation. By travelling through Sartre's early philosophical works in detail, I will shed much light on the magical nature of personal reflection (ego), emotion and the imaginary, as well as argue for how Sartre's early preoccupation with magic was actually ontologized in *Being and Nothingness*, not least in the structures of value, possession and language. Then, a second, applied part will show how Sartrean magic is highly relevant for a number of concrete cases, namely the arts, advertising, racism and stupidity and certain instances of psychopathology. In short, Sartre's magical being is important for any contemporary philosophical anthropology because it is essentially at work at the heart of many of our most significant experiences, both creative and damaging.

Sartre's concept of magic was not plucked out of thin air, of course. He grew up in a period where anthropology had magic as 'the core of the new discipline' (Davies 2012: 21) to the extent that it 'shaped its development' (ibid.). Indeed, major figures of the French intelligentsia of the time, including Durkheim, Marcel Mauss (Hubert and Mauss 1902–3), as well as Lévy-Bruhl, were certainly all figures – and even texts – that Sartre was well aware of. Richmond (2011: 147) has already noted how Sartre took particular interest in Lévy-Bruhl's idea of 'pre-logical mentality', which for the anthropologists of the time was more or less restricted to so-called primitive societies and certain elements of children's behaviour. Sartre, as we shall see, extends magic way beyond this, to a universal human dynamic.

Another very dominant discipline at the time was, of course, psychoanalysis. This discipline partially inspired the surrealistic movement and ran alongside its doppelgänger phenomenology. Here, although Sartre is known to have been critical of Freud, we will see how Sartre's understanding of these phenomena covers various forms of magical thinking and behaviour, not least in psychopathology.

On top of this, it is well known that Sartre was an avid reader of Bergson in his early years. Bergson had already criticized the anthropology of the time for opposing so-called primitive and refined cultures too starkly (cf. Bergson [1932] 2012: 176; Richmond 2011: 148). Here, the key claim that the feeling of distance is radically altered in magical thinking and behaviour was something Bergson was already at pains to express. It is also something that Sartre took up, as we shall see.

Finally, the influence of Alain (Émile-Auguste Chartier) on Sartre is equally well known (cf., for instance, Breeur 2010: 66–7). Moreover, one only needs to read Alain's *Propos sur le bonheur* ([1928] 2007) to see the centrality of the lived body and its passions, magic and incantation, as well as a vital place for the imagination in his thought. Sartre, more than any other, continued this discourse in a more systematic manner well into the 1940s and beyond.

Such being the intellectual climate of Sartre's early years, all of this was of course coupled with his pointed phenomenological interest that stemmed from the 1930s. Sartre is one of *the* phenomenologists of the twentieth century. Further, he has a phenomenology in which, I contend, magic has a crucial role, ultimately culminating with his 'phenomenological ontology' of 1943 (i.e. *Being and Nothingness*). Considering this, although there was diverse and concentrated interest in magic at the time, this work will show that it is actually in Sartre's early philosophy where a highly technical and multifaceted concept comes to the fore with full force. Indeed, although the word itself – like many of Sartre's technical terms – often appears sparingly, the concept nevertheless governs much of what is said. In fact, I would go as far to say that magic is one of *the* concepts at work in the complex portrait of human being which Sartre is at pains to express between 1936 and 1943.

Sartre's earliest philosophical works include phenomenological investigations into the nature of the ego (1936), emotion (1938) and the imaginary (1940). All of these works utilize a multifarious concept of magic that nevertheless has an underlying structure. Such a structure, I contend, led to Sartre's magnum opus, *Being and Nothingness* (1943), too. Indeed, I will show that Sartre's early preoccupation with magic necessitated much of this latter work's underlying structure and spirit. In this manner, Sartre's theoretical system in *Being and Nothingness* has not abandoned anything from his earlier works, but has, in fact, pushed the logic of these latter to its full limit. Thus *Being and Nothingness* is the culmination of many years of careful thought; it is a work borne out of Sartre's intense preoccupation with the magical being that we are.

I will already give a hint: Sartrean magic explicates how consciousness, in certain forms (personal reflection, emotion, imagination and valuing), manages to empower originally objective phenomena to the extent that they come to have force of their own and can thereby bewitch us, the original subjects. In short, Sartrean magic reverses the order of things; it involves modes of consciousness where the mind comes to inhere in, and thus enliven, previously inert things and phenomena.

I will show that such a discourse ultimately means we are in a tireless pursuit of an impossible synthesis, a synthesis that can take on many forms, but one that ultimately boils down to the contradictory dynamic between categories of being which are diametrically opposed in their ontological nature. Such a *passion inutile* is responsible for the rather nauseating caricature of Sartre's thought that is, by now, well known. Less well known, however, is the fact that such a dynamic *also* constitutes us as spontaneous creators that can celebrate as much as commiserate.

Sartrean theory is quite tough-going, especially if one wishes to represent it clearly in its full import. Moreover, even when this is done its concrete relevance to some contemporary issues might still remain unclear. Therefore, once I have fully explicated Sartre's concept of magic, as well as its underlying structure, in the first part, a second part will seek to show the theory's import in a number of cases. All of this should show that we are of a nature quite unlike any other known, one that allows for an infinite amount of spontaneity and creativity, as well as contingency and absurdity, all at once.

I believe such a work has a number of contributions. The first two are completely internal to Sartre and the scholarship on his philosophy. Firstly, it is not at all clear what Sartre means by magic, and there is, moreover, very little concentrated scholarship on the issue. I engage with the secondary sources that are directly relevant of course, but overall there has been a veritable and crucial gap that I believe I have now cleared up quite comprehensively here. Secondly, I also demonstrate that such an understanding of Sartre's early conception of magic shows why he was necessitated to produce his ontological system of 1943, with all its consequences for posterity.

I also believe there are a number of significant contributions that lie outside mere Sartrean scholarship. First of all, Sartre's concept of magic, through the method of applied phenomenology of the second part, can give a novel account of various issues that contemporary societies – not least in philosophy – are trying to understand and deal with, namely, artistic creation, advertising, racism and stupidity, and certain cases of psychopathology. Second of all, these analyses should also show us that Sartre's conception of human nature demonstrates a complex dynamic between emotion and value in general. This, finally, leads us to an intriguing philosophical anthropology (cf. Cormann 2012) which claims that any decent study of human nature needs not only to investigate the ego, emotion, the imaginary, as well as the nature of value, possession and language; it also must accept these structures, when phenomenologically studied, as having Sartre's magical being at their very heart.

# Part One

# Magic in Sartre's Early Philosophy (1936–43)

# Self- and Public Bewitchment:
# Sartre's Ego (1936)

In order to locate the magical dynamic at work in Sartre's theory of personhood, I will first need to outline his general phenomenological conception of the ego as an object pole of reflective consciousness. I will then need to explicate what Sartre means by states, actions and qualities of the ego. After this I will be able to hone in on the ego's magic. Finally, I will highlight what this means for personal reflection and interpersonality.

## The ego as object pole of reflective consciousness

One of Sartre's most important claims in *The Transcendence of the Ego* is that an explicit experience of one's own ego, including dimensions of 'I' and 'me', only originally appears to reflective consciousness. If one thinks otherwise, if one thinks the ego originally operates on a more basic, pre-reflective level, this is due, as we shall see, to its magic.

In order to explicate this general movement, I will start with some of Sartre's main arguments against an ego on the level of pre-reflection. Here Sartre goes against much of the philosophical tradition by arguing there is no transcendental 'I'; it is neither necessary nor desirable (cf. TE: 7/98). It is not necessary because the very nature of pre-reflective consciousness guarantees its own synthetic unity without any need of, or reference to, an 'I'. In Sartre's words, pre-reflective consciousness 'constitutes a synthetic, individual totality, completely isolated from other totalities of the same kind, and the I can, clearly, be only an *expression* (and not a condition) of this incommunicability and this interiority of consciousnesses'[1] (TE: 7/97). This means there is a basic coherence to the activity of pre-reflective consciousness that is in no need of an 'I'. In short, being a basic conscious self (*soi*) requires neither an 'I' (*je*) nor a 'me' (*moi*).

In fact, positing an 'I' or 'me' on this level does great damage to any theory of consciousness; 'this superfluous *I* is actually a hindrance. If it existed, it would violently separate consciousness from itself, it would divide it, slicing through each consciousness like an opaque blade. The transcendental *I* is the death of consciousness' (TE: 7/98) in the sense that consciousness in its most basic, pre-reflective activity must be completely transparent, with nothing inside it. Consciousness is the condition by and through which all else is perceivable, imaginable, thinkable and the like, and yet it is nothing – precisely nothing – in itself. This is because pre-reflective consciousness is a ceaseless transcendent activity towards phenomena it itself is not; it is that condition of non-coincidence by and through which all kinds of phenomena, from things to ideas, appear *to* it.

To posit a kind of fundamental 'I' as being in or behind such an utterly transparent activity would be to introduce 'a centre of opacity' (TE: 8/98) that weighs down the purely spontaneous and transparent nature of our most elemental form of being. Indeed, on the pre-reflective level everything is *for* consciousness in such an immediate manner that there is simply no time or space for 'I':

> When I run after a tram, when I look at the time, when I become absorbed in the contemplation of a portrait, there is no *I*. There is a consciousness of the *tram-needing-to-be-caught*, etc., and a non-positional consciousness of consciousness. In fact, I am then plunged into the world of objects ... this is not the result of some chance, some momentary failure of attention: it stems from the very structure of consciousness. (TE: 13/102)

How, then, does an 'I' come about? In a word, through reflection. 'Reflection' is when consciousness makes itself an object. This is the second level or moment of consciousness. First there is always pre-reflective engagement in and with the world. This needs no reflection – and therefore no 'I' – to occur. On the second, reflective level, however, we always take up aspects we have experienced and make them into an explicit subject matter; we make them into objects for reflective consciousness. For Sartre this necessarily produces a notion of 'I' that is nonetheless never directly cognized:

> The *I* only ever appears on the occasion of a reflective act. In this case, the complex structure of consciousness is as follows: there is an unreflected act of reflection without *I* which is aimed at a reflected consciousness. This reflected consciousness becomes the object of the reflecting consciousness, without, however, ceasing to affirm its own object (a chair, a mathematical truth, etc.). At the same time a new object appears which is the occasion for an affirmation

of the reflective consciousness and is in consequence neither on the same level as unreflected consciousness ... nor on the same level as the object of the unreflected consciousness (chair, etc.). This transcendent object of the reflective act is the *I*. (TE: 16/104)

This quotation shows that the ego 'gives itself *through* reflected consciousness' (TE: 15/103). It is an object pole that is constituted in and through every reflective act. These acts are always initiated by – and always take information or content from – the more spontaneous and pre-reflective level, not least our perceptions, as well as our pre-reflective affects and retentions.

The ego is very much real however. It may not be of the same reality as a chair, or even a mathematical truth, but it is nevertheless a transcendent *existent* (TE: 15/104) that always accompanies acts of reflection. Even so, such reality is, we have seen, only brought about in a secondary moment. Indeed, it is a grand reproach of Sartre that many theorists superimpose 'a reflective structure ... that is thoughtlessly claimed to be unconscious' (TE: 18/105) supposedly on or beneath the spontaneous, pre-reflective level. This, Sartre says, is a completely unwarranted move when one looks to basic phenomenological experience. In such experiences, Sartre thinks it is quite evident that pre-reflective, engaged acts always come first (e.g. running for a tram). These can then, in a second moment – but in a second moment *only* – be reflected upon ('I ran for the tram').

Another one of Sartre's own examples to prove this point is how one experiences the spontaneous desire to aid a friend. In such instances, 'I feel pity for Peter and I come to his aid. For my consciousness, one thing alone exists at that moment: Peter-having-to-be-aided. This quality of "having-to-be-aided" is to be found in Peter. It acts on me like a force' (ibid.). Here there exists a spontaneous, 'centrifugal' (ibid.) desire that 'transcends itself' (ibid.) in a non-ego-like manner; 'there is no *me*: I am faced with the pain of Peter in the same way I am faced with the colour of this inkwell' (ibid.). At this pre-reflective level there is an 'intuitive grasp of a disagreeable quality of an object' (TE: 18/106) – the whys and wherefores only come after such spontaneous feelings and desires. For Sartre, positing an ego supposedly underlying such autonomous and spontaneous behaviour is to pay ill attention to how we actually exist, feel and act on the immediate pre-reflective level.

This is not to say that reflection cannot influence one's desires and emotions. It is still however important to note that these latter items – notably in their spontaneous form – always arise first and can then be made subjects of reflection. If reflection does influence the spontaneous level, then Sartre's terminology for this is that reflection 'poisons' (TE: 20/107) pure desires in the manner whereby one takes one's spontaneous feelings and emotions and regards them – and no longer Peter – as a third person would. Sartre describes it as follows: 'If my state is suddenly transformed into a reflected state, then I am watching myself acting, in the same sense that we say of someone that he is listening to himself talking. It is no longer Peter who attracts me, it is *my* helpful consciousness that appears to me as having to be perpetuated' (ibid.). In this manner, reflection can put desires and emotions themselves under scrutiny, and it can even will to change those one does not like. However, all of this occurs for Sartre on a reflective level that is always already preceded by more spontaneous feelings and processes.

To sum up, the ego – and by corollary the 'I' and 'me' – appears only when one reflects upon one's pre-reflective feelings and actions. The I and me are, in fact, two sides of one and the same object pole, the ego, with the 'I' primarily concerned with actions and the 'me' with states and qualities (cf. ibid.). Just what Sartre means by these three terms – states, actions and qualities of the ego – is the next main step in his theory.

## States, actions and qualities of the ego

States, actions and qualities make up the three transcendent subcategories that are all ultimately unified by the ego (cf. TE: 21/108).

States are transcendent objects that appear 'to reflective consciousness' (ibid.). They are real in the sense that one can partake in them through undergoing certain affective and emotional experiences. Sartre's example is a state *of* hatred, where spontaneous feelings of anger, disgust, repulsion and the like towards Peter make me, upon reflection, state that I hate him, that I have for a long time, and even that I will continue to do so for all eternity:

> I see Peter, I feel a kind of profound upheaval of revulsion and anger on seeing him (I am already on the reflective level); this upheaval is consciousness. I cannot be in error when I say: I feel at this moment a violent revulsion towards Peter. But is this experience of revulsion hatred? Obviously not. … After all, I have hated Peter for a long time and I think I always will hate him. So an instantaneous consciousness of revulsion cannot be my hatred. Even if I limit it to what it is, to an instantaneous moment, I will not be able to continue talking of hatred. I would say: 'I feel revulsion for Peter *at this moment*', and in this way I will not implicate the future. But precisely because of this refusal to implicate the future, I would cease to hate. (TE: 22/108–9)

At work here is an important distinction between pure and impure reflection. Pure reflection simply witnesses what one is feeling in any given moment and does not go beyond it. Impure reflection, by contrast, takes such feelings and transcends towards objective states or thoughts (in this case hatred) that claim more than what is actually found in the original, spontaneous feelings. In Sartre's words, pure reflection 'stays with the given without making any claims about the future' (TE: 23/110), which means that it 'disarms unreflected consciousness by giving it back its instantaneous character' (TE: 24/110). With impure reflection, although it works with the same 'givens', it also goes beyond them by carrying 'out an infinitization of the field' (TE: 23/110) through creating a transcendent object (in this case a state) that serves as 'a letter of credit for an infinity of angry or revulsed consciousnesses, in the past and the future' (TE: 23/109).

A consequence of this is if one only ever had pure reflection, one would never have states. We do however have impure reflections and their necessary transcendent objects, states. In fact, they are probably the most common form for the vast majority of people by quite some margin. Counterintuitive as it may seem, focusing only on one's immediate experiences all the time is incredibly hard to do, and socially it would often come across as hyperpedantic. This does then mean that our personal reflections are filled with so many states, which always state more than any one instance can ever actually claim, precisely because the latter is an instance. I may, for example, have been annoyed by a certain person three, a hundred, even thousands of times – and yet, no matter the amount of individual instances, it is always a leap to state 'I hate so and so' in a blanket manner. This is because states, by definition, do not allow for any subtlety. If I remain on a purer level, then the discourse would always be, 'You annoyed me then because you' and so on. However, to make the blanket claim of hating someone tout court is to transcend towards and into the state *of* hatred, which is only accessible to emotive consciousness once it is reflected upon ('God I hate Peter so much!').

An important consequence of this theory is that states are originally 'passive' precisely because for Sartre all phenomena, whether physical or psychical, are relative to the absolutely spontaneous nature of original pre-reflective consciousness. In other words, consciousness lives its own spontaneity and even though everything else in the world can be seen as active in the sense that there is stuff happening, it is precisely because such actions are law-governed and thereby non-spontaneous that the causal nexus of things and forces remains 'inert' with reference to the absolutely active and transcending nature of consciousness.

In this manner, the 'entire psychology of states (and non-phenomenological psychology in general) is a psychology of the inert' (TE: 25/111). Reflective consciousness based upon spontaneous feeling builds a web of psychical states much like reflective consciousness based upon perception builds constellations of physical and natural laws. Indeed, like Hume's problem of induction ([1739–40] 2001: 1.3; [1748] (2007): chs 4, 5 and 7), Sartre's states automatically assume that the future will be just like the past.

The second subcategory of Sartre's ego is that of actions. Here he states that 'concerted action is before all else ... a transcendent factor' (TE: 26/112). Action of necessity 'requires time in which to be carried out' (ibid.). Corresponding to such actions are 'active, concrete consciousnesses' (TE: 26-7/112) that are, as usual, quite instantaneous and pre-reflective. Reflection, however, can apprehend 'the total action in an intuition which displays it as the transcendent unity of active consciousness' (TE: 27/112). In short, there are always spontaneous consciousnesses (cycling, writing, etc.) that through their realization can be grasped as total, completed actions in reflection (went cycling, wrote a paper, etc.). These latter are also, therefore, all transcendent reflected-upon objects belonging to the ego.

Equally succinct – and no less important – are Sartre's comments on qualities. These can form a kind of intermediary object between the ego on the one hand and states and actions on the other (cf. TE: 27/112–13). When, for instance, one has been angry at many people a great number of times, one then tends to 'unify these various manifestations by intending a psychical disposition to produce them' (TE: 27/113). Such a process often culminates in statements like 'I am an angry person', 'I have an angry disposition', 'You're a stresshead!' Being or having something like this is what Sartre means by qualities. They are not simply cumulative sums of all our past actual angers but are once again transcendent objects that we relate to *as* an angry person or *as* having an angry disposition. In this manner, Sartre's qualities represent 'the substratum of states just as states represent the substratum of *Erlebnisse* [i.e. spontaneities]' (ibid.).

To sum up, a state is 'the noematic unity of spontaneities' (TE: 28/113) in the sense that various spontaneous feelings give rise, in reflection, to states of certain things (of hatred, of happiness, of sadness and the like). An action is then some engagement or activity that one carries out in the world and is then solidified or encapsulated through reflection (e.g. 'I keep shouting at people'). A quality, in its own turn, is 'the unity of objective passivities' (ibid.). These latter can be either states ('I am a person who is full of hatred') or actions ('I have hated you for a long time now') or both ('I have been having feelings of hatred towards you for a long time now') – all of which lead to the idea that someone becomes or even is, for instance, a hateful person. In this manner, qualities are one conceptual step closer to the ego itself, although states and actions can bypass such qualities in unifying with the ego directly (e.g. 'I hate you'; 'I was shouting at him' – cf. TE: 28/113).

States, actions and qualities make up the whole logical language of personhood and interpersonality for Sartre. In short, personal reflection is necessarily a reflective activity, and its language always – and perhaps only – involves these three elements. Indeed, a challenge here would be to think of some description of yourself, or anyone, that would not fall into some combination of these three subcategories, some description of one's or another's personality that cannot be explained through Sartre's states, actions and qualities.

## The ego's magic

*The Transcendence of the Ego* is driven by a need to explain that most, if not all, theories on personhood have missed the essential phenomenological observation that states, actions and qualities are first and foremost objects *for* reflective consciousness. In this phenomenological sense anything one is explicitly conscious of is an object for that consciousness; objects are on the noematic side – the objective sense as opposed to the subjective modal (noetic) side – of the noesis-noema pairing. These objects of personhood only arise, moreover, on an impure reflective level, for indeed, spontaneous emotive engagements with the world always come first. These are then, through impure reflections, linked up with transcendent objects such as states, actions and qualities. Finally – and crucially – this order can be reversed through magic. In real time, of course, this can all happen in the blink of an eye, for thought (i.e. consciousness) is wildly quick (cf. Hobbes [1651] 2007: ch. III). However, with the powers of phenomenological analysis, which allow for a close, slow-motion inspection, we can uncover Sartre's crucial conception of magic with reference to the ego. This, I contend, is key if one wishes to anticipate the objection that we often think our feelings 'come from' our states, qualities and the like.

Sartre himself even goes as far to say that 'it is in exclusively magical terms that we have to describe the relations between the *me* and consciousness' (TE: 26/112). This means the problem with many psychologies is that they miss the more basic pre-reflective level provided to us through phenomenological analysis, with Sartre's variety now showing that magic is not only a real dynamic here but also an utterly crucial one. In short, psychology, like most empirical science, denies the existence of magic.

What is magic however? In these passages it is opposed to logical relations. Logical relations can – and must – be studied only from an objective, third-person perspective that necessarily takes its objects in an in-itself (i.e. 'is what it is') manner (cf. Goldie 2000: 1–2). Consciousness, on the contrary, is very often a spontaneous and pre-reflective engagement with the world that is anything but third-person, at least originally. This means that the two perspectives, the immediately engaged and the third-personally observant, are not on the same level as each other, and they would usually exclude one another at any given moment in the sense that it is difficult to act and reflect at the same time. With magic, however, this distinction becomes merged or confused, wherein objective, third-person-like aspects such as states are not only projected onto the spontaneous activities of consciousness but are, over time, conceived of as actually emanating from, or even constituting, this level. This has the result that spontaneity is covered over so much that it can even be denied completely, whereby one's spontaneous feelings and engagements are just so many signs of a deeply predetermined personhood (psychological determinism). Such magic of the ego thus transfigures original objects of reflective consciousness (states, actions and qualities) into the supposedly 'real' subterranean originating activities of all feeling, emotion and engagement; it allows one to go from pure phenomenological observations like 'I am currently feeling anger towards you' into more impure psychological reflections like 'I am angry at you *because* I hate you'. In this second instance, the anger seems to stem from the state of hatred itself, which has thereby been hypostasized and infused, through what Sartre calls magic, onto and into the more spontaneous level.

In this manner, 'original passivities' (e.g. a reflective state of hatred) are transfigured into pseudo activities ('I hate you'). States and qualities become conceived as the underlying source of all else. This displaces the original activities (e.g. feelings of anger), which are now considered only as conditioned effects of a supposedly more original disposition. In short, magic reverses the real phenomenological order of things. It makes primary feelings secondary and secondary reflected-upon objects primary. This has the consequence that although psychology does not believe in magic, it is precisely because of this that it falls victim to it most often.

Sartre's theory is thus quite subtle. The first level of consciousness is always spontaneous feeling (being-angry-at-Peter). Then, upon reflection the ego can be introduced in a manner that can be either pure ('I am angry at you at this moment') or impure ('I am angry at you because I hate you'). If one transitions from pre-reflection to pure reflection then no state or the like appears, but if the transition is impure – and often it is – then states, actions or qualities always arise. In both transitions, however, there are elements of magic: in pure reflection the 'I' is introduced as a hypostasized bearer – and even the origin – of the feelings and emotions, thereby causing it to cease to appear as the transcendent object pole *of* the emotion, and in impure reflection a state, action or quality (e.g. hatred, hating and a hateful disposition respectively) can be introduced in addition to the 'I'. Transitions from the first (pre-reflective) to the second (reflective) level always therefore involve some magic, turning originally transcendent objects into subjective bearers and pseudo instigators *of* the more original feelings.

Such magic can be fairly mild when limited to a mere use of the 'I' as a subject bearer of the present feeling, or it can be stronger when the 'I' is also accompanied by so many states, actions and qualities that ultimately come to be thought of as the actual origins to all one is feeling, or may ever feel.

All the foregoing distinguishes 'the "psychical"' (TE: 28/114) from consciousness: 'The psychical is the transcendent object of … reflective consciousness; it is also the object of the science called psychology' (ibid.). Sartre returns to this in *Being and Nothingness* (cf. BN/EN: 172–93/185–206), where many of the most significant points are reformulated although they remain the same in their essence. We also know (cf. Cabestan 2004a: 126) Sartre planned and started a much larger work in this period called *La psyché*, of which the *Sketch for a Theory of the Emotions* is said to make a part, and to which surely Sartre's main points from *The Transcendence of the Ego* would have applied. One may ask, however, in all of this: What of the ego itself? I have not really mentioned it directly.

The answer here is that one cannot really speak of the ego directly; it is only ever grasped *through* states, actions and qualities. The ego is the most transcendent, and therefore the most distant and opaque apex of the whole of reflective consciousness. In this respect, it is very hard, if not impossible, to capture it itself. Nonetheless, Sartre does have observations on it. First of all, the ego is the absolute object pole that 'appears to reflection as a transcendent object realizing the permanent synthesis of the psychical' (ibid.). In this manner, 'the Ego is to psychical objects what the World is to things' (TE: 30/115). In short, it is the ultimate unifying principle of all our psychical states, actions and qualities.

The ego does not actually add anything to these concrete aspects, however. It is, in fact, a relation of 'creation' (TE: 32/116) for Sartre. 'Creation' here means all states and actions can ultimately be 'attached directly (or indirectly, through quality) to the Ego as to its origin' (ibid.). Thus the ego, precisely because it adds nothing to such elements, can contain – and actually be felt as the creative origin of – everything psychical. Indeed, as just mentioned the ego is analogous to a physical object, which is also totally 'opaque' (cf. TE: 33/117) but is at the same time the unifying principle for all the possible *Abschattungen* (aspects, profiles, sides) that that thing can display – without, however, ever being fully and completely accessible itself.

Sartre also says the ego has a certain 'conserving spontaneity' (TE: 33/117). We have seen that consciousness is absolute spontaneity, so what is the difference between this and a conserving spontaneity? First of all, because the ego is necessarily passive at its core – it is essentially and primarily an object *for* reflective consciousness – any spontaneity it takes on can only be a pseudo one (cf. TE: 33/118). In Sartre's terms, 'real spontaneity must be perfectly clear: it *is* what it produces and cannot be anything other' (TE: 33–4/118). The ego, on the other hand, can only have a borrowed spontaneity. Borrowed from where? Consciousness. The ego, as the creation of reflective consciousness, is always originally an object for this consciousness. However, we have seen that this relation gets magically reversed; the original transcendence of the ego is hypostatized, allowing it to become a subject bearer as well as the supposed source of the more original spontaneities and feelings. In other words, consciousness creates this object, but it also crucially instils it with a power to act as if it had such power all on its own.

If one is aware of this, one can try to treat the ego phenomenologically, namely, as an object of and for reflective consciousness. However, the automatic tendency to reverse the trend is so ingrained in the activity of consciousness that this latter can, and often does, become bewitched by its own creation. This means the ego involves 'most of the time ... a magical procession' (TE: 33/117) where it is conceived as the actual root of so many states, actions and qualities of our personhood. Such a reversal is precisely what allows us to talk about ourselves as deep and long-lasting I's, conceiving ourselves as each having solid and even permanent underlying personae that we can believe to be the real root and structure of things, even though the 'I' is, phenomenologically speaking, only ever a more flighty and opaque object for reflective personality.

Such creation thus allows consciousness to believe in a solid form of personality that in turn allows consciousness to escape – to a certain extent at least – its own 'monstrous' spontaneity (cf. Breeur 2005: 24). Indeed, this latter is often too hard to bear:

> The Ego is an object apprehended but also *constituted* by reflective consciousness. It is a virtual foyer of unity, and consciousness constitutes it as going in *the reverse direction* from that followed by real production; what is *really* first are consciousnesses, through which are constituted states, then, through these, the Ego. But, as the order is reversed by a consciousness that imprisons itself in the World in order to flee from itself, consciousnesses are given as emanating from states, and states as produced by the Ego. As a consequence, consciousness projects its own spontaneity into the object Ego so as to confer on it the creative power that is absolutely necessary to it. However, this spontaneity, *represented* and *hypostatized* in an object, becomes a bastard and degraded spontaneity, which magically preserves its creative potentiality while becoming passive. Hence the profound irrationality of the notion of Ego.[2] (TE: 34–5/118–19)

Reversal, hypostasis and pseudo activity thus signify the magical capacities of relating to our own ego; a more elemental, pre-reflective consciousness instils its own creation with a pseudo power that allows consciousness to bewitch, escape and even suppress aspects of itself. This magical mixture of passivity and activity is the reason for the ego's 'irrationality', as well as its unintelligibility; the ego, as the origin of our actual spontaneities, does not make phenomenological sense, and yet it is nevertheless often experienced as so, rife throughout our daily reflections and words.

Because personal reflection is a massive dimension to human reality, and because the ego is a transcendent object that each and all have access to and can each and all transform in a magical manner, this leads Sartre to conclude that we are always 'sorcerers for ourselves' (TE: 35/119) as well as for others (ibid.). In this manner, we are always 'surrounded by magical objects which keep, as it were, a memory of the spontaneity of consciousness, all the while being objects of the world'[3] (ibid.). This 'irrational synthesis' (TE: 36/119) between activity (consciousness) and passivity (ego) produces a 'phantom spontaneity'[4] (ibid.) that allows the ego to be affected (i.e. to be passive – cf. TE: 35/119) *as well as* be the supposed cause (i.e. activity) of the *actual* causes (spontaneities; pre-reflective feelings; 'consciousnesses'). This means that these latter are often inverted onto the objective – that is, passive – side. Such a dynamic is never logical because activity and passivity, cause and effect, first-person and third-person perspectives are all here swapped, merged and even confused, thereby resulting in the magical relation that consciousness has with its own reflective self.

## Interpersonality and magic

The ego, as the child of reflective consciousness, is 'radically cut off from the world' (TE: 36/119). However, because reflection is always upon pre-reflective worldly events that act as the occasions for states and actions (cf. ibid.), the ego can and of course does still have a massive influence on our everyday (inter)personal lives. Engagement with the empirical world necessarily involves engagement with others, and here it is my contention, due to the 'public' (cf. O'Shiel 2015a) nature of Sartre's ego, that others might actually know aspects of ourselves better than we do. Running counter to this is the commonplace opinion that we somehow know ourselves better than others can or do.

There is a necessary interiority and individuality to a person, not only in terms of one's conscious awareness but also in physical terms – that is, the literal borders of one's skin. This observation should make it simultaneously clear that we never see ourselves as others do; there are objective aspects to ourselves that we cannot directly grasp or see. This can be on the perceptual level, like the fact that I will never be able to visually perceive the back of my head (using media like mirrors is already something else – image-consciousness (*Bildbewusstsein*)), but it can also be the case on a more psychophysiological level. Think of close friends and why you may love them. Here a load of pleasant images may spring to mind of how exactly they manifest their spontaneity, how they are to you and to the world at large. Indeed, from the side of that person there are so many spontaneities, but you, viewing them objectively from the outside, see their spontaneity manifest in a way that they themselves will never have direct objective access to (again media like videos are already something else). Thus there are aspects of people (e.g. a smile) that they can certainly enact spontaneously qua consciousness and as a *Leib* (a lived body) – and yet you see the concrete manifestation of such spontaneity (my-friend-smiling) in a manner that they, in their own turn, can only see through artificial media.

Such little instances can build up to the extent that the outside or second-person perspective can actually see aspects or whole character traits – that is, qualities – that the person might even be quite oblivious to. Hereby, thanks to such physical looks, one is aware of manifestations that the first-person perspective can never have; manifestations, moreover, that can tell one a lot about the person's way of being without however ever capturing their interiority as interiority. Thus in personal conversations others can provide information about you that you can never immediately grasp yourself, while you can provide the other side, namely, interior thoughts and processes when such manifestations were taking place. Such a matching up – or what Husserl calls 'pairing' ([1931] 2012: §51) – of spontaneity with how such spontaneity manifests itself is thereby a crucial dynamic of interpersonal relations. It is, moreover, always carried out through the reflective language of individual people (egos) that always have so many states, actions and qualities to express, reflect upon and share.

Considering these points, perhaps everything is 'other' for Sartre because, even when one is alone and wants to reflect upon one's own personality, one must of necessity make one's spontaneity an object and therefore try to view it as another would. On this note, however, it must be said that we cannot view our own consciousness as we can view another person in the world. Indeed, although when we view ourselves we have to objectify our own consciousness through reflection, we are nevertheless never completely separated from ourselves as we are from others. This is what Sartre must mean by the borrowed statement from Rimbaud that 'I is *an other*' (TE: 46/127); the very structure of reflective consciousness makes itself an object *for* such consciousness. This means the ego cannot be viewed as anything but a transcendent object, as an other, although *not* in the same manner as we view and relate to other people, who are external to us.

Of course the magic of the ego can make such objective aspects seem wholly subjective. This does not, however, change the phenomenological fact that they are originally pieces of reflected-upon information for us. In this manner, although such a process of magic is evident in all speeches and impure reflections, and although many can and do talk purely in magical terms about themselves and others, a person informed of the principles here being outlined would be able to struggle against the more serious pitfalls and dangers of magic that actually make one enter into overly bewitching and stringent relations with regard to oneself and others.

To briefly elaborate, through the magic of the ego there is always the danger of making blanket statements such as 'I am who I am' or 'no one gets me' in order to give one's I a privileged position at the heart of a supposedly deep persona that is no longer an object but a kind of profound subjectivity which no one can know or be except you (and perhaps not even you – for example, 'I'm nothing'). If the 'I' is magically hypostatized in these manners, individuals enter into bewitching relations with regard to themselves and others, creating an

'I' that is supposedly inaccessible to others ('Only I know who I am'), or is even pretended to be utterly non-existent ('I'm nothing at all'). Such sorcery has the consequence of covering over the dynamic relation *between* consciousness and the ego, both personally and publicly. Indeed, if one recognizes this dynamic one may start to struggle against the extremes of ego magic through a responsible and conscientious type of reflection that tries not to get overly bewitched by such blanket claims. For instance, if questioning what or who one 'really' is, then any answers, if they are to go beyond the banality of 'I am who I am' and the like, will have to start talking about states, actions and qualities. Now, although these must be talked about in their magical, hypostatized forms to some extent, they are nevertheless much more specific and, as a consequence, always ultimately betray their true objective origin. Indeed, precisely because the 'I' is absolutely opaque, if one wishes to describe it in (inter)personal terms then one must talk of states, actions and qualities. Such a discourse necessarily blends the objective origins of (inter)personality with the magical transformations that the borrowed spontaneity of the ego employs.

Further, and very importantly, such statements, although always imperfect because of their magic, are nevertheless, in theory, just as accessible to the listener as to the speaker (cf. TE: 43–4/125–6). This is precisely because they indicate an objective and universal structure of egoic consciousness that can, moreover, always be expressed through the reflective grammar of interpersonality, even if this latter is never perfect. This means if one reflects more honestly then any 'deep' 'I' is realized as a magical illusion that needs to be struggled against if one is to have more open and honest relationships.

In short, others do not have any access to our deep 'I' – but neither do we, because there is no such thing. It is a crucial Sartrean claim that we are always obliged to talk about ourselves from another-person perspective, even when we use 'I'.

Considering these points, one cannot really know oneself in one's absolute immediacy beyond a completely immanent interiority that can be captured only by rather rare moments of pure reflection. Nevertheless, I contend that a kind of conscientious reflection can still yield an open-minded conception of (inter)personality. Indeed, if one adopts responsibility and conscientiousness towards a Sartrean-informed reflection, one can remain aware of the more serious pitfalls of the ego's magic. This would allow one to have a flexible conception of personhood that is open to acts of pure reflection, conscientious acts of impure reflection, as well as influence from the opinions and judgements of others.

And indeed, others as friends can greatly help; their input can provide us with observations that we ourselves can only experience as pure spontaneity. Therefore, although memories are of course originally personal phenomena, through language and the objective reflective character of the ego, all is in theory just as accessible to another as it is to one's own 'I'; precisely because there are no profound personalities to be grasped all is up for grabs on a more superficial – and because of this – a more accessible, level.

The universal structure of reflective consciousness's relation to the ego, as well as its necessary language of states, actions and qualities, means that public bewitchment is as, if not more, commonplace as self-bewitchment. For example, couples can spend so much time together that they actually become the same persona, even to the extent that rigid appraisals are formed in a manner where the 'I' disappears almost completely and is replaced with a 'we' (for example, 'We won't come because we're tired'; 'We don't believe in eating meat'). Pushing this even further, the very real force of advertising (more on this in Chapter 6), propaganda and other social phenomena reinforces Sartre's point that the ego is a public phenomenon which can be greatly conditioned and moulded through all kinds of forces and pressures. In this manner, any form of social-personal magic that heads towards blanket claims that swallow up spontaneity on the one hand ('I cannot change'; 'It's who we are'; 'It's in my genes') and overly nihilistic claims on the other ('You couldn't possibly understand'; 'I'm nothing'; 'Everything's pointless') are both extremes to be avoided – and yet, the structure of the ego is such that the temptation towards such magic can never be eradicated, but only minimized.

To summarize, one cannot really know one's 'true self' precisely because of the flighty nature of spontaneous consciousness, which dictates that the 'I' can only be originally found on the reflective level and then, most often, as a hypostatized subject bearer. This ego, as completely opaque, can never be captured itself, and there are pitfalls of magic that need to be struggled against if one is to avoid bewitching extremes of affirming too much or too little. Such a struggle, it has been shown, can be done through a conscientious kind of reflection that tries to capture important elements of spontaneity on the one hand, and merge these with other people's observations on the other. This simultaneously teaches one what is important to one's own conception of personhood, as well as to interpersonality, and thus culminates in an interactive notion of personhood and friendship. Indeed, fruitful and lasting relationships, whether familial, romantic, intellectual or otherwise, seem to largely occur precisely when various sexual, emotional and intellectual resonances occur and develop in and between people, thereby promoting personal growth and exchange to their full potential.

On the flip side of this, if more damaging elements of the magic of the ego are given free rein, it can become responsible for self- and public bewitchments of all kinds, ranging from rather naive self-appraisals, to very pernicious social, political or religious phenomena (e.g. racism, as we shall see in Chapter 7). For now one should already partially see that Sartre's magic of the ego is as responsible for our lives' more pleasurable and fruitful captivations as it is for more destructive ones. The two seem to go originally together; it is a theme that is going to continue, and indeed it is elaborated upon further when Sartre embarks on that next grand realm of magical experience, emotion.

2

# Transforming Worlds:
## Sartre on Emotion (1938)

As has been noted in the first chapter, the standard psychological method regarding the ego misses the phenomenological perspective by treating consciousness's absolute spontaneity and fluidity as a stagnant, static thing that can be factually enumerated like so many physical things and forces. Psychological studies on emotion are no different, says Sartre; they 'try to confront their subject as the physicist confronts his' (STE/ETE: 1/7), where the subject matter comes as 'one chapter after the other chapters, much as in chemical treatises calcium might come after hydrogen and sulphur' (STE/ETE: 5/14). Why is this so? Because the psychological discipline 'tries to make use of only two well-defined types of experience: that which is given to us by spatiotemporal experience of organized bodies, and the intuitive knowledge of ourselves which we call reflective experience' (STE/ETE: 1–2/8). All of this is held together by 'an agreement upon one essential principle: that their enquiries should begin first of all from facts' (STE/ETE: 2/8). Elsewhere (BN/EN: 39–40/75) Sartre calls this 'the spirit of seriousness', which is very much akin to Dickens's Thomas Gradgrind in *Hard Times* ([1854] 1995: 9), where nothing matters but, indeed, the facts of the matter.

For Sartre this has the result that, because observations on physical phenomena (e.g. snapshots of facial expressions, brain states and the like) yield facts about the world and the mind as a physical thing (brain) and because reflective experience necessarily displays our experience from another perspective, psychologies of emotion are empirical and a posteriori through and through (cf. STE/ETE: 2–3/ 8–10). Such a method makes the categorial mistake of treating consciousness like a physical thing. Indeed, the old Cartesian issue of the fundamentally different natures of *res extensa* and *res cogitans* is ever-present here. This is because, for Sartre, one can perhaps translate the latter into the former (neurons firing, etc.), but in doing so one loses the experiential quality of conscious life by making it a physical thing. From a Sartrean perspective, although the physical body (*Körper*, including the brain) necessarily plays an essential role in emotion, to focus on this alone is to miss much of the essential phenomenological dynamic that is involved in each and every emotive experience.

In fact, psychological (and many philosophical) accounts of emotion fail to grasp the true essence of the subject because they, once again, overlook the essential magical nature of our lived emotions, which can never be grasped properly if one sticks to only enumerating physical data. Considering this, my task here is to show how Sartre, even in a supposed sketch, manages to capture the essence of emotive behaviour, namely, how it is actually lived from an immediate first-person perspective, as well as the rules and structures that necessarily pertain thereto. If one wants to attain this, one has to study the phenomena in their essence – that is, one has to attend to their fundamental manifestation, structure and signification, whereby one can explicate, 'by concepts, the content of this essence' (STE/ETE: 7/18) that we live every day. Not only will this explain the essential structure and dynamic of emotive experience, it will also demonstrate how all the facts fit into such a conceptual picture (cf. ibid.). The thread to carry all of this out is, once again, the magical core to emotive experience, which can be centrifugal or centripetal. I will now go through each element, starting with centrifugal.

## Transforming the world: Emotive consciousness

Through critiquing other dominant theories of his time, Sartre comes to state that one can only begin to understand the role of emotion in human life if one acknowledges its functional character (cf. STE/ETE: 25/50; also Zinck and Newen 2008). In other words, there is a 'finality' (STE/ETE: 22/45) to emotion that means it is essentially 'an organized pattern of means directed to an end' (ibid.). Moreover, such 'means are *summoned up* in order to mask, replace or reject a line of conduct that one cannot or will not pursue' (ibid.). This ultimately means that emotive experience runs counter to more pragmatic lines of conduct in its very essence. Once one considers this seriously, 'the diversity of emotions becomes easy: they represent, each one of them, a different way of eluding a difficulty, a particular way of escape, a special trick' (ibid.). Sartre notes that of course not all emotion is purely an escape in the normal sense of the term; emotions can signify (cf. STE/ETE: 30/60) moods, values (cf. Deonna and Teroni 2014) and desires that matter to us, and that therefore condition us in many different ways.

Sartre does not really enter into these subtleties directly in his *Sketch*, although it will be important for me to highlight the fact that ways of 'escape' are broad and technical here, and therefore do not preclude values and desires that are not only being lived out in the very fibres (cf. ibid.) of emotive experiences on the one hand but also implying a more general backdrop of affectivity on the other (as I shall get to in Chapter 4).

Actually, for me Sartre's work is of such note precisely because it shows how our values and desires are lived out most immediately in our emotions. To capture this one does need the colourful phenomenological method of Sartre, which is able to walk the line between assigning instinctive autonomy to the emotions on one extreme and an over-rationalized form of calculation on the other (cf. also Tappolet 2016). This is an opposition which characterizes the crux of the history of philosophies of emotion – in two words, sentimentalism versus rationalism.

Take the case of anger, for example. Sartre states that it 'is not an instinct, nor a habit, nor reasoned calculation. It is a brusque solution of a conflict, a way to cut the Gordian knot'[1] (STE/ETE: 25/50). How may one situate such comments? First of all, it is important to note that emotions are spontaneous 'conducts' (*conduites*) that occur in order to deal with the difficulty of the world and its events. This is because many worldly events follow their own deterministic laws in a – to us – cold and dispassionate manner. In Sartre's words, 'This world is *difficult*. The notion of difficulty here is not a reflexive notion, which would imply a relation to oneself; on the contrary it is out there, in the world, it is a quality of the world given to perception' (STE/ETE: 39/78). In short, the worldly courses of events often do not follow our wishes; every day there are problems to be solved and dealt with, and emotion is a main mode in and through which consciousness can meet and engage with such difficulties.

Indeed, for Sartre emotion is always opposed to a more pragmatic, deterministic attitude towards the world, wherein an individual can stoically accept the facts and events that run their course in their own autonomous manner. Here, living the pragmatic attitude would be precisely when one aligns oneself with the necessary practical steps that must be carried out if one is to attain one's goals. Emotion, on the contrary, is when consciousness spontaneously and pre-reflectively incants psychophysiological perturbations that do not want to face or accept the world as brutally deterministic, thereby making it magical.

Considering this, for Sartre emotion is ultimately a 'transformation of the world' (STE/ETE: 39/79) whereby psychophysiological incantations (e.g. shaking limbs) replace a more deterministic and cold appraisal of the world. These are incantations, moreover, through which the world and its objects also become impassioned.

Getting angry is a good example, where one does not meet a problem with calm collection but on the contrary proliferates a frustrated and boiling temperament to the world at large. Of course the causal structure of the world remains; it even must do so in order to fuel the emotion. However, it remains in a covered-over, transformed manner, wherein the world (in anger) *becomes* hateful, even though strictly speaking the world, qua causal nexus, can never actually be hateful. Thus, through such psychophysiological incantations (shaking one's fist, stamping one's foot, shouting) one's own psychical misgivings and rages can come to inhere in the world, ultimately showing how the world and its beings are not bending to what one wants and values. One of Sartre's own examples is tearing up a piece of paper in frustration because one cannot solve the problem written on it:

> Being unable, in a state of high tension, to find the delicate and precise answer to a problem, we act upon ourselves, we abase and transform ourselves into a being for whom the grossest and least adapted solutions are good enough (for example, tearing up the paper on which a problem is stated). Thus anger now appears as an escape; the angry subject is like a man who is unable to untie the knots of the cords that bind him, and who writhes about in his bonds. And the 'angry' conduct, though less well adapted to the problem than the superior – and impossible – conduct that would solve it, is still precisely and perfectly adapted to his need to break the tension, to shake the leaden weight off his shoulders.[2] (STE/ETE: 25-6/50-1)

Here there is a problem to be solved on a page. We try and try and the tension builds, until finally one loses one's temper and destroys the problem in a surge of anger that wishes the problem annihilated immediately. And it is annihilated in a manner of speaking, for such an action breaks the tension, even if only momentarily. The problem is 'destroyed' because it has been torn into a million shreds. Now, of course the problem was not actually torn into a million shreds. Nevertheless, such an expression is yet another little instance of the magical nature of emotion, which is often expressed, through language, in a magical – that is, inexact, hyperbolic – form.

To actually solve the problem, one would have to reprint or stick the sheet together once one has calmed down, namely, once one is prepared to re-enter the pragmatic attitude. With a cool, steadied reflection it would perhaps have been better to sit through the problem until the solution came or to wait for another hour when one would have been in calmer spirits. All this said and done however, anger (as opposed to a reflective state of hatred) is pre-reflective, spontaneous and surges upon and through us often in ways that we have little control over. Indeed, controlling one's anger – 'anger management' – is just another indicator to show that the anger is *already* there, whether we like it or not. Here, although it is always possible to try and calm down and meet the disagreement in a slow and steady manner, often our spontaneous feelings do not obey such rationalized reflections. Similar to Hume (cf. [1739–40] 2001: 2.3.3) again, passion often trumps reason.

Of course there are rational, reflective and justified angers, fears and the like – but this again is on the secondary egoic level. On the more primary, pre-reflective level, emotion is inherently magical for Sartre because, even if it does not completely fly in the face of the deterministic world, the strength of Sartre's conception means that it always at least blurs this world to the point where one cannot think fully straight. This point is made even clearer when one thinks of a truly courageous person, who is precisely she who is able to think straight – namely, remain in the pragmatic attitude – in situations where most others capitulate. One example is a war hero; a better one might be how surgeons are taught to control their emotions, whereby they can focus on the problem in a calm and collected – indeed in quite a cold – manner. In short, they can be the machine-like pragmatic attitude par excellence.

In this manner, one sees that emotions are a consuming form of consciousness that blur or even temporarily eradicate the pragmatic attitude. Moreover, when they are especially violent, they can cripple the world of determinism altogether (e.g. a nervous breakdown or a serious trauma).

One can often give reasons why one is sad, angry, resentful and so on. However, this, as we have already seen, is always a secondary moment of reflection upon the spontaneous emotive feelings, which are always already meeting a difficulty in one's world through more basic and primary tears, cries, shakes and the like. Therefore, just like with Sartre's ego, any claims such as 'You hurt me because ...' are always based upon more spontaneous, emotive incantations that consciousness invokes in instantaneous manifestations and upsurges that do not always make clear sense. To try and make sense of them is the job of reflection (cf. STE/ETE: 53/103). However, if this does not work – which is often the case – then one must often simply sit through it until the emotion subsides just as spontaneously as it arose (cf. ibid.). Here, serious traumas, anxiety complexes and the like would then be the cases where the unsettling emotions do not disappear but on the contrary persist in a manner that makes one unable to rationalize such disconcerting feelings away; emotions can become habitualized or sedimented in a manner that forestalls pragmatic appraisals for quite significant portions of time, even for whole stretches of one's life.

We may now see what Sartre means by the finality of emotion; inbuilt within their structure is a spontaneous kind of psychophysiological conduct that gets confronted with events in the world that are too much to handle in a more studied, pragmatic way. This means consciousness 'degrades itself' into so many shakes and quakes that are automatically incanted precisely in order to meet the given problem in a non-pragmatic, emotive manner. Such shakes and quakes transform our consciousness, as well as our body and our apprehension of the world, thereby having the result that all of these lose their strictly deterministic character.

Thus, emotive consciousness is magical through and through; it blurs, or even temporarily cripples, the pragmatic world of determinism. The resulting emotive world of magic, because it always unleashes less pragmatic ways of behaving, can be of a highly diverse and unpredictable range, whereby one's personal history, values, character traits and wishes all contribute to form individuals that respond to factual events (e.g. someone shouting) in equally diverse and unpredictable ways (in this example either with an emotion (anger, sympathy, fear, consternation) or without any emotion whatsoever, to name the two extremes). The main point here, once again, is the importance of this immediately lived and pre-reflective manifestation of emotive consciousness. Indeed, just like with the ego it is a constant reproach of Sartre that most theories start the study of emotion where they should in fact end, namely, on the level of reflection (cf. STE/ETE: 34/69–70). An important consequence of such a point is that it makes little sense to study emotion without incorporating considerations regarding the world and its objects. For example, fear as an emotion is always manifested as a fearful consciousness *of* or before something; 'Even if it is a case of one of those indefinite anxieties that one feels in the dark, in a sinister and deserted alley, etc., it is still *of* certain aspects of the night, or of the world, that one is afraid' (STE/ETE: 35/70). This is quite clearly a critique of Heidegger's (cf. [1927] 2006: §40) theory of *Angst* as 'objectless'. Indeed, Sartre notes psychology has admitted 'that emotion is touched off by some perception – a representative signal, etc.' (STE/ETE: 35/71), in phenomenology what is called an object (a thing, a person, an idea, etc.). However, psychology then makes a move in its studies whereby 'emotion then parts company with the object to become absorbed in itself' (ibid.), which for Sartre can only occur on a secondary, reflective level. Such a move loses sight, for Sartre, of the fact that on the original, instantaneous level 'emotion returns to the object every moment and feeds upon it' (ibid.). In this manner, 'the emotional subject and the object of the emotion are united in an indissoluble synthesis' (ibid.) whereby to play down either pole, or to abstract from the object altogether, is to fail to capture all the tonalities and dynamics of the complete emotive experience.

Even further, this inherent connection between emotive consciousness and objects of the world – or certain ideas or values – has great consequences for how the former constitutes these latter. We have already seen that emotion is a transformation of the world. However what, more specifically, does Sartre mean by this? First of all, emotion often arises when a 'pragmatic intuition of the determinism of the world' (STE/ETE: 39/77) is thwarted, frustrated, blurred or even breaks down. In the pragmatic attitude, 'the world of our desires, our needs and our acts appear all furrowed with straight and rigorous paths leading to such and such a determinate end'[3] (STE/ETE: 39/78). In short, we are more or less in control, and the way of getting where or what we want is neatly and practically laid out. However, because of the aforementioned difficulty of the world, along with its unpredictability, there are many scenarios in which such pathways are not so straightforward. Reactions here can range infinitely, from non-existent or mild tension on the one hand to complete nervous breakdown on the other. This is because the absolute spontaneity of pre-reflective embodied consciousness never ceases, even when one may wish it to do so. In this manner, even under moments of self-control where one takes a breath or a time out, consciousness can still incessantly transcend towards the material world, as well as towards a whole realm of mental objects, not least images, values and ideas. Such ceaseless activity can never be stopped (while one is alive, naturally). Thus, when difficulties arise – and they often do – the projects and desires of an individual have to be lived through in some way or other. When more pragmatic and practical options are barred or not liked, emotion results. Here, our lived, bodily consciousness spontaneously manifests itself in a psychophysiological manner and tries, through such manifestation, to transform the world in a way that perpetuates the continuous transcending activities of such consciousness. Here, consciousness realizes that pragmatic and predetermined ways of being are off limits (for now), due to a given state of affairs that one cannot – or does not want to – deal with in such a manner. In short, emotion transforms a world of determinism into a world of pseudo or non-determinism – magic – whereby emotive actions occur in order for consciousness to somehow deal with the

frustration or impossibility of living out a particular project right then and there
in all its practical facets:

> When the paths before us become too difficult, or when we cannot see our way,
> we can no longer put up with such an exacting and difficult world. All ways
> are barred and nevertheless we must act. So then we try to change the world;
> that is, to live it as though the relations between things and their potentialities
> were not governed by deterministic processes but by magic. But, be it well
> understood, this is no playful matter: we are cornered, and we fling ourselves
> into this new attitude with all the force at our command. Note also that our effort
> is not conscious of what it is, for then it would be the object of a reflection. It is
> above all the seizure of new relationships and new demands. To put it simply,
> since the seizure of one object is impossible, or sets up an unbearable tension,
> consciousness seizes or tries to seize it otherwise; that is, tries to transform itself
> in order to transform the object.[4] (STE/ETE: 39–40/79)

In order to further explicate this theory, take a very simple example: running
for and missing a bus. Perhaps you have been late a few too many times for
work and are therefore on your last warning. This accentuates the need to catch
the bus. You sprint and shout, but the bus pulls off and disappears around the
corner. This is a fact. You have missed the bus. However, due to the felt need to
be on time for work and thus keep your job (which you also need and want), this
failure becomes too much. You become enraged, shaking your fist at the bus as
it disappears, shouting and cursing. And when it has gone around the corner
your rage does not just disappear; the whole world has become hateful because
of this 'stupid' bus (which, of course, cannot actually be stupid, it being a bus).
Even this lamp post next to you becomes stupid and irksome, and so you kick it
in frustration. This hurts, fuelling your rage even more, until finally the pain in
your foot makes you sit down and you start to breathe. Only now do you reflect
upon what has just happened. Your toe starts to hurt so much that you think you
may have broken it. This fact makes you feel angry, sad and stupid all at once.
You feel like crying, feel sorry for yourself, but this time you control such urges a
bit better while you look for a new bus to take you to a hospital.

Why is all of this called magical? It is because a simple factual event (a bus
driving off) has gone so much against your wishes that you cannot merely accept
it as other people – or you in other circumstances – would. Indeed, in a less tense
mood it would not have bothered you so much ('Oh well, I'll get the next one').
However, in this particular instance your project of making it to work on time
had a weight and meaning for you that made catching the bus a very important
moment in the day. Missing it is therefore quite intolerable, and although one

could just as spontaneously blame – which is to say be angry at – oneself for not leaving enough time to catch it, in this particular manifestation the anger was so strong that it spontaneously flew out as so many shouts and gestures that assigned emotive qualities (stupid) to the detested object (disappearing bus), as well as to the surroundings (lamp post) in general.

In such fits of emotion the whole world becomes hateful, and unless one regains control such actions as kicking a lamp post can have yet more factual consequences (broken toe), which are yet more worldly difficulties that must also be met with either more emotion (crying) or a return to the pragmatic mode (looking for a new bus to the hospital). Thus, in emotion, consciousness seizes the world and its objects (bus, lamp post) in new ways because the cooler, calmer way of apprehending the world has broken down, been hijacked or suspended. All of this is pre-reflective, moreover, precisely because it is a spontaneous engagement with the world that actually makes the world itself, through psychophysiological incantations (shouting, shaking a fist, kicking), hateful and annoying. In this manner, emotion is magical consciousness, spontaneously instigating a magical phenomenal dimension because it tries to no longer accept the brute facts of the world as determined causal processes. Indeed, emotion transforms the world and its objects by assigning the latter with new qualities that do not actually belong to them originally and in themselves (e.g. 'stupid' bus):

> Emotional conduct is not on the same plane as other kinds of conduct; it is not *effectual*. Its aim is not really to act upon the object as it is, by the interpolation of particular means. Emotional conduct seeks by itself, and without modifying the structure of the object, to confer another quality upon it. ... In a word, during emotion, it is the body which, directed by consciousness, changes its relationship with the world so that the world should change its qualities. If emotion is play-acting, the play is one that we believe in.[5] (STE/ETE: 41/81–2)

The concept of 'belief' is vital here, for emotions without spontaneous beliefs therein 'are false emotions which are nothing more than conduct'[6] (STE/ETE: 48/94). Sartre's example (ibid.) is receiving a gift one is not actually moved by, but one acts so nevertheless. Here there is conduct without belief in such conduct. This is a false or simulated emotion, in this case supposedly for the benefit of the giver. It is not genuine because the gift has precisely not been experienced in a transformative way. In this manner, emotion proper needs not only bodily behaviour (conduct) but bodily behaviour that is genuine and spontaneous, and thereby incantatory. In other words, emotions need behaviour that one really believes in as significant to one's actual feelings, wishes and values.

It is crucial to note that such belief is neither propositional nor primarily reflective; it is more in line with Humean and Husserlian conceptions of belief (or *doxa*), which happens quite automatically and pre-reflectively (cf. also Hervy 2014). In Sartre's words, '*To believe* in magical conduct one must be deeply moved'[7] (STE/ETE: 50/98). This can only occur if consciousness automatically incants its – in this case – joy into so many psychophysiological actions (raised heartbeat, shaking limbs, clapping hands, a beaming smile) that actually mean – that is, signify – something for that same consciousness.

There are of course other variations of emotion. Sartre notes two. First are 'subtle emotions' (*les émotions fines* – STE/ETE: 55/105), where emotive conduct as externally manifested is 'hardly noticeable' (ibid.), as well as the fact that the person only feels and grasps the emotive quality in a vague manner (cf. ibid.). This is different to 'weak emotions' (*des émotions faibles* – STE/ETE: 55/106) for Sartre, which are actually 'seized with a lightly affective character regarding the thing'[8] (ibid.), as opposed to apprehending the (strong) quality in a vague or subtle manner in the former instance.

Even considering these subtler and weaker types, for Sartre the theory of emotion always involves magic at its heart; 'All emotion comes back to the constitution of a magical world, by making use of our bodies as instruments of incantation. In every case the problem is different, and the conduct is different. To grasp the signification and the finality, one would have to know and analyse each particular situation'[9] (STE/ETE: 47–8/93). It is thus an endless task, and must also be the case with the more positive emotions such as joy.

Here, Sartre distinguishes between emotive joy and a merely satisfactory feeling (cf. STE/ETE: 46/90), where the latter lacks the transformative characteristics that all of the main strong emotions (anger, fear, disgust, joy and the like) contain. The case of joy is significant because Sartre is aware of a possible objection that the positive emotions do not confront a 'difficulty' in the world. However, for Sartre they do, although this difficultly is a rather strange one. In joy, for example, the 'difficulty' is naturally not manifested as irksome or hateful; it is more about the structure and nature of the world as a causal, successive state of affairs that cannot actually be captured all at once – except through emotions such as joy.

What does this mean? What does one actually do and experience in joy? In joy one can get so excited that one actually leaps and dances around. What does this signify? Take, for example, receiving good exam results. At bottom, in front of you, is only a list of numbers (or letters). That is all. And yet these numbers have such significance for you that you can dance with glee. Here, therefore, is an instantaneous, magical release of all the gruelling effort that has gone into studying, a release of all the worrying and obsessing before and after each exam, and it is an equally gleeful anticipation of the celebrations that will be carried out tonight with one's friends and beyond. Joy thus manifests as jumping, skipping, smiling and the like because it is consciousness's spontaneous way of grasping past efforts and future events that in the present situation are only indicated factually on a black-and-white list. This list, *through* joy, however takes on a magical significance for you; the black and white actually signify, in joy, all the past efforts and future prospects in a manner whereby one is able to positively and colourfully overflow the pure pragmatics. For indeed, there are some people who meet good exam results with little or even no joy, simply viewing it as one more expected step in an ongoing logical project. For those who do leap, however, it is what Sartre means when he characterizes joy as 'a certain impatience' (STE/ETE: 46/90), a 'magical conduct that tries, by incantation, to realize the possession of the desired object as an instantaneous totality'[10] (STE/ETE: 46/91). All the past efforts and pains, all the future prospects and celebrations, which are – causally speaking – impossible to grasp all at once, can nevertheless be grasped altogether *as* joy. This makes joy an emotive consciousness that allows one to leap and laugh and clap in a manner that transcends and enchants everyday black and white.

Further, joy also brackets or suspends more pragmatic considerations of what such results will necessitate in the future – more studying, job applications and the like. This shows that joy swallows up, in one moment, all that is blissful about one's existence, taking time out from future pragmatic and more serious considerations. This is exemplified in Sartre's own example, where one's joy at being told, for the first time, that you are loved by someone you love, allows the newly beloved to 'turn his mind away from the prudent and difficult conduct he will have to maintain if he is to deserve this love and increase it, ... turn away even from the woman herself who represents, as a living reality, precisely the pole of all those delicate procedures'[11] (STE/ETE: 47/92). Joy thus 'is possessing the object by magic' (ibid.) because it consolidates a whole person's hopes and dreams into blissful incantations whereby one sings, skips and dances in a manner that brackets all the more practical considerations (getting a job, buying a home, raising a family) that such an event *also* harbours. In short, in joy it feels like the whole world is singing too, thereby putting any more serious and pragmatic considerations on the backburner.

I believe these explications and analyses show that emotion always involves elements of the world, as well as qualitative additions thereto, and transformations thereof. Moreover, the examples should also show a form of captivation that consciousness enacts spontaneously upon itself and its surroundings (cf. STE/ETE: 52–3/101–2). Indeed, through events of the world consciousness is able to bewitch itself in a manner that allows it to behave in ways that augment a given concrete state of affairs in a whole variety of magical forms, from infuriated rages on the one hand to rapturous celebrations on the other. Such experiences, both good and bad, are thus only possible because of emotion and its inherent magic. In short, whatever the emotion, it is 'undergone' (STE/ETE: 53/102) in a manner where consciousness initiates the incantations to deal with a given situation, and in doing so it can and often does 'perpetuate itself' (ibid.) in a world that has become hateful, sad, joyful, exasperating and so forth.

## The world transforming: Others and emotion

The preceding is not however the full story; the world, always peopled by others, is magical too. Indeed, we have just seen how consciousness can captivate and bewitch itself with regard to certain phenomena. This is a bewitchment that necessarily transforms the whole world into a magical – that is, non-deterministic – one. The other side to this is when the world itself 'reveals itself to consciousness as magical just where we expect it to be deterministic' (STE/ETE: 46/107). How is this possible? Chiefly because of others. Indeed, 'there is an existential structure of the world which is magical' (ibid.); because of people's inherent freedom, always already instantiated in their language (bodily and verbal), we can be greatly moved by their actions and behaviour precisely because the latter are often quite unpredictable. In Sartre's language, 'the category of "magic"' governs … interpsychic relations between men in society' (STE/ETE: 56/108) because our apprehension of others can always be experienced in a manner that does not abide strict causal laws. Of course the other as a physical body has to abide such laws, but the way in and through which others live their spontaneous lived body (*Leib*) as freedom, choice, language and behaviour can always have the capacity to mesmerize and captivate, from extremes of horror, disgust and consternation on the one hand to wonder, admiration and love on the other (cf. STE/ETE: 55/106). In this manner, although it of course is not 'impossible to take a deterministic view of the interpsychological world or to build rational superstructures upon it' (STE/ETE: 56–7/108–9), once again our everyday interpersonal lives are filled with more primary instances and phenomena that often cannot be predicted, and that often deeply affect us.

Even Sartre's aforementioned example of a woman telling a man she loves him has elements of this sort of otherworldly magic, precisely because it is a free, unpredictable action on her part, which the man can then, in a secondary moment, celebrate as his own emotive joy (or they together of course).

On the other extreme, sadness because someone has committed an action that hurts you is also emotive through and through, precisely because it usually cannot be completely foreseen. Here, instead of brutally accepting the event in a matter-of-fact manner ('It has happened; it's done; it doesn't matter'), through sadness one pines for and splutters over the person, thing or event in a manner whereby consciousness tries to deal with the wrong that has been done by, in a certain sense at least, actually making it a wrong – that is, by not being able to accept it as a raw factual event. Any kind of rationalization thereupon is therefore, as always, a secondary moment that signifies entry onto the reflective realm. An extreme here is of course stoicism, the practice of constantly trying to live on the level of reflection (judgement), thereby trying to pre-empt every emotion through rationalizing reflections. Most of us are not so stoic however, and almost never all the time. Indeed, most often 'man is always a sorcerer to man and the social world is primarily magical' (STE/ETE: 56/108). This is precisely why interpersonal relations are nearly always involved in the highest, as well as the lowest, moments of people's lives. Because such joys and hurts are freely given, often in highly unpredictable and unrepeatable manners, it means great emotive events are often felt and then recalled with particular strength.

Although interpersonal relations can always be rationalized and turned into deterministic structures ('Love is a chemical reaction in the brain'), at bottom these structures 'are ephemeral and unstable ... [and they] crumble away as soon as the magical aspect of faces, gestures and human situations becomes too strong'[12] (STE/ETE: 57/109). Such strength is primarily lived on the pre-reflective, interpersonal level, although it can also be endlessly discussed on the reflective level as well (thanks to the nature of the ego, as we have seen).

Nevertheless, considering these points one may ask what, more precisely, is the phenomenological structure of such magic on the pre-reflective level? Here, once again, it fundamentally involves a strange mixture of activity and passivity. Indeed, starting from Alain's definition of magic as 'the mind crawling among things' (STE/ETE: 56/108), Sartre immediately translates this into his own terms: 'An irrational synthesis of spontaneity and passivity' (ibid.). A smiling face (cf. ibid.), for example, is both passive – that is, a physical thing – because it abides by

certain physical laws (movements of certain facial muscles and the like), and yet
it is also active in the sense that a particular smile emanates from the absolutely
spontaneous nature of a certain person. This is what Sartre means by his technical
notion of 'degradation' (cf. ibid.); in everyday life consciousness is never purely
psychical but is always already instantiated in a certain *Leib*. This living person,
viewed from another perspective, appears as a 'special object', namely an object
which is an object, indeed – but an object who is also a person and can thereby
surprise us by displaying their spontaneity at every turn. Such magical being is
'irrational' because from a scientific, strictly empirical perspective this strange
synthesis between passivity and activity does not really make sense. In short,
these analyses give credence to a psychophysiological dynamic that goes beyond
mere causal mechanics. This is why phenomenology is useful for capturing its
details.

A smile that grabs our attention in an emotive manner is just one little
instance of Sartrean magic where there is 'inert activity, a consciousness
rendered passive' (STE/ETE: 56/108). This includes the physical manifestations
of a certain formation of lips, eyes and the like on the one hand, and the same
phenomenon points to and automatically imbues the freedom (i.e. activity) of
a certain individual person on the other. Such a combination always has the
potentiality to move us in an emotive manner.

The world as magical does not stop here; the world as such can also always
surprise, horrify and enrapture us in quite astounding ways. For instance,
so many physical phenomena can be magical in the sense of having surprise
elements that one can react to with a whole host of emotions – horror, disgust,
wonder to name but a few. In this manner, the world is not magical only because
of others, although Sartre does maintain they are normally the main triggers.
Indeed, with the augmentation of scientific knowledge the world has, in a way,
become less magical than in supposedly more 'primitive' times precisely because
more can be predicted. However, matters of fact (e.g. faeces) can still produce
emotions (disgust) where one's experience of an object goes against how one
would like the world to be, even though it is factually not so. Sartre's passage
goes as follows: 'Naturally, magic, as a real quality of the world, is not strictly
limited to the human. It extends to things also, inasmuch as they may present
themselves as human (the disturbing impression of a landscape, of certain
objects, or of a room which retains the traces of some mysterious visitor) or bear
the imprint of the psychic' (STE/ETE: 58/111). Hereby, thanks to existence of
others the world and its things can imbue magical aspects too (e.g. a cherished
item of clothing given to you as a present and a favourite place where you used

to spend time with a close friend). This makes the world of emotion one where either consciousness transforms the world, through bodily incantations, into a world of magic that flouts the laws of determinism and causality or the world itself, inhabited by others and their things, can equally captivate and enchant, both positively and negatively, transcending and transfiguring a world of facts into a one of captivation and surprise.

Finally, by saying that one 'returns' to the magical attitude of emotion (cf. STE/ETE: 61/116) Sartre even suggests that the magical world of emotion is ontogenetically the most primary. This is evident from the world of children, who must learn determinism and pragmatism – as in Dickens's *Hard Times* – in order to restrict and control their more original and often very pure emotional desires. It is thus no coincidence that when someone is undergoing strong emotions they are often criticized for acting like a child, because indeed the pure emotion of children shows that parents and society must prepare them for the more pragmatic world of adulthood. In short, society usually dictates that it is necessary to give into the more passionate and violent emotions less and less as one grows up and matures (cf. also Freud [1905] 2010: 141).

## Centrifugal and centripetal: Magic as the unifying element to Sartre's emotive consciousness

Sartre's *Sketch* is an enduring piece with a richness that we are still coming fully to terms with. Indeed, there has been a resurgence of interest in the work in anglophone scholarship, although there are quite a few contrasting accounts and interpretations. One of the main debates has taken place between Richmond (2011 and 2014) and Hatzimoysis (2011 and 2014), although others have also now added their thoughts (Elpidorou 2016).

Richmond's position is that Sartre vacillates between two theories of magic in his work, one the 'dominant line of thought' (2011: 151), the other the 'innovative' (id.: 153). The first, according to Richmond, is nothing new; other thinkers of and near Sartre's time, including Lévy-Bruhl, Bergson, Alain and Freud (id.: 147–50), all recount elements of such magical behaviour, where people introduce magical qualities (e.g. a 'hateful' computer when angry) into the world through a kind of bad faith fooling of oneself. This is in place of a more rational or pragmatic appraisal and engagement with the same objects (cf. id.: 151–3). Moreover, just as Richmond aligns this type of magic with bad faith, the second, 'innovative' type is aligned (id.: 157) with Sartre's well-known theory of 'the look' (*le regard*) as it is ultimately presented in *Being and Nothingness* (BN/EN: 276–326/292–341). Here, magic is not introduced by someone spontaneously trying to escape a difficult situation; for Richmond it is rather that the possibility for emotive qualities to inhere in objects to the point of captivation (e.g. a horrifying face when scared) is already present in the world in such cases. This supposed type happens, as we have seen, primarily through others and is more centripetal.

Richmond's claim that there are two types of magic leads her to claim that there are likewise two – moreover 'inconsistent' (cf. Richmond 2014) – theories of emotion at work in the *Sketch*: one that (irrationally) introduces magic into the world (e.g. anger); another that reacts to a form of magic that is already there (e.g. horror at a face in the window). Although it is a good insight that there are precursors to both bad faith and the look in the *Sketch*, this does not have to mean that there is inconsistency.

Indeed, Hatzimoysis's position (2011: 72–7) counters Richmond's; there are not 'two different theories of a single kind of thing, but … two different kinds of thing' (Hatzimoysis 2014: 82). Emotion is one thing with two kinds – or what I have referred to as centrifugal and centripetal. This is because these two kinds share 'the presence of magic' (ibid.). Although Hatzimoysis admits that the issue of magic is complex (cf. 2011: 74), he nevertheless maintains that at bottom the single structure to emotion is 'magical behaviour'. This latter 'purports to change one's situation not by effecting changes in the world, but by changing the meaning of the situation; the behaviour is "magical" because the agent, by means of his body, affects the way the situation is laid out before him, without acting on it' (Hatzimoysis 2014: 82). Hereby, emotion is where the agent changes the meaning of his or her own situation through their body. This means, even in the case of horror, that magic does not really emanate from the world alone (as Richmond maintains); the agent is still heavily involved for Hatzimoysis, even to the point where she freezes in terror in order to freeze the 'imminent threat' (2014: 82) as well. Richmond would maintain that the threat the agent is reacting to is already magical; however, I believe that it is very possible to react non-emotively to someone at a window, and thus the threat, as Hatzimoysis claims, is at least partially constituted by the person.

Although Hatzimoysis is correct in noting that Sartre was not interested in a kind of chicken-and-egg, what-comes-first question (the agent or the world) – precisely because the two are always already intermingled (cf. Hatzimoysis 2011: 74) – his emphasis on a kind of agency or behaviour in veritable cases where the world shocks and startles seems a bit forced. I do agree there is one underlying structure to emotion, but it is not magical 'behaviour'. For me the more basic thread is that of transformation; whether in its centrifugal (e.g. anger) or centripetal (e.g. fright) form, I have tried to convey that both are transformations (cf. STE: 39) of an instrumental use of the world, whereby objects accrue captivating qualities (annoying, frightening and the like) that were not there before, thereby arresting and concentrating one's attention. In one case consciousness transforms the world; in the other the world transforms consciousness. The terms are the same; there is consistency in transformation, although the direction, trigger or 'source' (cf. Richmond 2014: 613) can be experienced as centrifugal or centripetal. In other words, the structure remains the same in the sense that an object of the world is charged with non-deterministic qualities and is thereby transformed, even though the trigger and movement can be outward- or inward-flowing. Regardless of the direction, the crucial elements are that one has been captivated by the object (an annoying computer; a scary face) because there has been a transformation from determinism to non-determinism.

Actually, even when the bewitchment seems to come 'wholly' from within (e.g. anger) or without (e.g. fright), there are *always* two terms, consciousness and world, in a fused dynamic. This, actually, is nothing other than the phenomenological principle of intentionality (consciousness *of* such and such), with subject and object always necessarily together in an intrinsic experiential bind. Sartre himself states that 'this distinction between two main types of emotion is not absolutely rigorous: there are often mixtures of the two types and the majority of emotions are impure [i.e. mixed]'[13] (STE/ETE: 58/111). The important point is that these two main types, centrifugal (I am angry *at* something or someone) and centripetal (something or someone is scaring *me*), are still two types *of* emotion; emotion at bottom has the same underlying structure because it is always a magical transformation of the world that explicitly experiences emotive qualities in a certain object (or group of objects) to the point of captivation, mesmerization and psychophysiological incantation.

Hatzimoysis himself notes (2011: 74) that the role of Sartrean magic – especially in relation to emotion – has not been fully clarified. I believe I have rectified this. Indeed, the two dimensions to Sartre's emotive magic – consciousness and the world each enchanting the other – must, for me, ultimately be considered as two poles of the same fundamental dynamic. This is because, although Sartre does state that there are 'two forms of emotion' (STE/ETE: 57/109), we have just seen that he also admits the majority are mixed with aspects from both poles. In this manner, although we can have more centrifugal and centripetal movements, because consciousness is always already transcendence towards a world that also always already conditions and possesses us in various manners, these two origins or directions are on two sides of one and the same structural dynamic. In short, there is always a magical mixture of activities (consciousnesses) with passivities (objects in the world) in emotion; regardless of whether the trigger originally stems from consciousness or the world, emotive magic is still always when consciousness – our own or other people's – spontaneously and pre-reflectively inhabits things, objects and people in a way that is often unpredictable and always captivating.

Still missing from a complete picture might be a proper role of affectivity. Here, one might realize that an original form of affective connection to the world, its things and people could allow conscious elements – certain affective qualities – to be put into non-conscious things to the extent that these things gain a pseudo activity that might ultimately be characterized as a kind of 'reverse intentionality' in episodes of magic. Thus affectivity would be a condition of possibility for emotion and its magic, with the latter able to arise precisely because the world is always already being affectively charged, much like in Heidegger where *Dasein* is never completely unattuned (cf. Heidegger [1927] 2006: §29; also O'Shiel [2016] 2017). Here, then, the world and consciousness are always already interacting in a complex dynamic that needs to be further elaborated. I shall be able to do this in Chapter 4. First of all, however, these reflections do not complete the Sartrean discourse on magic leading up to *Being and Nothingness*, for there is still one massive element that needs to be investigated for a much more complete picture: Sartre's 1940 work *The Imaginary*.

# Evoking Absence: Sartre's Imaginary (1940)

For Sartre, acts of imaging consciousness are equally magical, by their very nature. In fact, although the word itself appears sparingly in *The Imaginary*, when it does Sartre states that the whole imaging act is magical: 'The act of imagination ... is a magical act' (IM: 125/239). It is going to take some time to see what this means precisely, as well as how such magic might differ from, or introduce new elements into, the other two forms of magic we have already seen (i.e. ego and emotion).

First I will need to situate Sartre's imaginary in a rather static way; we will need to see how he defines imaging consciousness and how it is delineated from other forms of consciousness, most notably from perceiving and conceiving.

On the basis of such delineation I will then, second, be able to consider Sartre's imaginary in a more dynamic and genetic way, which is to say I will be able to consider precisely not only how it arises in and through our engagement with the world, but also how consciousness at the same time neutralizes this very same world in a manner that allows one to go beyond it and enter the irreal – that is, the imaginary – as such. Here the vital focus will be on how we are able to experience implicit absence in the world of perception, and how this, in a second moment, opens up a gateway that actually allows us to explicitly evoke absence in imaging acts.

Such explication will lead, thirdly, to an understanding of why the imaginary is always magical, albeit to varying degrees. It will also show us why the imaginary is of vital importance for any conception of consciousness whatsoever, for indeed, Sartre goes as far to say that our capacity to imagine represents one of 'the two great irreducible attitudes of consciousness' (IM: 120/231), the other being perception. Even further, ultimately for Sartre there is no irreal (the imaginary) without the real (the perceivable), and vice versa. My analyses of these elements will finally lead us into why magic and its basic structures were ontologized three years later.

## Situating Sartre's imaginary: Between perception and concept

Sartre's 1940 work 'aims to describe the great "irrealizing" function of consciousness' (IM: 3/13) where the active, noetic and subjective side is named 'imagination', 'imagining' or 'imaging', while the activity's 'noematic correlate' (ibid.) is called 'image', 'the imaginary' or 'the irreal (object)'. Thanks to the phenomenological tenet of intentionality – consciousness is always consciousness *of* something – these two poles always necessarily go together; there is no irreal without the irrealizing activity of consciousness, and there is no irrealizing activity without a correlative irreal (i.e. imaginary) object. Indeed, at bottom imaging consciousness's essential characteristic is its ability to irrealize reality.

In order to alight upon this insight, Sartre in fact has four characteristics that all help towards delineating imaging consciousness from some other basic forms. These four characteristics have been dealt with in detail by other scholars (for instance, Bonnemann 2007: 77–96). However, this has been done with differing foci and aims, and none I am aware of have thoroughly discussed the role of magic, as is the case with the other chapters in this part too. This is why it is important to go through the basic elements under this new light, in quite some detail.

Before explicating these four factors, I must already distinguish imagination from the forms of consciousness we have seen in the first two chapters, namely, personal reflection (ego) and emotion. In this present text under scrutiny, Sartre claims that 'to perceive, to conceive, to imagine: such are indeed the three types of consciousness by which the same object can be given to us' (IM: 8/22–3). Now although emotive consciousness can be seen as a special form of perception, namely, a magical, non-pragmatic way of perceiving the world that automatically assigns emotive qualities (sad, horrible, scary, etc.) to things and people (cf. also Tappolet 2016), it does not seem clear where reflection would fit in this tripartite division. I may say that it does not, at least at this stage, because Sartre is here discussing the three forms of *pre*-reflective consciousness through which objects may be given. To perceive, to conceive and to imagine, these form the three chief ways through which objects are given to us on a pre-reflective level, where consciousness itself is not made an object – as it is in reflection – but precisely things, concepts and images are. Such a focus therefore brackets considerations of worldly judgements and remembering, not to mention presupposing the more general role for retention in many, if not all, of our perceptions, conceptions and imaginations.

Be this as it may, there is a consequence that all such modes of givenness (perceiving, conceiving, imagining) may be taken up, as always, onto the reflective plane – but only, as always, in a secondary moment. Indeed, outlining Sartre's four characteristics will actually show us that, while he engages in a comparison of imaging consciousness with the other two primary ways of pre-reflectively experiencing objects, some nice delineations are made. Such distinctions are however complicated later when pure concepts in fact end up on the reflective level. These nuances notwithstanding, my central aim will remain fulfilled, namely, to demonstrate that imaging consciousness takes a conceptual middle position between pure perception on the one hand and pure conception on the other.

Sartre's first characteristic (cf. IM: 5–7/17–22) is that 'the image is a consciousness'. This is of vital importance for Sartre because much of the history of philosophy falls victim to an 'illusion of immanence' (IM: 6/19). In this latter there is only a difference in degree, and not in kind, between perceiving and imagining. Such theories thereby fail to grasp the phenomenological fact that perception and imagination present two radically different modes of consciousness, even consisting in different structures and laws.

For philosophers like Hume, images – that is, certain ideas – seem to be merely watered-down perceptions inhabiting the psyche and are therefore, moreover, exact copies of their more 'forceful and vivid' impressions (cf. Hume [1738–40] 2001: 1.1.1; also IM: 5–6/17–18). For Sartre, to the contrary, absolutely nothing can inhabit consciousness; consciousness is a perpetual transcending activity towards objects it is not. In short, there is utterly nothing 'in' consciousness for Sartre (cf. IM: 5/17). This yields the curious but profound Sartrean insight that, because consciousness is complete transparency and non-coincidence, it is that active, transcending being by and through which various objects appear *to* it, as well as by and through which one is able to experience different objects through various different modes. Perceiving and imagining are two such utterly distinct modes for Sartre.

As just mentioned, the Humean conception of imagination leads to grave errors for Sartre because imagining, although always aiming at the exact same object as a (possible) perception, does so in such a different manner that the image is by no means a faded perception but is on the contrary a completely different way of relating to the object. We can imagine everything that we have perceived, but not vice versa (e.g. a unicorn). This is precisely thanks to imaging consciousness's irrealizing and creative capacity.

In short, perception is realizing by nature, imagination irrealizing. They both can aim at the same object (e.g. Pierre), but they do so in radically different ways. In perception, Pierre is actually there, given concretely, and his presence, moreover, does not depend on me. In imagination, on the contrary, an absent Pierre is evoked through various physical (e.g. a picture), psychophysiological (e.g. a feeling) or psychical (knowledge – memories – of Pierre) materials that are indeed present to me. Even if Pierre is right in front of me, to imagine him properly would require a suspension of the perceptual situation (e.g. by closing my eyes) in order to evoke an irreal appearance of him. If in doubt, try it; try to imagine and perceive an object at the very same time. I think one will find that one does either one or the other, or one will kind of hesitate between the two and end up not really doing either.

This makes imaging consciousness a type of consciousness in its own right – one that, moreover, obeys different laws. Regarding such laws, one main difference is Sartre's second characteristic, 'quasi-observation'; 'In perception I *observe* objects ... the object, though it enters whole into my perception, is never given to me but one side at a time' (IM: 8/23). This is the tried and tested Husserlian observation that although the perceptual objects is given as such, at any given moment only a particular aspect or side (*Abschattung*) of it is actually visible, touchable and so on (cf. Husserl [1918–26] 1966: 3). In this manner, objects of perception do not appear 'except in a series of profiles [i.e. aspects, *Abschattungen*] which calls for and excludes at the same time an infinity of other points of view' (IM: 8/23). This makes the objects of perception truly, truly inexhaustible, whereby 'one must *learn* objects' (ibid.) by making endless tours and investigations of them, and more generally by recognizing that they have a nature and independence all of their own. In this way, all objects of the realm of perception have their concrete forms and properties, and they obey strict natural, causal laws. In short, they do not depend on consciousness for their ex- and subsistence.

To conceive, on the other hand, is to be 'at the centre' (IM: 8/24) of an idea for Sartre; it is to 'apprehend its [the idea's; the concept's] entirety in one glance' (ibid.). For instance, when 'I *think* of a cube by a concrete concept' (ibid.) I grasp all its essential properties (six sides, right angles and the like) in one snap ('a cube'). Here there is 'no apprenticeship to serve' (ibid.) like in perception, for the concept is understood quite instantly, once and for all, and does not change.

This is very Cartesian of course. However, Sartre has additional interesting phenomenological insights, like the claim 'we can never perceive a thought nor think a perception' (ibid.) because conceiving is 'knowledge conscious of itself, which places itself at once in the centre of the object' (IM: 8–9/24). Perceiving, on the other hand, is 'a synthetic unity of a multiplicity of appearances, which slowly serves its apprenticeship' (IM: 9/24). In short, the apprenticeship in the concept is already complete (or it never took place); in perception it is unending.

For Sartre the image or imaging act is an intermediate between perception and conception. Here, although it seems to mix aspects of both the preceding, it does so in a wholly new manner, thereby making it distinct from the other two forms. To explicate, Sartre states that 'the image is a synthetic act that [like perception] links a concrete, not imaged, knowledge to [like conception] elements more properly representative' (IM: 9/25). Imagining a cube, therefore, has the pseudo appearance of a perception in the sense that one can represent, for instance, a particular side, but it also approaches – without being – a concept because one can also get a general sense of a cube through an image of one.

Further, the image does not have an infinite potential for learning as perception does, nor the already-completed attainment of a concept. Indeed, it has its own unique characteristic whereby I 'will never find anything there but what I put there' (ibid.). Thus imaging consciousness can create objects that resemble things in the world, as well as things that do not. It does so, however, in a manner in which it is wholly constituted through what one puts into it, through precisely what one thinks of, imagines. This means the inexhaustibility of the perceptual world, perhaps counterintuitively, is no longer included in the imaging act. 'Counterintuitive' because everyday opinion often rates the imaginary as not bound by reality and therefore richer and inexhaustible, with perceptual experience often being considered as limited, dull and monotonous. Phenomenologically speaking, however, perception has a structural inexhaustibility – an actual infinitude – that the imaginary cannot have. Indeed, the world as real, external and endlessly horizonal and temporal can never be fully grasped by us, whereas what I imagine (even considering the fact I can imagine so long as I live) is always already limited by precisely what I – and I alone – can put there. Sartre's realism is evident here: the things of perception are endless and do not need us; our images are not and totally do.

This point is corroborated when Sartre states that the image 'is a kind of essential poverty' (IM: 9/26); it is wholly dependent on the conscious act that creates and maintains it. The imaging act is therefore by nature isolating and isolated from the comparatively rich nexus of the perceptual world and all of its infinite possibility. Of course one can imagine many things that have never actually existed (yet). However, such images are always 'impoverished' because they have 'no relations with the rest of the world and maintain only two or three relations between themselves' (ibid.). Here, then, images are not less vivid perceptions but are phenomena of a different kind; images can 'in no way exist in the world of perception; they do not meet the necessary conditions' (IM: 10/26), for indeed, objects of perception 'constantly overflow' (IM: 10/27) consciousness in a manner where they have reality and autonomy of their own.

An object of imaging consciousness, to the contrary, is 'never anything more than the consciousness one has of it; it is defined by that consciousness' (ibid.). This ultimately means, once again, that one cannot learn anything wholly new from one's imaginings because they are wholly constituted by the imaging act and its concomitant knowledge (i.e. memories). Indeed, one either knows, for example, how many columns the Pantheon has or not (cf. IM: 86–8/171–5); all the imagining in the world is not going to alter this piece of knowledge – only a direct perception, an image-based one (e.g. a photograph) or recalling a forgotten memory will.

In this manner, imaging consciousness is quasi-observation because 'it is an observation that does not teach anything' (IM: 10/28). This has 'the paradoxical consequence' (IM: 11/29) that the imaged object is both external and internal. It is external because I observe what I create, from a distance, so to speak. It is internal because it is the imaging act that has created it, thereby making it depend on my consciousness utterly. It is this latter aspect of internality that gives the object, although always poor in comparison to perception, 'a rich and profound sense for me' (ibid.). In this manner, when one compares images to perceptions, barring certain limit cases like illusions and hallucinations (cf. Smith 2002), the former are always only mere wisps of actual colour and form – and yet, because it is a creation that is wholly dependent upon its creator, it has an intimacy and indeed a privacy that the world of perception often does not.

There is more to Sartre's characterization of imaging consciousness as quasi-observation than has just been said, especially to the extent that the term 'observation', even if it is only quasi, can be misleading. In fact, one does not observe an image like one can observe an object in perception. On the contrary, in imaging the matter of observation is itself taken into the act. Thus, one can watch – which is to say perceive – a tennis match by actually going to it and by actually moving one's head and eyes to and fro, following the ball and the players. This is how one observes in the perceptual realm. To imagine a tennis match, however, it is only necessary for similar psychophysiological movements (e.g. eyes moving to and fro) to be enacted, this time with one's eyes closed, in such a manner that these very movements facilitate and actually *become* the basis for imagining the irreal tennis match itself, along of course with one's knowledge of tennis and even memories of particular matches. Indeed, try to imagine a tennis match – especially the ball flying through the court – without moving one's eyes at all. Sartre's claim here is that imaging acts are 'quasi-observations' because they take up bodily actions (eyes moving) in a manner that does not actually – that is, perceptually – observe anything; on the contrary the movements *produce* the imaging, whereby it is again *as if* one is perceptually observing something when one in fact is not.

Sartre's crucial concept of the 'analogon' is already at work here, of which we shall see more a bit later. For now we need to move on to Sartre's third characteristic, which is stated well in his next subtitle: 'Imaging Consciousness Posits Its Object as a Nothingness' (IM: 11/30). Here, for example, 'the transcendent consciousness of a tree as imaged posits the tree. But it posits it *as imaged*, which is to say in a certain manner, which is not that of perceptive consciousness'[1] (IM: 12/31). Indeed, 'every consciousness posits its object, but each in its own way' (IM: 12/32). For perception the object is always automatically posited as existing (cf. ibid.). There is no other way, it being the very nature of perceptual consciousness. Imaging consciousness, on the contrary, posits its object as 'a nothingness', which is to say either 'as non-existent, or as absent, or as existing elsewhere' (ibid.) or 'it can also "neutralize" itself, which is to say not posit its object as existent' (ibid.). Such positing, whether perceptual or imaging, is not some after-effect of the act – it is in the intentional, noetic fibre of the constituting act itself.

Considering these points, perception always witnesses the existence of a concrete object – a thing – while 'concepts and knowledge posit the existence of *natures* (universal essences) constituted by relations and are indifferent to the "flesh and blood" existence of objects' (IM: 13/32). It is, however, only in imaging consciousness where an actual evocation of nothingness is involved. This is to say, if I imagine something it is necessarily 'given as absent to intuition' (IM: 14/34); imaging consciousness always presupposes the absence of the object to perception. If I imagine a unicorn, it is evidently not there. However, even if I imagine someone real like my friend in Berlin, it is because she is not here, in Brussels. And even if she were, it is still one thing to perceive and another to imagine her. All this has the important consequence that imagining presupposes consciousness's inherent capacity to evoke nothingness or absence, which is to say transcend the concrete world, take up material and psychophysiological aspects (a picture, a feeling, a piece of knowledge) and spontaneously create images therefrom.

Sartre's fourth characteristic is indeed that the spontaneity of imaging consciousness is decidedly more spontaneous than the spontaneity of the perceptual attitude. Here, although it is the case that consciousness qua original activity and transcendence is always spontaneous, in the perceptual attitude consciousness nevertheless 'appears to itself as passive' (ibid.). This is because the perceptual world of objects does not depend on any individual consciousness; such objects have reality of their own, in relation to which perception is often felt as a mere witnessing of such reality. It is such witnessing that gives perception its passive character, because here there are laws and concrete properties that can indeed be manipulated, but only if one enters the pragmatic attitude, thereby obeying the causal laws and chains of their natural relations.

In the imaging attitude, by contrast, there is no such necessary reality. One can of course imagine causal chains of events. However, in this case one does so alone and in phantom form, which means the independence of the events themselves has already been stripped. Indeed, although the content may still be considered real, the imaginary only arises through spontaneous irrealizing acts that by definition are not part of the perceptual realm and that can thereby flout the laws of causality and mechanics altogether, representing objects in ways borne out wholly by the individual consciousness that creates and sustains them.

Not listed as an essential characteristic, but nevertheless as an important consequence of the characteristics, is what Sartre calls the peculiar '*flesh*' (IM: 16/38) or 'intimate texture' (ibid.) of the imaging act. Here, as we have already seen, images are not watered-down inhabitants of the psyche; they form a consciousness all of their own with their own particular laws, dynamics and textures. Indeed, objects of perception are 'constituted by an infinite multiplicity of determinations and possible relations' (ibid.). By contrast, 'the most determinate image possesses in itself only a finite number of determinations' (ibid.) that are wholly reliant upon what consciousness has put there. It is because of this 'poverty', as compared to real-world inexhaustibility – as well as the concomitant total reliance upon the creative intentional act – that there always exists a 'discontinuity at the very heart of the object of the image, something jerky, qualities that spring towards existence and stop halfway'[2] (IM: 16/39). This insight shows there is often a staccato-like texture to one's imaginings. On this note, I think one need to only inspect one's own perceptions and images to see that the latter almost always have something quite frivolous and evanescent, awkward even, to their very fibre and texture. This makes it freer in a sense, of course, but it also makes its 'flesh' less solid, more elusive, and almost ghost-like – especially when compared to a thing that is right in front of you in all its utter physicality, presence and complexity.

Such are Sartre's 'statics of the image' (IM: 16/39). Imaging consciousness finds its place between pure perception on the one hand and pure conception on the other. However, in later sections this apparently clear tripartite distinction gets more complex. Here, although perception is still very much delineated from thought in general, images and concepts in fact seem to come to form two subcategories of this more general realm. And they can often become blurred. In fact, Sartre even seems to change his stance somewhat, in that the concept can either manifest itself as 'pure thought on the reflective terrain' (IM: 114/219), where consciousness is conscious of being in the presence of some truth; or the concept can manifest itself pre-reflectively, which is to say that it is manifested, through an image, in a way that 'degrades' the pure concept (cf. IM: 34, 51, 67, 105/75, 108, 134, 204). Now, concepts that utilize images on such a pre-reflective and 'degraded' terrain come, themselves, in three gradations. The first grade almost haphazardly imagines a particular instantiation (e.g. a particular man, Pierre) in order to represent the more general concept (man), and thereby only attains to the concept quite imperfectly and indirectly (cf. IM: 113/218). The second 'directly grasps the concept itself' by representing the object man as such in a spatialized but necessarily indeterminate form (image of 'man as such') (cf. ibid.). Finally, the third gradation turns away from objects altogether and merely imagines the necessary 'system of relations' (IM: 113/218) of the class under consideration, in what Sartre calls 'a symbolic schema' (ibid.).

Thus concepts can be imagined in many ways, and they attain pure, reflective knowledge only when there is a conscious presence to some in-itself truth that no longer requires imagining. This leads Sartre to suggest that the concept, although always possible of being pure on a reflective and logical level, more often than not becomes – or remains – 'degraded knowledge' (cf. IM: 67/134) through the use of imaging consciousness. Thus, here for Sartre thought first 'naturally takes the form of the image' (IM: 111/214). Because we are so immersed in the world of the sensible, thought, when sparked, also has the natural tendency to approximate towards the sensible too; 'the image is like an incarnation of unreflective thought … imaging consciousness represents a certain type of thought: thought that is constituted in and by its object' (IM: 112/216). In other terms, when one leaves concrete perception most of us most of the time carry out imaging acts that only in rare cases entirely enter pure conceptual thought.

Under this conception thought is like a sliding scale where you have so many images of individual and concrete things on one extreme, and then purely logical and mathematical concepts that have no need for – or cannot even have – any remnants of sensibility on the other. In a word, 'naked thought[s]' (IM: 116/223) without any imagery at all are rather rare events because they require ideas that are 'entirely transparent' (ibid.) to themselves.

Sartre does allow that 'the habit of reflection can curtail' (IM: 111/214) the more natural tendency to think of concepts in terms of specific images. However, often this does not happen for most of us. For example, many people 'asked about the nature of beauty produce in themselves the image of the Venus de Milo, and this is as if they responded "Beauty is the Venus de Milo"' (IM: 111/214–15). Considering this, a great number of our thoughts on average contain something of the imaginary, where Sartre's use of such terms as 'degradation' and 'incarnation' already shows that, even on this conceptual level of delineation, we already see signs of – and Sartrean vocabulary for – magic within the phenomenological structure of imaging consciousness. For we can already see that imaging consciousness is essentially a process of making the real irreal – already quite a magic trick – whereby one enacts free and spontaneous acts of imagination that evoke images not only in order to approximate towards certain concepts but also to evoke a more general attitude of (artistic) creation. Indeed, imaging consciousness, as that great realm between pure perception on the one hand and pure conception on the other, forms a mighty one that can help not only in matters of understanding but also in many other matters, from works of artistic genius to the less appealing – but by no means mutually exclusive – dangers of possession, captivation and insanity (more on these issues in the second part). Just how such variety is possible still needs further explication throughout large remaining portions of this work. We must first, however, understand precisely how our capacity for the imaginary arises dynamically out of, and is sustained by, consciousness's relation to the world and its materials. This makes up the aforementioned dynamics – or 'genetics' in a Husserlian sense – of Sartre's theory of the imaginary.

## Experiencing and evoking absence: Perception, imagination and the analogon

To understand how the imaginary arises out of our engagement with the world, I will need to give a phenomenological account that revolves around consciousness's capacity to both implicitly experience and explicitly evoke absence, with the latter relying wholly upon Sartre's crucial concept of the analogon.

We have already seen that consciousness is an absolutely necessary condition by and through which a world and all its objects can appear. In order for this to occur, consciousness must also be defined essentially as non-coincidence. The very fact that a world and its objects appear *to* a conscious subject already demonstrates that such 'consciousness of ...' is not itself the world and its objects. In this sense, the advent of consciousness means a kind of phenomenal gap is introduced that allows for a basic and all-pervasive awareness, by and through which all does indeed appear *to* such fundamental awareness. This, again, is the language of intentionality, whereby the elemental activity of consciousness constitutes a general phenomenal ground out of which consciousness can be conscious *of* something.

A well-known Sartrean example highlights this point; when I look for Pierre in a café, the café is automatically constituted as a 'ground' (BN/EN: 33/44) out of which objects arise through the direction of my gaze, with each individual one being 'thrown back to nothingness' (BN/EN: 35/45) when I realize that they are not what I am looking for, Pierre. If Pierre is there, I would be 'suddenly arrested by his face and the whole café would organize itself around him as a discrete presence' (BN/EN: 34/44). In short, I would perceive Pierre, greet him and sit down.

However, Pierre is not there, and once I have searched the whole café this place is 'thrown' in its own turn, because I have seen that the café does not contain him. In other words, I experience Pierre's absence 'from the *whole* café' (ibid.).

I have already hinted that in the realm of the imaginary proper, absence is not simply and implicitly experienced but is explicitly evoked in a manner that transfigures reality precisely through irrealizing it. Extending upon Sartre's own example, I may here say that after I have left the café, I, while walking down the street, start to wonder where Pierre is, and here I may imagine him on a bus. In an instant I evoke an image of Pierre on a bus while I myself am walking down the street. Such an imaginary act is a spontaneous creation of my consciousness that has no necessary link with my very real act of walking – though it does, in this case at least, have a non-strict causal link to the preceding events, namely, looking for Pierre in the café and not finding him. This is a small example to show that the imaginary arises through consciousness irrealizing the real. Clarifying this further will require another example.

Sartre claims that it is one thing to perceive that an arabesque continues behind a cupboard and another to imagine what the arabesque behind the cupboard might actually look like. In the first case it is quite clear, says Sartre, that there is always, in any given perception, an 'emptily intended' (cf. IM: 121/233) project of perceiving that continues beyond the actually given content of the present perception. In other words, there always exist elements that are not actually perceived in the present moment but are nevertheless always implicitly there. Moreover, they can always, if we so choose, be perceived (in this example, by looking behind the cupboard). This is completely in line with Husserl and the inherent horizonality of all perceptual consciousness, with the underside of an ashtray on a desk being one of Sartre's own examples (ibid.).

With regard to the arabesque, it means that if I perceive only half of it on the wall, then, according to the phenomenological laws of perception, I automatically have an 'empty intention' of the hidden half in the one and the same perception of the visible half. Such empty intentions have their basis in our knowledge, Sartre says. More specifically, our knowledge has its source in memory or in implicit – that is, 'unformulated' or 'antepredicative' – inferences (cf. ibid.). In simpler terms, such knowledge always has to do with being actually or memorially present before a certain object or truth.

Perception and knowledge thus essentially revolve around presence for Sartre, whether actual or intellectual. Imagining the arabesque behind the cupboard, on the other hand, is an act of positing that radically excludes any emptily intended perception of it. Moreover, it tries to make something which is absent, present. Here the part of the arabesque behind the cupboard is no longer a mere empty continuation of the present perception but is now directly aimed at, although crucially not as perceived but as imaged. In other words, I isolate the absent part of the arabesque and aim, often with the help of memory, directly at it through my imagination. Such an act involves a neutralization of the perceptual attitude in order for an imaging one to spring up. In this manner, imagining an object necessarily excludes emptily intending it because the object is now directly aimed at, albeit as imaged.

Even further, imagining also neutralizes acts of perception in general. Indeed, although the world does not completely disappear when we imagine, it should be clear that the details within a normal perceptual attitude, as well as its objects and many of their particulars, take a back seat – a more marginal significance – when one is properly imagining something. There are comical (and painful!) examples of this, like walking into a lamp post while lost in some image or thought. Also think of daydreaming more generally, where someone might be 'miles away' from their immediate surroundings, 'staring into space' because they are consumed by their own imaging.

All in all, imaging consciousness is here an act where I both make explicit *and* impoverish my (empty) perception in a spontaneous act that posits, in this example, the arabesque behind the cupboard in a complete though irreal manner (cf. IM: 122/234). In short, I do not emptily intend the arabesque behind the wall but 'see' it through my imaging consciousness *of* it. Perception and the imaginary therefore necessarily exclude one another for Sartre because reality must be neutralized and irrealized if an imaging act is to arise at all.

How, more specifically, is such irrealizing made possible? Sartre's answer is that absence – or more generally nothingness – can be evoked only through materials that *are* present to us. Such materials form an 'analogon' for absent or non-existent – in short irreal – objects. Under this heading one needs to think of all the materials that can be used to evoke something not existent or there. These can be physical and external (e.g. a painting, a photo, an actor – cf. IM: 17–53/40–112), psychophysiological (affectivity (viz. feelings) and kinaesthetic sensations (e.g. moving one's eyes in order to imagine a tennis match – cf. IM: 68–83/135–64)) or psychical (knowledge (i.e. memories) of something – cf. IM: 57–68/115–35). Let us read Sartre on the matter: when trying to 'capture' my absent friend Pierre, I try to (1) think of (i.e. internally imagine) him, (2) look at a photo of him and (3) look at a caricature of him:

> We have employed three procedures to give ourselves the face of Pierre. In the three cases we found an 'intention', and that intention aims, in the three cases, at the same object. This object is neither the representation, nor the photo, nor the caricature: it is my friend Pierre. Moreover, in the three cases, I aim at the object in the same way: it is on the ground of perception that I want to make the face of Pierre appear, I want to 'make it present' to me. And, as I cannot make a direct perception of him spring up, I make use of a certain matter that acts as an *analogon*, as an equivalent of perception. (IM: 18/41–42)

Imaging acts, whether they use external objects (e.g. pictures), psychophysiological phenomena (mainly feelings and bodily movements) or even more purely psychical materials (non-affective memories and knowledge), all ultimately have the same structure: to show that an 'object is given, when absent, through a presence' (IM: 85/170). Such presence is nothing other than the specific analogical material (a feeling, a photo) used to constitute the particular imaging act (missing my home, seeing my grandmother). Indeed, the analogon contains all the present materials used in order to make an absent, non-existent or reality-neutral object appear before consciousness in a way that denotes 'consciousness of an *object as imaged* and not consciousness *of an image*' (IM: 86/171–2). The image, therefore, is an active form of consciousness through which an object is given as imaged and not as perceived or conceived.

The analogon, moreover, need not be made up of one specific type of analogical material of course. On the contrary there more often than not exists 'a plurality of differentiated qualities in the analogon' (IM: 85/168). For instance, a photograph of my grandmother *and* a concomitant feeling of sadness that she is gone often co-constitute my imaging experience of her. More generally, although these elements, such as pieces of knowledge, movements, affectivities and so on, can all be distinguished in the abstract through analysis, in the actual imaging act they form the analogon entirely, once and for all, each and every time, in the 'unity' (IM: 137/263) of the whole act. The analogon therefore neutralizes or modifies aspects of reality (first moment) so consciousness can then use this material to evoke its imaginary object (second moment). Indeed, a feeling of sadness as real is the precise tonality of the feeling, made possible by an immediate pre-reflective or reflective consciousness thereof; a feeling of sadness in missing someone who is not there uses this feeling as analogical material *for* the missing and missed person. This is what Sartre means when he states that the feeling, portrait and the like all cease to be objects of perception (cf. IM: 22/51); they here function rather 'as matter for an image' (ibid.). In other words, there are always materials of the world and of consciousness that are experienced with all their immediate and real force. However, a great number can also be used to evoke something that is not there, and might never be (again). It is in these latter cases that such materials, because they are presences used to evoke absences, come to stand in for something else, and thus become irrealized, incorporated into and co-constitutive of a structurally new act of imagination.

In Sartre's terms, 'the imaginary and the real ... are constituted by the same objects; only the grouping and the interpretation of these objects varies' (IM: 20/47). Such groupings and interpretations are thanks to the two different structures of perceptual and imaging intentionality, where the former is soaked through, in its very phenomenological fibre, with reality, the latter with irreality.

Thanks to the real materials that are capable of being used by imaging consciousness in an analogical way, a whole irreal realm opens up, which is full of both enchantments and pitfalls. Indeed, imaging consciousness is '*constituting, isolating,* and *annihilating*' (IM: 181/348) all at once. It is that 'great irrealizing function' (cf. IM: 3/13) as Sartre himself stated. It is thus no wonder that it is wholly magical too.

## The magic of the imaginary and its complications

For me, until now surprisingly little has been made of the inherently magical nature of Sartre's imaginary. I find it even more surprising given that I think it can provide important insights into a number of contemporary issues, as we shall see in Part 2 of this work. For now, this section plans to highlight the main and underemphasized elements, as well as some potential theoretical tensions that stem from the imaginary and its magic. Such tensions will ultimately also highlight how Sartre had to ontologize his multifarious concept in the culmination to his early philosophy, *Being and Nothingness*.

Hopefully it is already clear how the irreal depends upon the real, for I cannot possibly imagine something without utilizing some real materials (photos, feelings, memories and the like). However, the claim that the real equally presupposes the irreal might be less obvious, and yet it is a claim that Sartre maintains (IM: 185–8/356–61). For instance, in the previous section it was shown that experiencing absence (not finding Pierre) and evoking it (imagining Pierre) are distinct – and yet, to what extent do our experiences of absence in the real world presuppose the imaginary in general? Can one know something is real without implicitly supposing it is not irreal at the same time? In short, can one have one category without the other?

Another issue to highlight is the fact that the imaginary seems to have a power of its own, and if this cannot come from the inert and passive created image, where does it come from? Finally, can the real not be conceived as often completely infiltrated with, or even contaminated by, our imaginary creations, even to the extent that to speak of some unmixed reality is difficult, if not impossible?

Sartre does have answers to these questions, but they will take some time to go through. Here I will be able to answer a number of them as we journey through the important but often implicit discourse on the magic of the imaginary.

It seems, to me at least, that Sartre's imaging consciousness can be outlined as magical in a fourfold manner. First of all trivially so, which is to say as a spontaneous creation of consciousness that does not need to obey the world's causal laws. Secondly, like previous forms of Sartrean magic there is a strange mixture of activity (spontaneity, freedom) and passivity (inertia, objectivity) in all imaging acts, where, thirdly, in certain cases (artistic creation, dreaming and madness in particular) imaging consciousness can, like with the ego and in emotion, captivate itself so much that – this time – the real can be completely transfigured, suspended or even corrupted. This third point culminates in the problem of possession, where one's imaginings can become so powerful that a kind of 'reverse intentionality' could be said to be at work. Fourthly and finally, the fact that the imaginary can seem to infiltrate the world at every turn not only corroborates Sartre's claim that 'every concrete and real situation' (IM: 186/358) of consciousness in the world is already 'pregnant with the imaginary' (ibid.), but also seems to generate some conceptual problems when considering some of Sartre's other claims and stances.

First, then. Trivially so, the imaginary is magical because it is a free creation of an individual consciousness. For instance, when I imagine Pierre on a bus after having looked for him, one could of course say that such an act springs up because you are wondering where he is after not having found him. In short, here the implicit experience of absence (not finding Pierre in the café) leads to an explicit evocation of absence (Pierre on a bus). Nevertheless, although there is a link between these two events, there is not a strict causal one: it is just as possible to imagine Pierre on a bus without having just looked for him; it is also perfectly possible to imagine something completely else after having left the café; or to imagine nothing at all. In this way, although one can, once again, construct reflective superstructures explaining why one imagines such and such, these come, as always, after the more primary pre-reflective event. This latter, considered simply as it is, is a quite spontaneous creation that has no strict link to the present causal events.

This is not all; the imaginings themselves flout the standard laws of causality. Time, space and everything else are all irrealized in and through the imaging act by very definition (cf. IM: 125–36/239–61). In fact, irrealized time and space are made integral to the internal fibre of the image, which always has something irreal and therefore often something quite whimsical and frivolous about it. Here is Sartre on the matter:

> The act of imagination, as we have just seen, is a magical act. It is an incantation destined to make the object of one's thought, the thing one desires, appear in such a way that one can take possession of it. There is always, in that act, something of the imperious and the infantile, a refusal to take account of distance and difficulties. Thus the very young child, from his bed, acts on the world by orders and prayers. Objects obey these orders of consciousness: they appear. But they have a very particular mode of existence. (IM: 125/239)

We have already seen something similar with regard to Sartre's account of emotion, especially with regard to the short-circuiting of dealing with difficulties and distances in more patient and practical ways. Here the imaginary is also able to deal with difficulties – and particularly distances – in a magical manner, thus showing why Sartre does indeed see magic as quite synonymous with his own brand of action at a distance (cf., for instance, STE/ETE: 57/110). What is of particular note here is that objects of the imaginary appear on demand, precisely because consciousness can create and sustain them all by itself. In the real, perceptual world this is not so; there is an infinite world of physical restrictions, determinations and possibilities that one often has little control over, and so one must meet such aspects and demands with a pragmatic attitude if one is to enact any real – which is to say causal – change.

Such spontaneous action also means that, although one can will certain images, the issue of spontaneity runs much deeper. Indeed in Sartre's thought the will is a merely reflective and bastardized version of a more monstrous, impersonal spontaneity of brute pre-reflective consciousness (cf. TE: 47/128). Here it helps to think of 'spasms' of spontaneity (cf. IM: 126, 154/241, 298; also Breeur 2005: 124) whereby images just spring up, often out of nowhere and therefore not in one's wilful control. In short, the will belongs on the reflective plane for Sartre, and is thus often quite powerless with regard to the more primordial spasms of irreflective activity.

This is what creates the curious twist of fate in the imaginary too. Indeed, although images are usually quite spontaneously created, and moreover are without any real care for the causal nexus of the world, the imaginary can actually appear – especially in dreams, obsessions and the like – in a manner whereby everything is fixed, repeated or even preordained. This is in stark contrast to the real world, where, just like any compatibilist theory, there is always a real dynamic – a real to and fro – between real, factual and determined events on the one hand and one's free (re)actions thereto on the other. This is because in the real world there are infinite possibilities, choices and determinations, wherein one must also simultaneously be aware that there are very real consequences to one's own (in)actions. Imaginary life, by contrast – and Sartre does maintain that many (e.g. an artist) predominantly live such a life – 'is *without consequence* in the strong sense of the term' (IM: 135/250). This is because more often than not nothing actually – which is to say physically and causally – happens in the imaginary; contrary to rather stereotypical accounts of the richness of imaginary life, for most people such life is quite 'scholastic' (IM: 145/282), banal and repetitive. Think of any normal fantasy (sexual, of power, of fame). These can indeed be a pleasure to create, and can even be met with a kind of personal glee. However, when actually studied they usually amount to the same old same old – themes precisely of sex, power and fame wherein there is a tendency to repeat and exhaust.

Of course, a great novelist has a very rich imaginary life. This, however, merely corroborates Sartre's point; it is precisely why we admire such great creative works because we implicitly realize the wonderful effort and talent that must have been involved to attain such richness, which goes over and above the more widespread impoverishment and banality of most of our imaginary lives. Thus, rich imagination is the exception not the rule; put most people in a room with only a pen and paper, and little interesting will result.

Furthermore, things can, and often do, turn fatal in a more decided sense. Indeed, because of the crucial idea that I do not learn anything from the imaginary in the sense that I only get what I put into it, the freedom of the imaginary can come full circle, translating the absolute spontaneity of imaging acts into a kind of fatality. Actually, one might even say it is precisely because of the immanence of the spontaneity that makes the imaginary fatal. Sartre comments on the fatalism of the imaginary with reference to the dream:

> Contrary to what one might believe, the imaginary world is given as a world without freedom: no more is it determined, it is the inverse of freedom, it is fatal. Thus it is not by conceiving other possibilities that the dreamer is reassured, saved from embarrassment. It is by the immediate production of reassuring events in the story itself. The dreamer does not say 'I could have had a revolver', but all at once has a revolver in hand. But too bad if at that very moment there occurs a thought that in the waking state would be expressed in the form 'and what if the revolver is jammed!' This 'if' cannot exist in the dream: this saving revolver, at the very moment when it is needed, is suddenly jammed. (IM: 169–70/327–8)

Here we already have a strange mixture of a spontaneously created act that nevertheless has a fatal content – precisely because it is so spontaneous, immediate and immanent. In the everyday world determinate events are needed for freedom to manifest itself as possibility and choice. This is another tenet of compatibilism. In Sartre's characterization of a dream, however, something else happens. Indeed, dreams as a subcategory of the imaginary are noteworthy – as we shall see more on later in Chapter 8 in the section 'Hypercaptivation: Dreams and psychopathology' – because a suspension of the perceptual world is almost complete; one is sound asleep (cf. IM: 165/319). Precisely because of this there can be a very strong immersion and self-captivation where one's point of reference to something real has been totally bracketed in these moments. This means any imaging intention can appear immediately and precisely as it is intended – and this is why conditions and choices cannot really exist here; such is the immersion and immanence of the imaginary in dreams that there is no space for hesitations, ifs and the like. All appears as instantly as it is produced, without gap.

Going further, in psychoses fantasies can come to dominate waking life too, whereby subjects seem to abandon the difficult, practical world in order to create and control images that may indeed torment, but that are at least sequestered away from the often very frightening unpredictability of the real world. We will see a particular case of this later in Chapter 8 in the section 'The case of Schreber: A Sartrean reading'. More generally however, Sartre is quite extreme in this and even claims that the one who loves in the imaginary to a pathological degree only does so because he is 'no longer' (IM: 148/285) – or never was – 'capable of loving' (ibid.) in a real way.

More technically – and this is the second issue – the imaginary is magical because of a strange mixture of activity and passivity. Imagining is active because of the creative act on the side of consciousness (noesis), while it is also passive because of the inert quality of the image on the more objective side (noema). However, because of intentionality noesis and noema are always closely interlinked, which in Sartre's magic means the objective, passive side to the image can be instilled with a pseudo power – that is, a pseudo activity – from the originally more active, noetic side. This can of course take on varying degrees; there is an inherent elasticity to such a principle. However, in general it is quite clear for Sartre that the imaging intention has the power to animate its noematic correlate by breathing a kind of 'feeble life' (IM: 125/240) into it.

It is the structuring intention that is all-important here, for, contrary to what one may assume in a more causal, common-sense attitude, the possibility of constituting an imaging consciousness, although necessarily needing analogons, cannot exist without the creative power of the act itself; 'If I see Pierre in the photo, *it is because I put him there*' (IM: 19/44). As a pure thing, the photo is a material object with certain colours and a spatial physicality. However, due to the nature of the imaging intention the colourful thing operates precisely as an analogon, where, based upon levels of knowledge and feelings one has, it is automatically posited as a photo, a photo of a man, a photo of Pierre, a photo of my best and dearest friend and so on – in short *always* as some kind of image (cf. IM: 18–19/43–4). Indeed, although it might be possible to view a photo as a mere material object of perception (with a certain texture, certain colours, etc.), this can normally only be done with effort or abstraction; the more automatic intention is always the imaging one which already constitutes it as an analogon ('Oh! That's a photo of such and such').

Such an intentional act is moreover magical because it is, once again, an 'irrational synthesis that is difficult to explain' (IM: 23/52). Why is this so? Because with a photo of Pierre he is both there and not. On the one hand this material object and my knowledge of Pierre (the analogon) are present, putting Pierre in the photo. On the other hand, the ultimate object of the act – Pierre – is not actually there at all. He might even be dead, and yet he is present as absent, through the analogical material. In this way the imaging act 'lend[s] life to these dry schemas' (IM: 28/61). Here, depending on how much life one lends, there can result the difference between quite normal imaging acts on the one hand and quite intense and consuming ones on the other.

More generally, because of the imaginary's inherent capacity for captivation, getting consumed by one's imaging acts is a constant possibility, and can indeed become quite obsessive and even pathological when such bewitchment either distances oneself from, or even completely corrupts, more ordinary and balanced engagements with the real. This is because, due to the fact that irreal objects can be instilled with a pseudo spontaneity, borrowed from the imaging act itself, the result is that certain imaginary creations can seem to have life – and even an autonomy – of their own. In short, the activity of consciousness and the passivity of images get mixed up in the captivating qualities of the imaginary. Such a characteristic means that 'the image carries in itself a spurious persuasive power, which comes from the ambiguity [i.e. the magic; the pseudo activity] of its nature' (IM: 120/231). Thus the image as a noematic correlate is originally a 'passive object' (IM: 126/241). However, it is one that can be 'artificially kept alive' (ibid.) through an imaging intention that 'nourishes itself' (IM: 125/242) through its own acts. This, in sum, is all language and themes similar to what we have seen with regard to the ego and emotion, with captivation and reversals of power and direction being key. These are, moreover, also issues that I will be able to flesh out further in the second applied part of this work.

One of Sartre's examples regarding such captivation might already help here: my real love for Annie revolves around the absolute inexhaustibility of her freedom and character; 'she overflows my desire completely' (IM: 147/283); 'with every person we love, for the very reason of their inexhaustible richness, there is something that surpasses us, an independence, an impenetrability, that demands perpetually renewed efforts'[3] (IM: 145/279). But then Annie is gone, has left me, and what am I left with? Nothing but so many memories and feelings that must go into constituting an image instead of feeding off the actual person (as would be the case in perception). Here there is an 'essential reversal, it is now the feeling that produces its object and the irreal Annie is no more than the strict correlate of my feelings for her' (IM: 144/277–8) – I evoke the absent Annie through my pinings and misgivings; I must now create and give life to the object of my desire all on my own.

If the feelings are strong enough, this can create intentions that seek to instil a formidable power and activity into the images themselves ('I can't get her out of my head'). Often, however, the weakness of the imaginary leads to a return to the real (finding a new girlfriend, for instance). The general point can still hold however; there are certain scenarios where one lets oneself be taken up and bewitched by one's own creations. Moreover, because one pines for that actual object who is evidently not there, one starts to give the images more and more power, where a pseudo autonomy seeps into them in a way that actually appears to reverse the intentional structure of the original act. If this occurs, one transfers from a rather normal act of missing someone to a more chronic form.

Indeed, certain psychopathologies are, for Sartre, nothing other than extreme imaginary attitudes where one's images have become sedimented and automatized with powers of their own. Voices speak and torment; paranoia sets in; one comes to live in a disparate imaginary world almost entirely, repeating images with strict regimen, even ultimately claiming that such phenomena now have a reality of their own, or are even 'more real' because they are yours, wholly yours, and no one else's. One can find it incredibly hard to control such possessions by this stage precisely because the monstrous and spasmodic spontaneity of consciousness has surrendered its powers to its own creations. Extreme cases can actually fragment the solidarity and integrity of consciousness altogether (cf. IM: 155/299; also Laing [1960] 2010), thereby bracketing – or even corrupting – the real attitude for great spells, or even for the rest of one's life. This we shall return to in Chapter 8.

For now I wish to focus on possession in the imaginary, the third main theme in this section. At first glance it seems different to concrete possession (owning something), as well as to being in love with, and around, a particular person who is there and utterly inexhaustible. Indeed, with the possession of the imaginary (and perhaps in extreme cases of ownership) one becomes possessed by one's own creations or things, whereby a *reverse intentionality* sets in a manner that makes the image or thing the agent and the subject the patient ('The voices are making me do it!'; 'That car is everything to me!'), thus making the person *dis*possessed by the very possession (cf. Visker 1999: 142 and [2004] 2008: 79–82). Such creations – in the imaginary at least – do allow us to 'escape from all the constraints of the *world*' (IM: 136/261). However, they also lead to a form of self-captivation that can be quite torturous, where one cannot or will not let go and rejoin the world, spasmodically and fatally preferring to be bewitched by one's own torturous creations and possessions.

Here, it is not as if a person wilfully chooses to be tormented. Although to some extent one is still always responsible for one's explicit choices, because of the automatic spontaneity of basic consciousness just how much one can remain in control is not at all that clear. For now, suffice it to say that the spontaneity of consciousness is ceaseless and can be extremely hard to bear. Nevertheless, a conscientious reflection – just like with the ego – that notes a good balance between real and irreal should be able to avoid the more serious pitfalls of such magical hypercaptivation, at least in most cases.

A more general insight is that consciousness necessarily lives in and around irreality and possession, where the real, practical world can fall victim to methodical and often very banal – or even dangerous – forms of captivation. The cases of advertising and racism in Chapters 6 and 7 respectively will show elements of this. More generally, however, it is now time to ask whether the two planes – namely, the real and the irreal – are always so disparate and conflictual? Leaving the amazing capacity for artistic genius aside for now, here I want to focus more on mundane examples where the irreal seems to condition the real to a great extent – even to a limit where it seems to have already infiltrated within the very fabric of the real itself. This is the fourth element to Sartre's magic of the imaginary.

Central to this point is Sartre's main concluding argument in *The Imaginary* that the real presupposes the irreal just as much as vice versa. Of course consciousness, when engaged with the world and its projects, can seem to operate on a purely perceptual basis. Just because, in a game of tennis for instance (cf. IM: 182/349), there are always immediate moments to come (i.e. protentions in Husserl's terminology) as well as always moments that have just past (retentions), this in no way means these moments are absent in the sense that they are irreal and imaginary. Here Sartre takes Husserl's conception of time-consciousness very seriously; there is a perceptual anticipation (e.g. an immediate going to hit the ball) that is different from isolating the future for itself and thereby irrealizing it, just like there is an immediate just-past moment that is not itself a proper and explicit act of remembering. In this way distinct planes still remain: a perceptual one where consciousness is a constant surpassing, where 'all real existence is given with present, past and future structures' (IM: 182/350); and remembering and imaging ones where past, implicit and possible elements can here be posited explicitly for themselves.

This leads Sartre to a 'metaphysical question' (IM: 179/343) in the closing pages of his work; 'this fundamental absence, this essential nothingness of the imaged object, suffices to differentiate it from the objects of perception' (IM: 180/346). This means that, although nothingness might be required for perception to exist as such in the sense that consciousness here too creates a phenomenal gap for things to appear *to* this very consciousness, it is only in the imaging act where nothingness *itself* (an absent, inexistent or reality-neutral object) is explicitly and actively evoked through a presence – through an analogon. For Sartre, an 'essential condition for a consciousness to be able to *image*' (IM: 182/351) is that 'it must have the possibility of positing a thesis of irreality' (ibid.), which by necessity 'include[s] the entire category of negation, though in different degrees' (IM: 183/351). However, such total negation can only be enacted on something, namely, the real; 'To posit an image is to constitute an object in the margin of the totality of the real, it is therefore to hold the real at a distance, to be freed from it, in a word, to deny it' (IM: 183/352). This can also imply, importantly, that the real might only be recognizable *as* real because it stands in automatic contrast to something else that has negated it, namely, the irreal.

It is such closing reflections that necessitated a more concerted effort to fully explicate the 'problem of nothingness' three years later. Already, however, it is clear that the nothingness involved in perception allows the world to appear as such. Moreover, the (same?) one involved in imagining allows us to always be able to stand back from, neutralize and indeed irrealize this very same world. Indeed, the two actually go necessarily together for Sartre: consciousness's most basic activity is responsible for both our capacity to implicitly experience and explicitly evoke, absence; *both* the real and irreal arise out of such fundamental activity, where the irreal 'is always double nothingness: nothingness of itself in relation to the world, nothingness of the world in relation to it' (IM: 186/357).

A consequence of such argumentation is that it makes little sense to speak of the real all on its own, for both, the real and irreal alike, are defined in contradistinction to each other, and they both ultimately arise out of the spontaneity of fundamental consciousness. This is what Sartre means when he states the following: 'We may therefore conclude that imagination is not an empirical power added to consciousness, but is the whole of consciousness as it realizes its freedom; every concrete and real situation of consciousness in the world is pregnant with the imaginary in so far as it is always presented as a surpassing of the real' (IM: 186/358). Real and irreal necessarily go together for Sartre, then. However, his previously clear-cut distinction where either one perceives or imagines at any one moment now seems blurred. Indeed, in the remaining comments Sartre gets even closer to saying that the irreal is always already pseudo present in our everyday worldly engagements; it always already conditions them (cf. ibid. ff.). This might be the very reason why we can experience absence in the world, which then often leads to more explicit evocations in the imaginary. However, does it not also mean that absence has infiltrated the world to the extent that the imaginary is always already operative in it, whether implicitly or not?

In his introduction to the translation, Webber shows (2004: xxvi) with a simple example that the capacity to imagine means the real is often, if not always, conditioned by our imaginings; 'It is because I can imagine a tidy office that piles of paper and other objects can look to me like mess that needs to be cleared away.' And take, for example, a more complicated case: I had a St Christopher's medal, a rather cheap thing that nevertheless held great sentimental value for me. My Dad bought it for me one day on Grafton Street when I was younger and I cherished it for many a year. From time to time I discovered it again in a drawer, and it was only with a real wilful effort that I could perceive it as a mere thing. Of course on the front was an image of St Christopher, the patron saint of safe passage. However, for me the image of St Christopher was not of that much significance; the medal rather symbolized my father's care and affection, and it was something I was loath to lose.

Now, although it is clear that the affective memories and images it evoked were significant, did I really irrealize the thing? Is the medal some kind of powerful analogon? I think it could be claimed that although there clearly is a symbolic – and hence imaginary (cf. IM: 97/189) – power inhering in the thing, the intention seemed to be of the reverse current, meaning I did not irrealize it but, on the contrary, the affections and past memories seem to be in, or emanate from, the object itself. Now that it is lost, the memories and feelings as merely imaged – as not instantiated in that particular, unique medal – have to some extent remained. It is no longer, however, the same experience. Indeed with the medal I was not transported onto the imaginary plane but I rather remained with the present, significant item itself, which imbued, then and there, more than its mere material qualities in quite a powerful manner.

This would open the possibility of the irreal being realized, through me and the thing, just as much as it could be the real irrealized. It would, in fact, perhaps open the possibility for a kind of virtuality (i.e. irreal tending towards real) within Sartre.

Now of course Sartre could say that whenever I looked at this object I nevertheless still irrealized it, just merely in a manner where I magically projected sentimental qualities onto or into it, thereby lending it strong pseudo powers that caused the reverse intentionality. However, I still think the question remains whether certain irreal – or even ideal – qualities or values can actually inhere quite singularly in particular objects (cf. Breeur and Burms 2008: 139), a loss of which would then mean a loss of the real affective import of the experience. For if it were mere projection, how would the loss of the thing change the whole experience? In this case the analogon would change from the medal mixed with feelings and memories to only the latter two. However, even these latter seem more impoverished with the disappearance of the medal.

Here we are approaching the idea that many values and feelings can inhere, over time, almost essentially in specific physical things, although of course the link to us remains essential as well. In other words, we are approaching a scenario where the irreal may come to inhabit real physical things and give these latter a significance and value over and above their physical qualities. In this manner, although we have seen how the real is often irrealized, I am now pointing to the possibility that, indeed, the irreal can be realized in acts and things in their own turn. This is to say, it seems that the irreal can often infiltrate – at least implicitly – the real to such an extent that some values and feelings become so imbued that there does not seem to be much explicit irrealization taking place. In fact, certain irrealities and images might even become permanent symbolic significations of values, feelings and the like, which actually always automatically instantiate themselves, still through our intentions, into the very things themselves.

To sum up, although we are still necessarily involved, of course, such objects come to imbue values to the extent that they now have the power; *they* reach out to us with a pseudo or reverse intentionality that affects us with an influence seemingly all of their own. This actually is another strong idea of Sartrean magic, this time in the context of the imaginary, where images are automatically incanted into specific physical things. It might, however, blur the other Sartrean thesis of only perceiving or imagining at any given moment.

Perhaps, with regard to this latter issue, it is more about an immediate first-hand phenomenal experience on the one hand, of either perceiving or imagining at any given moment, over against more of a third-person discussion regarding a metaphysical backdrop of real and irreal in general, not least their complex and dynamic interrelation and interaction in our lives (cf. Heidegger [1931–2] 1997: §44). It is an ongoing issue that is only going to widen with growing virtual technologies. For us, now and in this context, a deepening of these issues can only proceed onto an ontological level, which is precisely where Sartre went, and where we shall follow.

# Magic Ontologized: *Being and Nothingness* (1943)

With the ego we saw magic entails a reversal and hypostatization of originally second-order, reflected-upon aspects of our psyche, which, through such reversal and hypostatization, come to be treated as supposedly first-order, deeply subjective elements, and are thereby instilled with a pseudo power and originality quite bewitching to ourselves and others. With emotion we saw magic entails a standard, pragmatic attitude being frustrated or breaking down, whereby psychophysiological incantations transform a world of pragmatism into a world of feeling, ranging from crushing despairs to jubilant celebrations. Finally, with the imaginary we have just seen magic there entails spontaneous creations of images that are also instilled with pseudo powers of their own, even to the extent that one can lose oneself in them quite completely, as well as the curious eventuality that irreality, in certain cases, seems to infiltrate the real. These are, in nutshells, the crucial findings so far regarding Sartre's highly technical and multifaceted concept of 'magic'.

A first reading of *Being and Nothingness* might suggest that such preoccupations have largely faded. Further, even if some explicit use of magic does remain, it remains so only in a marginal and 'pejorative' (cf. Richmond 2011: 158–9) form. I am going to demonstrate the opposite; it is precisely due to Sartre's preoccupation with humans as magical beings in the 1930s that necessitated him to form his ontological system of 1943. Under this understanding, magic may not be explicitly mentioned that much, and yet it still is highly significant. Indeed, we have just seen with the imaginary that although magic is explicitly mentioned rarely, when it is, Sartre says that the whole of this form of experience is magical.

I am not going to say that the whole of our being and nothingness is magical. I will however argue that there are very significant elements to the work – not least affectivity, value, possession and language – which all contribute towards various elements of magic being ontologized into a system. Actually, magic can be seen as in the very architectonics of our being and nothingness, which is precisely why it crops in so many – but by no means all – of our various forms of experience. Indeed, it is through such dynamic structures as value, possession and the like that Sartre's magic finds its roots all the way down in and between his basic ontological categories. In this manner, by focusing mainly on affectivity, value, possession and language, I will show that all either facilitate or play out various elements of magic between two or more of Sartre's three basic ontological categories of being-in-itself, being-for-itself and being-for-others.

*Being and Nothingness* is, for me, a work in phenomenology, quite obviously – but it is also one in transcendental philosophy. Actually, it is one of the last philosophical systems, which is to say it is a work where there is either a direct answer to any question one might have in its pages, or at least an indirect one. More pointedly, *Being and Nothingness* provides the ontological preconditions for understanding phenomenological life. Thus, if magical experiences are occurrent in our personal reflections (ego), emotions and acts of imagination – which I have shown they are – then their roots must find a place in this system.

One may say that Sartre's descriptions and conceptions of magic, until now, have largely utilized a cluster or family of concepts or dynamics, including hypostatization, reversal, non-pragmatism, incantation, non-rationality, non-determinism, projection, captivation, action at a distance and more. I find that such a cluster or family gets crystallized into a basic structural dynamic in 1943, which one then realizes was present all along. In short, magic is when objects of consciousness are given qualities and powers that those objects cannot originally contain in or by themselves. The original and quite automatic activity of consciousness imbues objects with non-naturalistic qualities and powers to the extent that such objects can come to hold significant sway over that which imbued them in the first place. It is thus a reversal, an inversion of order, where explaining through physical laws of nature is often not sufficient to capture the phenomenological reality and details of these experiences. Actually, it is precisely through magic when such laws are momentarily bent, suspended and flouted; we inject our experiences with personal reflections, emotions, images, values and the like to the extent that many of these experiences do not follow any strict logical or causal chain. Magic is hereby, at bottom, our inherent capacity to flout nature, both for good and ill – it is that gap opened up in nature by our spontaneous freedom, explicitly lived out through our feelings, values, (dis)possessions and expressions.

This is of course not to say that all human endeavour or action is magical. It is however to say that magic is always possible and takes up a significant portion of our lives, thanks to our very ontological makeup. In short, Sartre's magic makes up a part of our existential fibre.

In order to explicate and demonstrate these points, there are five sections to this chapter. First, I will explicate the most pertinent points regarding Sartre's three ontological categories. Of course many scholars (e.g. Catalano [1974] 1985; Daigle 2010; Gardner 2009) have already given quite detailed introductions and commentaries on many of these issues. It is still however necessary to present my own understanding because none have been guided by the concentrated thread of magical being. Then, second, I will turn to a significant and largely neglected theme I name the trinity of ontological affectivity, which I will specifically relate to what we have seen with Sartrean emotion. Third, I will focus on the phenomenon of value and valuing, and how this relates to our facticity and magic. Fourth, I will turn to possession, quality and the magic of being (dis)possessed by our own possessions and experiences of certain – primarily evaluative – qualities. Finally, I will look to language and the magic of the other, also relating these developments back to what we have already seen with others and interpersonal relations.

## Sartre's three ontological categories

I look at this white page on my table. I perceive its shape, its colour, its position. These different qualities have common characteristics: first they give themselves to my gaze as existences that I can only bear witness to ... and whose being does not depend on my caprice in any way. They are *for* me; they are not *me*. But nor are they *others*, that is to say, they do not depend on any spontaneity, neither mine nor that of another consciousness. They are at once present and inert. This inertia of sensible content, which has often been described, is existence *in itself*. It is useless to discuss whether this sheet of paper can be reduced to an ensemble of representations or whether it is, and must be, *more* than that. What is certain is that the white that I bear witness to ... cannot be produced by my spontaneity. This inert form, which is set back from all conscious spontaneities and which one must observe and learn little by little, is what is called a *thing*. In no case could my consciousness be a thing because its way of being in itself is precisely a *being for itself*. To exist is for it to have consciousness of its own existence. It appears as a pure spontaneity facing the world of things, which is pure inertia.

> We can then posit from the beginning two types of existence. Indeed, it is insofar
> as they are inert that things escape the domination of consciousness; it is their
> inertia that protects and preserves their autonomy. (Sartre [1936] 2012/2012:
> 3–4/1)

This quotation comes from the opening lines of Sartre's very first significant
philosophical work, and it shows that he was concerned, from the very
beginning, with three fundamentally different forms of existence, as well as with
their interrelation. In *Being and Nothingness*, some seven years later, this relation
is spelled out in full. I will go through each now in their own turn.

## Being-in-itself

The opening pages of *Being and Nothingness* seek to establish a primordial form
of being that is the absolute precondition for all beings as such. This being-in-
itself (*être-en-soi*) is proven by a phenomenological approach that, through a
study of the immediate nature of phenomena and consciousness alike, uncovers
an essentially transphenomenal being that simply is what it is.

'Transphenomenal' means categories of being that are the transcendental
conditions for phenomena as we experience them. Such categories are
transcendental because they are those ontological structures we must
theoretically presuppose and explicate in order to make sense of our everyday
experiential lives. With Sartre, they are discovered through phenomenological
pathways that necessarily lead back to these structures. Being-in-itself is the first
such category.

Sartre's point of departure is a study of the world of appearances. Here he claims
that any given appearance (e.g. a cup) 'refers to the total series of appearances'
(BN/EN: 1/11–12) – the table, the floor, etc. – and not to a kind of noumenal
hinterland to which we have no real access (cf. BN/EN: 1–2/11–12; also Barnes
1973: 49). For how can something essentially noumenal, which is to say non-
phenomenal, give rise to phenomena? By dispensing with such a thought Sartre
claims that any given appearance is a 'full positivity' (BN/EN: 2/12); 'the being
of an existent is exactly what it *appears*'[1] (ibid.). Sartre therefore adheres to a
main dictum of phenomenology, to go back to a description of phenomena as
they appear themselves. Here, a phenomenon is 'absolutely, for it reveals itself *as
it is*. The phenomenon can be studied and described as such, for it is *absolutely
indicative of itself*' (ibid.). In a word, the phenomenological method allows for a
collapse between existence and appearance; phenomena exist precisely because

they appear. This means any metaphysical queries as to how such things might ultimately be beyond our experience of them is bracketed, put out of play.

Under this conception, a phenomenon is, therefore, its own essence, and its existence is incorporated into this essence to the exact extent that it always refers, at any given moment, to its own (infinite) series of appearances (cf. BN/EN: 2–3/12–13). Essence therefore implies existence for the phenomenon, which moreover maintains a fundamental transcendent character in relation to me, in that, a cup, for instance, has its own reality as appearance, which at the same time necessarily means that 'it *is not* me'[2] (BN/EN: 3/13). In this manner, the phenomenon is always outside me and I forever transcend towards it (cf. ibid.).

Sartre goes even further; there is an intrinsic element of 'the infinite in the finite' (ibid.). This signifies that, although being and appearance have been equated, the appearance, as *Abschattung* ('aspect', 'adumbration'), means that the object is '*within*' (ibid.) the aspect as well as 'altogether *outside*' (ibid.) it. Precisely because of this the finite appearance is the object, and yet it also always implicitly refers to an infinite series of appearances which, qua infinite series, can never actually all appear at once. This is of course reminiscent of Husserl's initial paradox of external perception (cf. Husserl [1918–26] 1966: 3) – that we have a sense of the object as such even though, strictly and phenomenologically speaking, we only ever immediately perceive one aspect or side at a given moment.

With such a conception, has Sartre really escaped the noumenal? Is this infinite series of appearances not just another reformulation of the same old problem? Sartre is well aware of the danger and in fact proceeds to show how it may be avoided. Here, further phenomenological analysis will provide ontological foundations that are not noumenal but transphenomenal. This transphenomenality cannot come from the conscious subject, for this latter has a different, unique transphenomenality of its own (as we will see shortly in this and the next subsection). Moreover, consciousness even demands a transphenomenality in addition to its own, one that is not itself.

In order to reach this point, Sartre makes an important distinction between the being of the phenomenon and the phenomenon of being. This distinction ultimately yields an ontological proof that allows us some access to being-in-itself, as well as gives us a first glimpse into the ontological nature of consciousness.

A '*phenomenon of being*, an appearance of being' (BN/EN: 4/14), such as in cases of boredom, nausea and the like, is where being is 'unveiled to us'[3] (ibid.).

The being of the phenomenon, on the other hand, is where there exists a more primal category of being as such. This latter is a category, moreover, that constitutes the ontological conditions for our experiences of the former. Further, 'the being of the phenomenon cannot be reduced to the phenomenon of being'[4] (BN/EN: 6/16) precisely because in the phenomenon of being there exists an ontological call, a demand for being that cannot be explained by the phenomenon itself. Therefore, 'the phenomenon of being requires the transphenomenality of being' (ibid.) – that is, the being of the phenomenon (cf. BN/EN: 5–6/15–16). This transphenomenality of being is moreover defined not as some being 'hidden *behind* phenomena' (BN/EN: 6/16) nor as something distinct from the phenomena. No, it is characterized as a more general form of being that, 'although coextensive with the phenomenon' (ibid.), nevertheless 'must escape the phenomenal condition'[5] (ibid.).

Sartre goes on to demonstrate how this transphenomenality of being cannot stem from the conscious subject, which is (as will be seen) of an utterly different nature to the being of the phenomenon. Idealism is hereby avoided, because although the essence of an appearance is manifested in that very appearance of which we are conscious, the appearance at the same time refers to a transphenomenal form of being that is ultimately independent of consciousness.

With regard to consciousness more particularly, any perception of a thing introduces 'a center of opacity for consciousness' (BN/EN: 7/17). Here it is vital to understand that such opacity is *for* consciousness, not 'in' consciousness. This is because Sartre picks up another cornerstone of Husserlian phenomenology, namely, that of intentionality; 'All consciousness, as Husserl has shown, is consciousness *of* something' (ibid.). Such intentionality is constituted for Sartre as a pervasive, spontaneous and pre-reflective transcendence towards that which is not consciousness. Nothing strictly speaking is 'in' consciousness; all consciousness of objects – whether they be perceptual things, states or qualities of character, images and ideas and so on – are intentionalities for Sartre. This means there always exists a movement towards that which is not itself pure, spontaneous consciousness. This movement is, in fact, the basic and ceaseless activity of pre-reflective consciousness itself. Consciousness is pure spontaneity towards things it is not.

On top of this, there exists a simultaneous and implicit awareness (of) one's own consciousness. This is, in fact, an absolute condition for any form of intentionality (i.e. consciousness of X) whatsoever, for how can consciousness be consciousness of something if it is not at the same time implicitly self-aware (of) being this consciousness of something? The 'of' is bracketed by Sartre because although he wants to adhere to the rules of grammar, consciousness (of) self is not intentional, in that such awareness is absolutely immediate and immanent – completely implicit on the pre-reflective level. This ultimately means that no form of intentionality can exist without the pre-reflective aspect of the *cogito*, namely, consciousness (of) self (cf. BN/EN: 10–11/19–21) – which can be made an object and reflected upon in a second moment, as we have already seen with the ego.

In this manner, any transcendence towards that which is not consciousness necessarily implies a simultaneous and immediate consciousness (of) self. This latter is, in fact, *'the only mode of existence which is possible for a consciousness of something'* (BN/EN: 10/20). Consciousness *of* something and consciousness (of) self thus form two sides of one and the same intentional coin.

Such analyses have far-reaching consequences, of which I may, at this point, highlight a few relevant to my purposes. Firstly, the pre-reflective *cogito*, as consciousness (of) self, is the spontaneous transphenomenal nature of consciousness as such – and of consciousness *alone*. This has the additional consequence that the transphenomenality of consciousness is of an opposite nature to the transphenomenality of the being of phenomena. Although the phenomenon (appearance) as essence implied, or even demanded, a concomitant call to existence, consciousness's transphenomenal, spontaneous being simply is before any possible essences (e.g. a past) can be constituted (cf. BN/EN: 11/21). In short, with the phenomenon essence implies existence; with consciousness existence implies essence.

There is, as mentioned, another aspect of pre-reflective consciousness: consciousness of X. This aspect is spontaneously aware of things it is not, thereby strengthening the call for a form of being that consciousness does not found but on the contrary needs to exist in order for its own transcending nature to be comprehensible. This means that consciousness's first of two dual fundamental aspects, consciousness (of) self, cannot account for the transphenomenal being of the phenomenon, and consciousness's other fundamental aspect, consciousness of X, in fact demands an additional call for a transphenomenal being that is not itself consciousness. This being will therefore be the absolute precondition for consciousness, or any beings, as such.

To summarize, the automatic reference to an infinite series of appearances through any given finite appearance does not depend on my *bon plaisir* (EN: 13).

Moreover, there exists a non-conscious being that cannot be explained through an articulation of the basic nature of consciousness, because this latter, once studied in its basic transcending movement, in fact demands the former even further. In Sartre's words, 'The transphenomenal being of consciousness is not able to found the transphenomenal being of the phenomenon'[6] (BN/EN: 15–16/26). This discourse therefore culminates with an 'ontological proof' of the being of the phenomenon; because a study of the phenomenon demands a transphenomenal being and because consciousness cannot be 'constitutive of the being of its object' (BN/EN: 16/27) and moreover always transcends towards such being itself, then there is a demand for a universal '*plenitude of being*' (BN/EN: 17/27) that is the condition of possibility for both phenomena and consciousness alike. Such is the ontological proof, in which 'consciousness implies in its being a non-conscious and transphenomenal being' (BN/EN: 18/28).

Such a discovery immediately leads to another question, however: What, more precisely, is this primordial non-conscious being? In a word, it is in-itself.

'Being is. Being is in-itself. Being is what it is' (BN/EN: 22/33). Being is; it is beyond all talk of possibility and necessity – 'uncreated, without reason for being, without any connection with another being, being-in-itself is *de trop* for eternity' (ibid.). This is the fundamental contingency of being. It simply is, without rhyme or reason, and is thus the root of our basic facticity (as we shall see). Also being is in-itself; it is beyond assignations of activity and passivity, beyond affirmations and negations – it is again uncreated, in-itself (cf. BN/EN: 20–1/31–2). Finally being is what it is; '*massif*' (BN/EN: 22/32), 'full positivity' (BN/EN: 22/33), it is 'not subject to temporality' (ibid.), 'has nothing secret' (ibid.) and 'knows no otherness' (ibid.).

Strictly speaking one can say no more than these few points about being-in-itself, for it is beyond most, if not all, of our human assignations. Being-in-itself tests the very limits of our language (cf. BN/EN: 21/32). Being is, it is in-itself, it is what it is. These few truisms are formulated so simply because to add more descriptions would be to assign human characteristics to a type of being that is primordial, which is to say non-human. Being-in-itself thus forms the absolute and vital ontological basis of all reality, human or otherwise. Being-in-itself simply is.

This conclusion, Sartre warns us, is only 'provisional' (BN/EN: 19/30). The more complex dynamic between the simple in-itself and human reality will only start to come about through an investigation into Sartre's second ontological category, being-for-itself.

## Being-for-itself

This second category has already been provisionally analysed in the foregoing comments on consciousness. One must remember however – and this is Sartre's second warning – that although a rudimentary analysis of consciousness allowed us to discover being-in-itself, this by no means implies that consciousness is some kind of being-in-itself, or precedes it. Such a stance is a continual source of reproach for Sartre against other thinkers who have always taken consciousness as some kind of original substance. According to Sartre, all here make the same fundamental mistake of thinking consciousness in terms of an in-itself. Indeed, for Sartre consciousness ontologically defined must be a being-*for*-itself (*être-pour-soi*) that is necessarily dependent upon being-in-itself, but is also of a very different ontological nature.

It should already be clear that being-in-itself and -for-itself can be thought, at least to some extent, separately from each other, in the abstract. Such abstractions will not, however, suffice for discovering the true natures of, and dynamics between, the two categories. For this, one must turn to the concrete 'synthesis' (BN/EN: 27/37) of the Heideggerian-inspired rubric of 'man-in-the-world' (BN/EN: 28/38). The question there becomes how such a synthesis is constituted or indeed even possible, given the utterly simple nature of the in-itself.

A first important glance at this riddle is that human beings, as they exist in the world, have an essentially interrogative attitude towards being(s) in general (cf. BN/EN: 28/38). By the fact that humans have the capacity to question, one must assume 'a being who questions and a being which is questioned' (BN/EN: 28/38). Moreover, crucially for Sartre a question '*on principle*' (BN/EN: 29/39) allows for a negative answer. This is absolutely vital because, if being-in-itself is full positivity and is thus without the least shred of negation, how can the latter come into the world at all? One answer is that, by the very fact of the question, there exists a 'permanent possibility of non-being' (BN/EN: 29/39–40) in the world. Further, such a possibility is real in that 'to destroy the reality of the negation is to cause the reality of the reply to disappear' (BN/EN: 29/39).

Questioning and a general interrogative attitude (the French is *interroger*) therefore allow for some negation in the world. Now our question must be the following: Whence, more generally, does this stem? Firstly, because negation has to do with a questioner, and because it also implies non-being, 'it is evident that non-being always appears within the limits of a human expectation' (BN/EN: 31/41). This is not to say, however, that negation only surfaces on the level of human judgement. On the contrary, this latter form is only possible on the back of a more fundamental, 'pre-judicative' (ibid.) form. This is very akin to Husserl's passive and active syntheses, where every active judgement (e.g. negation) has its pre-logical roots in the immediately lived – which is to say passive – world of perception. An example (cf. Husserl [1918–26] 1966: 26–7) is turning a red ball around and realizing that it is neither red nor round on the other side, as was being passively expected.

Sartre gives a number of examples to highlight his own points. I will briefly highlight one: a notion such as destruction, Sartre argues, can only come into being through human reality. A storm, considered in itself, does not 'destroy' anything; 'There is *no less* after the storm than before. There is *something else*' (BN/EN: 32/42). A storm, from an in-itself perspective, does not, strictly speaking, destroy anything. There is simply a rearrangement of matter. In this manner, the fragility of being, which is experienced in many phenomena, only 'comes into being' (ibid.) through us. 'Thus it is man who renders cities destructible, precisely because he posits them as fragile and as precious and because he adopts a system of protective measures with regard to them' (BN/EN: 32–3/43). Humans are responsible for the delicacy and fragility of many things in the world; being-in-itself does not care in the slightest. It cannot possibly because it is not conscious.

In fact, such phenomena as interrogation and destruction fall into a category of pre-judicative *négatités*. This is a neologism by Sartre used to categorize those types of experiences that have elements of negation or nothingness in their very fibre (cf. BN/EN: 48/58–9). Such instances are crucial for Sartre because they necessarily point towards a pervasive and permanent possibility of non-being or nothingness. We are hereby again on the road to an ontology that goes beyond particular phenomena. Sartre corroborates this explicitly when he says there is 'a transphenomenality of non-being as of being' (BN/EN: 33/43). In short, negation at heart involves a 'double nihilation' (BN/EN: 34/44) in which 'a being (or a way of being) is posited, then thrown back to nothingness' (BN/EN: 35/45). 'Nihilation' (*néantisation*) is another word coined by Sartre. Quite similar to Heidegger's use of *nichten*, nihilation is neither simple negation nor complete annihilation – it is something subtler and in between. In short, it is consciousness's basic ability to automatically cover being with nothingness, which allows consciousness to be conscious in the first place. Moreover, dwelling on such activity leads one to a transphenomenal non-being that needs to be articulated in terms of an automatic and spontaneous production of nothingness.

What, more precisely, might Sartre mean by nothingness? Also, what is its relation, if any, to being-in-itself, which cannot contain the slightest element of it? Sartre ends his section with the rather elusive claim that because we see non-being as 'a perpetual presence in us and outside of us' (BN/EN: 35/46), nothingness must always 'haunt' being (cf. ibid.). Curious as this may seem, we may already see that non-being or nothingness are, under Sartre's conception, logically posterior to being-in-itself, for the simple reason that for non-being to be possible one must assume being in general in order to then negate it (cf. BN/EN: 38/49). This seems to be a general expansion of Bergson's (cf. [1907] 1912: 312) idea that, in order to have judicative negation some kind of judicative affirmation must be presupposed. Moreover, because such negation is only made possible through the interrogative capacity of a human subject, non-being 'supposes a [*sic*] irreducible mental act' (ibid.). This makes it absolutely inconceivable for nothingness to be some kind of 'original abyss from which being arose' (BN/EN: 39/50). On the contrary, being-in-itself is precisely in-itself because it has absolutely 'no need of nothingness in order to be conceived' (BN/EN: 40/50). In this manner, being-in-itself establishes the necessary 'ground' (ibid.) for the possibility of nothingness. Going against Hegel therefore – or at least Sartre's reading of Hegel (cf. BN/EN: 36–40/46–51) – Sartre claims that being and non-being are not logically contemporaneous, because nothingness in its most general sense is the total undifferentiated negation *of* total undifferentiated being-in-itself (cf. BN/EN: 38/49). A consequence of this is Sartre's realism; nothingness possesses a 'borrowed existence' (BN/EN: 40/51) because it depends upon a logically prior being-in-itself. It is in this manner that nothingness haunts being because 'it is from being that nothingness derives concretely its efficacy' (ibid.).

Although nothingness haunts being then, it is, nonetheless, never totally beyond a world. Indeed, even the world itself is due to a confluence of, as well as an – often opposing – interaction between the two forms of being. The world cannot be the in-itself alone, nor can it be mere consciousness. Webber ([2009] 2013: 32) summarizes this well: 'Sartre uses the term "world" to denote not the mind-independent stuff that our bodies and surroundings are made of, "being-in-itself", but that stuff as it is organized into the complex of instruments, obstacles, and positively and negatively valued objects and events that we encounter.' In fact, to extend upon Webber the world arises through the basic nihilative activity of consciousness. This is important because, in discussion with Heidegger (cf. BN/EN: 40–5/51–6), Sartre rejects the former's claim ([1929] 1978: 113) that 'das Nichts selbst nichtet'. This is because nothingness for Sartre has to be a nihilating process of or by (a) being and not a negation carried out by nothingness itself. This latter thought is absurd for Sartre because nothingness, precisely because it is nothingness, cannot do anything itself. On the contrary, it must be the ontological consequence of a process of being. Nihilation must hereby be carefully distinguished not only from simple negation but also from total annihilation; nihilation neither simply denies (negation in the normal sense) nor completely obliterates (annihilation). Nihilation negates in a more complicated sense by coating being or an element of being with a film of nothingness, while at the same time keeping an element of that which it nihilates at its very core. Nihilation is, therefore, always linked in some kind of relation to being-in-itself, or elements thereof, for the simple fact that being-in-itself is the logical precondition of all talk of negation and nothingness, the latter of which also both presuppose an inherent nihilating process of or by some being. Beyond this there seems to be no real – at least strictly causal – link between nihilation and being-in-itself, for this latter simply is and is in no need of any other being to exist (cf. BN/EN: 46/57).

With this in mind, nihilation, at this stage, seems to coat being with nothingness, while still retaining a borrowed element of such being. This latter aspect is what Sartre means when he says 'nothingness carries being in its heart' (BN/EN: 42/53), which is the other aspect to the previously explained fact that nothingness haunts being. Such carrying being in its heart ultimately leads to Sartre's conception of facticity, as we shall see presently in this subsection. For now, it is important to understand the double aspect to nihilation; it both coats being with a veil of nothingness (nothingness haunts being) and carries elements of this being in its heart (being within nothingness). Nothingness therefore surges up into being by this double nihilative process that may be already characterized as a strange kind of disparate synthesis in the sense that such a process directs itself towards (synthesizes), as well as simultaneously separates itself off from ('disparates'), the world it co-constitutes. Because such nihilative activity is conceived as an incessant process, moreover, it also means that there is a constant surpassing of the world in a kind of perpetual flight from *and* towards it – a flight which also always keeps some elements of being at its very core.

Such nihilation is, in fact, the necessary precondition for any form of negation (cf. BN/EN: 45–6/55–6). There remains a great problem however; although nothingness seems to have a close relationship to being in an extremely general sense, this latter, at least in the sense of being-in-itself, can in no way be the origin of the former. Being-in-itself simply is, and can never have the slightest atom of negation. So what precisely produces this nothingness?

Although we have seen that nothingness seems to be the outcome of the nihilating process by or of some being, 'we must first recognize that we cannot grant to nothingness the property of "nihilating itself"'[7] (BN/EN: 46/57); 'We must admit that only *being* can nihilate itself, because, however it comes about, in order to nihilate itself it must be'[8] (ibid.). There must therefore be a being other than being-in-itself through which nothingness comes into the world. Such a being must not, on the one hand, receive this nothingness from elsewhere because this would make it wholly passive – it would be contradictory because of the inherent activity involved in nihilation (cf. ibid.). On the other hand, such a being cannot '*produce* nothingness while remaining indifferent to that production'[9] (ibid.) because 'the being by which nothingness arrives in the world must nihilate nothingness in its being'[10] (BN/EN: 47/57). In more concise terms, nihilation must be a part of this being's ontological structure (cf. ibid.).

'Being can generate only being and if man is inclosed in this process of generation, only being will come out of him' (BN/EN: 48/59). However, human reality can question being, which also means it 'can modify' (ibid.) its '*relation*' (ibid.) to being without annihilating it. This is because 'for human reality to put a particular existent out of circuit is to put itself out of circuit in relation to that existent. In this case human reality escapes the existent, it is out of reach, the existent cannot act on human reality, for the latter has retired *beyond a nothingness*'[11] (ibid.). In this manner, human reality has the inherent capacity to 'secrete a nothingness which isolates it' (ibid.). In a word, freedom.

At this point it is only a word; Sartre goes on to comment that we can only, at this stage, give a provisory account of freedom (cf. BN/EN: 49/59–60). Let us nonetheless give this provisory account. Firstly, freedom is not 'a faculty of the human soul' (BN/EN: 49/59) to be described apart, nor is it a '*property* which belongs among others to the essence of the human being' (ibid.). On the contrary, freedom 'precedes' (ibid.) all talk of essences and in fact makes the latter possible as such. Freedom, as manifested in questioning and the like, is moreover the 'requisite condition for the nihilation of nothingness' (ibid.) in general, and so, ultimately, it is 'impossible to distinguish' (BN/EN: 49/60) freedom from the '*being* of "human reality"' (ibid.). Human reality *is* freedom therefore. As an original ontological upsurge consciousness possesses a double nihilative structure that constitutes both a world and a self by never fully coinciding with either. Coincidence, for Sartre, means is what it is – i.e. in-itself – like a stone is a stone. Consciousness, as a free double nihilation, can never be what it is because through coating being with a fundamental nothingness consciousness is separated off both from the world it co-constitutes and from its own self, by precisely nothing. Nihilation is thus the essential structure of freedom, or original consciousness; it is responsible for the incessant activity, as well as the absolutely spontaneous character of pre-reflective consciousness. Indeed, the curious thing with Sartre's conception of freedom – and I think this has often been misunderstood – is that it is a ceaseless nihilative process on a very basic, pre-reflective level. This means that there is often a fatalistic tone to it in that it is impossible not to be one's freedom – it is impossible, as a human consciousness, not to be ceaseless spontaneity and transcendence. This is what Sartre will later call 'the facticity of freedom', the fact that we, whether we like it or not, cannot not be free.

Moreover, such basic freedom is an automatic process that runs much deeper than any reflective freedom of the will. As previously mentioned, Sartre views the latter as a bastardized version of this more spontaneous and primordial form. Thus consciousness, ontologically defined – that is, as a being-for-itself – is nothing other than a ceaseless nihilative process that always already transcends us towards a world and objects that it itself is not. This, furthermore, often occurs quite outside of one's wilful, reflective control. In a word, being-for-itself is consciousness ontologically defined as a ceaseless, utterly spontaneous and free nihilative transcending activity towards beings and objects it is not.

Sartre further develops his ontological conception of consciousness through an analysis of bad faith. Bad faith is of vital importance for Sartre for one chief reason; 'If bad faith is to be possible, we should be able within the same consciousness to meet with the unity of being and non-being' (BN/EN: 69/80). In other words, if consciousness is capable of bad faith, we may be led through such a phenomenon to what precisely consciousness is in its most basic ontological structure (cf. ibid.).

Sartre's chapter on bad faith starts by comparing it with lying. For Sartre, negation is everywhere in relation to consciousness. Just as seeing a cup automatically implies I am not this object; just as the question posits something which must by necessity be capable of being denied; and just as destruction posits a thing as fragile and therefore destructible, the liar 'is in complete possession of the truth which he is hiding' (BN/EN: 71/82). Sartre grants that this is 'the ideal lie' (BN/EN: 71/83). Nevertheless, lying in general must know something of the truth; to lie about something one does not know is not lying but ignorance or experimentation (cf. BN/EN: 71/82; for the latter cf. Visker 1999: 263).

With regard to bad faith, Sartre initially states that it is a 'lie to oneself' (ibid.). Here the crucial difference is, whereas the lie is directed outwards, bad faith is a lie to oneself that necessarily assumes 'the unity of a *single* consciousness' (BN/EN: 72/83).

In order to explain bad faith correctly, one must introduce the vital notion of facticity. Simply put, one's facticity is all the facts of one's life and existence that one must relate to *through* one's freedom. For example, it may be a fact that I am quite short. However, it is an issue of facticity when considering how I relate to my shortness at any given moment.

More generally, as a free original upsurge that constitutes both a (past) self and a world, consciousness has two primary poles integral to its structure: freedom and facticity. These two poles are always inextricably connected. However, if one is fled through an extreme preference for the other, the result is bad faith. Bad faith is thus when one tries to live either one's free transcendence as an absolute fact or one's facticity as an absolutely free transcendence (cf. BN/EN: 79/91). Going further with facticity, it always involves contingency, which is the state that our being simply is, without any real (rational) rhyme or reason, though we may try to rationalize it through reflection. In point of fact our facticity as contingency is nothing other than our inextricable relation to the absolutely brute fact of being-in-itself, though crucially in a nihilated – that is, free – form (cf. BN/EN: 105–6/117–18). Being-in-itself is contingent but cannot feel it; human reality, due to its essential nihilative link to being-in-itself, is also contingent, and it can most certainly feel it.

That there are facts about ourselves and the world is necessary so long as we exist. An important existential addition is, however, that the particular details are always tainted with a feeling of arbitrariness. This is due, as said, to our facticity as contingency, as well as to that second fundamental aspect of our being, namely, our transcendence. This is our freedom, which recognizes, through an immediate sense of possibility (cf. BN/EN: 119–26/132–9) and our capacity to imagine, that the given state of affairs could always be otherwise. In short, by ceaselessly surging up into the world as a freedom that forever surpasses itself, our transcendence both constitutes the world as a particular state of affairs that relates to me (facticity) – and, at the same time, our freedom has always already surpassed this particular state of affairs in a perpetual nihilative movement.

Freedom and facticity therefore go necessarily together; they are of a piece, in tandem.

Bad faith entails the failure to recognize the dynamic between these two fundamental aspects of our being. By trying to cling wholly to either side, one always at the same time tries, always futilely, to deny the other, and actually one becomes aware of such a failure in the very attempt of denial.

The waiter is the famous example of one who tries to cling to his facticity without acknowledging his freedom – or, more precisely, he tries to live his freedom as absolute fact, for he thinks he is a waiter and nothing else. He therefore tries to live his job – and by corollary his whole existence – in an 'I am what I am' manner.

The woman on the date is one of Sartre's main examples of one who tries to cling to pure transcendence by trying to ignore a factual state of affairs. The man on the date, by taking her hand, makes an obvious action with a clear intention, Sartre says. The woman recognizes this, leaves her hand in his, but then 'draws her companion up to the most lofty regions of sentimental speculation' (BN/EN: 79/90). She is in bad faith because she lives her facticity – that is, an object of sexual desire – through transcendent speeches about how romantic everything is. The whole world becomes romance, beauty, exquisiteness, and not simple desire (cf. BN/EN: 78-9/89-91). Bad faith thus has a curious character such that either facticity is affirmed as '*being* transcendence' (BN/EN: 79/91) or transcendence is affirmed as '*being* facticity, in such a way that at the instant when a person apprehends the one, he can find himself abruptly faced with the other' (ibid.).

Ultimately these analyses show that the being that we are is not an in-itself, but on the contrary one that is inherently non-coincidal. In fact, there must be such an ontological non-coincidence for consciousness to exist as such. In short, consciousness *is* non-coincidence by definition. Through bad faith, consciousness seeks to eradicate this; it seeks to be certain aspects of what it is in an absolute manner. Such projects always fail because consciousness, being perpetual nihilation, can never coincide absolutely with itself; it can never eradicate the non-coincidence in the manner of pure fact or pure transcendence, even though it is wont to try.

The fact that consciousness is a free and spontaneous flight away from itself towards a world that it is not shows us there is 'an inner disintegration in the heart of being' (BN/EN: 93/105). This is what consciousness is, and bad faith reveals this most explicitly. Consciousness therefore has both a spontaneous freedom and a factual relationship to the world, one's own embodiment and past. These two fundamental aspects, freedom and facticity, always go necessarily together therefore, for the act of nihilation, which can only occur concretely and in an embodied manner, brings about a world as well as consciousness's concomitant flight from and towards it. This double movement hereby allows consciousness to relate to things it is not (i.e. facticity), which simultaneously allows it to not be what it is (i.e. spontaneity).

These analyses also show that consciousness is inherently related to being-in-itself through this process of nihilation. This means although consciousness is incessantly haunted by the in-itself, it can never actually be it, at least not before one's death.

All roads have been leading here; we have increasingly discovered a form of being that slides nothingness into the world and itself. Such a double nihilation is our freedom, which constitutes a world and a self precisely by incessantly separating itself off from them, and in which nothing can bring about a cohesive permanence. Considering this, one comes to the ultimate ontological formulation of human consciousness as being-for-itself: 'The being which is what it is not and is not what it is' (BN/EN: 119/158). Being-for-itself is an essentially double nihilative structure that both perpetually constitutes and transcends from and towards the world – and precisely through such transcendence it is capable of separating from itself too. Bad faith shows the two extreme cases of this dynamic, where one wishes to either be utterly absorbed in facticity, or try to escape it completely. However, because such attempts are just that, we come to see that being-for-itself is diametrically opposed in nature to that which it nihilates. In short, it can never be what it is, either as pure facticity or as pure freedom. Being-for-itself, so long as it is, must be both; it must be what it is not (facticity and passivity) *and* not be what it is (freedom and activity).

This completes the analysis of the main points in Sartre's second ontological category. There remains one, being-for-others. This comes later in the work and relies on the two preceding.

## Being-for-others

Sartre is concerned with the issue of being-for-others (*être-pour-autrui*), quite logically, for the whole third part (BN/EN: 243–452/257–471) of the work. This is broken up, in its own turn, into three main chapters: 'The Existence of Others' (BN/EN: 243–326/259–341), 'The Body' (BN/EN: 327–82/342–400) and 'Concrete Relations with Others' (BN/EN: 383–452/401–71). The second chapter on the body articulates three 'ontological dimensions' (cf., for instance, BN/EN: 375/392). The first dimension (BN/EN: 330–62/345–78) is how we experience our lived bodies in an immediate, first-hand manner. The second (BN/EN: 362–74/379–91) is how other people's bodies appear to me, and mine to them, in an everyday and interpersonal – as well as 'special' (cf. Van der Wielen 2014) – manner. The third (cf. BN/EN: 375–82/392–400) is when I am actually made an object for another subject. Therefore, if the first dimension is how consciousness spontaneously acts as always already embodied, and if the second is our everyday engagements, relations and communications with others as special embodied psychical objects, then the third, deepest dimension – *being a mere object for another subject* – is where the veritable ontology of our being-for-others lies.

The principle that holds this ontological category together is the look (*le regard*). In the first bodily dimension I look out as a subject without any real or immediate consideration for others as other subjects. On the second level there is interpersonality and engagement, but this is only possible because of a more basic, ontological principle of intersubjectivity (cf. O'Shiel 2015a). This latter is only possible, in its own turn, because of the look in Sartre's technical sense. Indeed, if every category of being has its main principle or ontological characteristic – being-in-itself contingency and being-for-itself freedom – then the look and the ontological 'shame' it gives rise to is the main one for being-for-others.

I believe that once the look is understood, Sartre's main notion of being-for-others can be grasped, at least in its essentials. The look is Sartre's solution to the 'the reef of solipsism' (BN/EN: 247/261); there must be an internal, ontological negation within my being that makes me immediately and patently aware of the existence of others (cf. BN/EN: 256, 324/270, 340). 'Negation' here means there is an other; there is someone who is not me. 'Internal' means this immediately affects me in my ontological fibre. Indeed, one can say experiencing the other through the look transfigures my being from a mere for-itself to a for-itself-for-others.

The look in its most basic sense is a fundamental principle or process, 'an irreducible fact' (BN/EN: 281/296) that can be 'deduced neither from the essence of the other-as-object, nor from my being-as-subject'[12] (ibid.). To get its essence, we can look at Sartre's well-known example of the man at the keyhole. He is pre-reflectively glued to his activity. He is a *Leib* engaged in something in the world, in situation (cf. BN/EN: 283/299). In Sartre's words he is 'the for-itself in its isolation' (BN/EN: 284/306) where 'irreflective consciousness cannot be inhabited by a me'[13] (ibid.). To consider oneself as a 'me' one normally does so on the level of reflective consciousness, namely, as an ego (cf. BN/EN: 283/299–300). However, in this phenomenon there is something that allows the 'me' 'to haunt irreflective consciousness'[14] (ibid.). This is very significant because a 'me' cannot arise without being constituted in contradistinction to another subject. Thus there is already a preliminary conclusion that 'the other is the indispensable mediator between me and myself'[15] (BN/EN: 246/260).

How, though, is it possible that the other can be present on this pre-reflective level? In a word, through the look. The look is that basic principle which haunts being-for-itself and makes it realize that it is not alone in the world; there are other for-themselves that, through the look, make one deeply aware of an ontological aspect of one's being that one cannot ever fully grasp oneself, namely, my being as an object, an in-itself, *for* another subject. This is the internal, ontological negation Sartre was looking for; through the look I am affected in my very being by the presence of another subject. So much so, in fact, that my being as a simple for-itself is transfigured into a for-itself-for-others.

Of course the look can be actual, physical looks that act as concrete occasions for the principle. For instance, in this example a person coming up the stairs and seeing me spying. However, this need not be the case. Indeed, the look may be described as metaphysical because, in its generality, it does not need the actual physical presence of an individual, let alone physical eyes looking. In fact, Sartre explicitly states that physical eyes disappear when the look is in full force; 'If I apprehend the look, I cease to perceive the eyes' (BN/EN: 282/297). In this manner, the look operates as a pervasive force that there are other subjects who can view and transfigure my being in a manner that is beyond my control. In fact, the look and all the other consciousnesses it implies are the very things that give me my objectivity. The for-itself, as a pure nihilating subject, and even as embodied, could never have given such a deep sense of objectivity to itself.

Concretely, the look can be occasioned by almost anything, from the rustling of a bush, to a laugh, to even, in this day and age, the sound of a text message. The same is the case with the ontological recognition of the look, shame. Of course shame can have the normal, everyday meaning of feeling embarrassed that someone caught me spying. Additionally though, shame has deeper ontological roots and in its essence 'refers to my loss of transcendence' (Visker 1999: 335–6). In fact, and as just mentioned, shame in its most general sense is nothing other than the ontological recognition of the look itself; through shame one is inherently aware, in one's very being, that there is always a 'permanent possibility' (BN/EN: 281/297) of being looked at, of being turned into an object. This is thus another technical term; as Sartre puts it, there is 'an internal hemorrhage' (ibid.) that makes me an object for another subject. The look and its necessary consequence of shame is therefore a petrification or alienation of my conscious being; it makes me an ontological slave to another being's transcendence, even if only momentarily (cf. BN/EN: 287, 291–2/302, 306–7).

Being made an object means one's transcendence is transcended by the transcendence of another subject (cf. BN/EN: 287/302). This implies that the looker still knows the subjectivity (i.e. transcendence) of the person but has – often quite unintentionally – simply transcended it and thereby turns the person into an object. In this manner, by being made an object for another I can never fully grasp what I am for them, as they precisely see me. The other, through the look, is responsible for an objective aspect of my being that I do not constitute myself, and that I cannot grasp myself as the other does. Shame is therefore at the bottom of the ontological awareness of an 'omnipresent and inapprehensible transcendence' (BN/EN: 294/309) of a 'pure subject' (BN/EN: 294/310) that destroys 'all objectivity for me' (BN/EN: 293/308) precisely by making me an object.

A further important consequence is because at the limit the look is a metaphysical principle that goes 'beyond the world' (BN/EN: 294/309), it also goes a long way in formatting this world for us in a way that is beyond our control. Indeed, the world as peopled is just so many instantiations of this principle of the other as 'infinite freedom' (BN/EN: 294/310). Even on a more mundane level the look highlights the fact that we are now well beyond a simple, innocent and single *Leib*. The look makes it possible on an everyday and interpersonal level that 'instead of a grouping toward me of the objects, there is now an orientation which flees from me' (BN/EN: 254/300). Our being for and with others is instantiated in the world through a principle that makes us aware of ourselves as objects for a whole host of other subjects. We are no longer – and never really were – at the centre of everything (cf. also: Zahavi 2014).

One can look back of course. Sartre calls this, again technically, 'arrogance' (BN/EN: 314/330). This means, at bottom, to reaffirm one's transcendence by transcending the look of the other in its own turn, thereby recuperating one's subjectivity and simultaneously reducing the other to an object of my look. This is the grand 'circle' (BN/EN: 386/404) of Sartre's intersubjective relations, where a kind of ontological 'seesaw' (Visker 1999: 334) occurs, ceaselessly oscillating between looking and being looked at.

Such is the basic ontology of our being-for-others. It is important to note, however, that these were ontological considerations. Indeed, Sartre was not interested in everyday interpersonal and anthropological issues in these pages (cf. BN/EN: 306/322; also Van der Wielen 2014: 63). Furthermore, even his 'concrete cases' (BN/EN: 383–452/401–71) could be viewed as extreme instances used to highlight the basic ontological seesaw. Indeed, I think this has often been misunderstood to imply that *all* relations must take place on the extremes of the seesaw. Hell is the other and such. However, there is of course a whole world of possibility in between (cf. also: O'Shiel 2015a), possibilities that are nonetheless only possible because of this basic ontological dynamic which constitutes our existence for others without, however, being necessarily felt at every moment. In short, there are everyday good looks where one does not feel objectified; these more middle-of-the-road possibilities occur more often for most of us in daily life than the ontological extremes underneath.

This is why *Being and Nothingness* is veritably a work in phenomenological ontology – or equally a piece of transcendental philosophy; it provides the basic conditions of possibility for the most basic forms of being, reached through phenomena without however detailing all these latter. I even contend that the extremes of the look are not usually felt as often as a lot of readings of Sartre seem to suggest (e.g. Jackson 2013). The look does indeed make the extremes of our existence for others possible as such, and they can of course be quite strong and even chronic in certain instances, ranging from complete objectification to complete subjectification. This does not, however, make all everyday interpersonal relations hell within Sartre's system (again cf. O'Shiel 2015a).

## Sartre's trinity of ontological affectivity: Nausea, anguish and shame

There has been no mention of magic, yet. This will remain the case for a little while longer. Indeed, now that the basic ontological categories of being have been delineated, I need to articulate largely overlooked dynamics that occur in and between them. Here I am talking about what I term Sartre's trinity of ontological affectivity, namely, how the for-itself relates to being-in-itself originally through nausea, to itself originally through anguish, and to the other originally through shame. Such an emphasis on this trinity will show how being-for-itself is ontologically connected to other forms of being and itself in a primarily affective manner, and it will also provide the roots that allow for explosions of magic in and between the categories.

Unlike Sartre's emotion, which has been significantly analysed by various scholars (see, for instance, Fell [1965] 1966; Hartmann 2016; Mazis [1983] 1997; O'Shiel [2016] 2017), Sartrean affectivity is rarely mentioned, and if so largely in passing (for instance, Barnes [1984] 1997: 135). Hopkins (2011) has a piece on how we can learn things about ourselves from our imaginations and the supposed affective states they give rise to. Such a focus on learning is not the main one under consideration here, however; here I rather wish to try and grasp a more basic, pre-reflective dynamic of affectivity, and how it in fact grounds Sartrean emotion and its magic, as well as any possible reflections thereupon.

This task is tricky because Sartre was working on a large work, provisionally entitled *La Psyché*, only for it to be set aside and subsequently lost. This is also why the *Sketch* is merely a sketch. I believe, however, that there are signs in the early, extant texts. I also believe that there are crucial developments, albeit couched in different terms, in *Being and Nothingness*. Such an approach would allow us to speculatively reconstruct a fuller theory of affectivity and emotion than each individual work provides on its own.

Affectivity and emotion occur on the pre-reflective level in Sartre's philosophy. As we have already seen, on the reflective, egoic level, affectivity and emotions are reflected upon as impure and transcendent states, actions or qualities. Here Sartre's vocabulary is that of *sentiments*, which is usually translated as feeling. Although I have used feeling very generally up till now, as is permissible in English, in this context *les sentiments* are more the reflected-upon, transcendent sedimentations that take explicit forms like 'I am sad' (a state), 'I was crying' (an action) and a sad person (a quality) over against more immanent, pre-reflective experiences. As already hinted, I believe Hopkins is already on such a reflective level when speaking of the affective states one can reflect upon during or after certain images (e.g. 'That film made me sad.').

The pre-reflective level precedes this, and is finally getting some recognition in contemporary philosophy of mind (cf. Miguens, Preyer and Morando (eds) 2016). On this level, *sentiment* is also used non-technically – which is to say loosely on the pre-reflective level – in the sense of feelings in general, like, for instance, in an immediate feeling (of) sadness. Nevertheless, Sartre's more technical language on this level is that of affectivity and emotion, which I believe form the two conceptual poles of one and the same dynamic on this plane.

Affectivity (*affectivité*) is the most original, most basic category of feeling in Sartre's *Sketch for a Theory of the Emotions*. Here, however, it also takes a back seat because Sartre's focus is, as we have seen, on more pointed and explicit emotional episodes such as anger, fear, joy and the like. Nevertheless, even in this very early work the crucial supporting and substantive role of affectivity is already acknowledged. Indeed, at one point, when discussing how the *Sketch* is only an attempt at a phenomenological psychology and not yet a full-blown phenomenology, this is, Sartre says, because the latter would have to give a full account of affectivity as 'an existential mode of ... human reality' (STE/ETE: 12/26–7). I find this crucial because it is already implied that consciousness has a basic, existential affective structure out of which more pointed and explicit emotional episodes can then arise.

This point may be corroborated further; the term 'affective' (*affectif/affective*) is also used in the *Sketch* (for instance, STE/ETE: 44, 51, 54/86–7, 98, 105) even though it is not the work's focus. Here, again, affectivity is always already presupposed for emotion to occur at all. This is confirmed in the brief conclusion, where Sartre states that one of the work's very limitations is that it 'postulates an antecedent description of affectivity so far as the latter constitutes the being of ... human-reality' (STE/ETE: 63/123). I believe this is very significant because it indicates precursory considerations for a more general ontologization that then took place in *Being and Nothingness*. Indeed, I see this is a common theme in Sartre's early work; a supposedly local study (ego, emotion, imagination) presupposes more general ontological issues that are more often than not mentioned at the beginning and the end of the very same works. For instance, the beginning and end of *The Transcendence of the Ego* focus on the nature of an egoless transcendental field of pre-reflective consciousness; and a part of the conclusion to *The Imaginary* is well known for its almost metaphysical discussion of the interrelation and mutual dependence between reality and irreality. Such discussions all culminate with *Being and Nothingness*.

Affectivity plays a more obvious, but confusing, role in *The Imaginary*. Here, Sartre does not use the term 'emotion' at all and seems to replace it with a discourse on a more general affectivity. He goes as far to make a principle that 'all perception is accompanied by an affective reaction' (IM: 28/62) even to the extent 'each affective quality is so deeply incorporated in the object that it is impossible to distinguish between what is felt and what is perceived' (IM: 139/268). It seems, then, that general feeling and perception always go together in the constitution and recognition of various perceptual qualities, and that Sartre terms the basic thing responsible for this 'affectivity'.

As we have also seen, affectivity also plays a crucial role for imaging acts. Indeed, affectivity here is one of *the* crucial psychophysiological materials that constitute the analogon and thereby allows us to evoke something absent (e.g. sadness partially constituting an image of home through homesickness). This ultimately means that a general, existential and structuring affectivity seems to lie at the base of both our perceptual and imaging experiences.

There is however an ambiguity in this text, in the section dedicated particularly to affectivity (IM: 68–73/135–45). Here Sartre speaks mostly of feeling (*sentiment* again), and it is very close to his previous account of emotion, even though he does not use this latter term here. Maybe, then, affectivity and emotion – and even feeling – are just synonyms for Sartre, at least in this work, in that he has replaced one term with another?

I think a more nuanced interpretation is required, which makes affectivity and emotion two poles in the same dynamic. Here emotion occurs precisely when affectivity crystallizes into an experience (1) which gives the object an evaluative quality (e.g. disgusting) that does not originally and essentially belong to it, as well as (2) thereby making this object an intense focal point with this standout quality (or set of qualities). Hereby the emotion would result from a general build-up – and sometimes a break or culmination – of one's affective engagement with the world, its objects and people. In other words, affectivity has already – and often lightly – charged objects with so many variable affective qualities (useful, desirable, pretty and so on), and then explicit, pointed emotion results when these qualities intensify into one object (or group of objects) to the point where an instrumental engagement with the world is transformed into a captivating, non-instrumental one, as has already been seen.

In this way, affectivity is the missing piece of the puzzle; the world is always already affective and therefore already has the capacity to bewitch us to varying degrees. Nonetheless, emotion as a proper magical transformation only arises when a quality takes on so much power that it overtakes any more balanced appraisal of various objects, whereby one or a small number of evaluative qualities consume one's whole current experience through that very emotion. In short, there is a general affectivity that often crescendoes and thereby becomes a concentrated emotion (cf. O'Shiel [2016] 2017). Moreover, whether this is triggered from within or without is rather beside the point, precisely because both consciousness and world are always already engaged in this more general affective dynamic.

I think this mechanism works for perception and imagination alike, that is, whether the object is real (perceived) or irreal (imagined). With perception, I think it is quite clear that general affective feelings of tiredness and stress can, for example, crescendo and result in a more pointed anger at someone or something delaying your route home, in traffic, for instance. With imagination, affectivity is one of the main analogical materials for our imaginary creations, to which we can then emotively respond (e.g. 'That film made me sad.'), as well as subsequently reflect upon and thereby learn something from, as Hopkins maintains. In short, affectivity, which has a decidedly psychophysiological character, is the general felt tenor out of which more pointed emotive experiences arise and subside back into.

It is true that some affective modes already act a bit like emotions in the sense of a strong feeling (e.g. being in a rotten mood) – and yet here the idea would still be that even stronger emotions (e.g. rage) result precisely from such strong moods. This means there is a correlation of greater intensity between the mood one is in and the possible (strengths of) emotions that can arise therefrom (cf. again, O'Shiel [2016] 2017). In short, emotions, both in perception and imagination, are here characterized as intensifications and crystallizations of a more general background of affectivity (cf. also, Ratcliffe 2008).

Cabestan (2004b: 82–7) echoes some of these main points when he finds a distinction between 'original' and 'constituted' affectivity in Sartre. The latter are more straightforward cases of Sartrean emotion for Cabestan, worldly transformations where an emotive quality gains power and inheres in an object to the point of captivation and reversal (cf. id.: 86). The former, original affectivity is characterized as a much more basic, passive and diffuse type of feeling. Indeed, it is equated with the immediate lived reality of the *Leib* and all of our 'coenaesthetic' sensations (cf. id.: 85), as well as with the more diffuse and background felt orientations of our moods that do not usually have specific objects or powerful emotive qualities (cf. ibid.; also Bollnow [1941] 2009: 21; Heidegger [1927] 2006: §29; Ratcliffe 2008). In this manner, Cabestan also shows there is a basic affectivity in Sartre which facilitates more pronounced and explicit emotional episodes, without however being the episodes themselves.

Actually, Cabestan includes 'the fundamental dispositions of nausea, anxiety, boredom, and shame' (2004a: 85) as belonging to original affectivity. Here, I believe three of them (not boredom) are actually three types of ontological affectivity that can be found through an attentive reading of *Being and Nothingness*. For indeed, although Sartre is somewhat loose at times with what he terms 'feeling', 'emotion', 'affectivity' and 'affective' in his early works, and although a supposedly crucial one is missing from our records (*Le Psyché*), an argument for three ontological forms of affectivity, plus a focus on value, possession, quality and language in *Being and Nothingness* will give sufficient evidence to the plausibility of this dynamic. In fact, I would go as far to say that such basic affectivity is the most primordial bond between being-for-itself with itself (anguish), with the in-itself (nausea) and with others (shame).

As I have already mentioned, there are only small signs (e.g. Cabestan 2004b; Fell [1965] 1966; Webber [2009] 2013) for the significance of three types of ontological affectivity – nausea, anguish and shame – with each one corresponding to a category of being in *Being and Nothingness*. Actually, here I will show that these three privileged forms of affectivity are on the ontological, transcendental level, which then make all more empirical affectivities and emotions – as well as their magic – possible as such.

I think now it is fair to say that *Being and Nothingness* inherits and employs the distinction between affectivity and emotion that was outlined in the earlier works, and which was most probably delved into greater detail in the lost work on psychology. With this work most likely forever gone, I focus on the ontological forms, which I can now go through one by one.

Firstly, 'anguish' (*angoisse*) is Sartre's term for our immediate recognition of our freedom (see also, Fell [1965] 1966: 61–2; Webber [2009] 2013: 74–87). Indeed, anguish is an essential characteristic of being-for-itself (i.e. consciousness). It is characterized as a certain 'vertigo' whereby 'I am in anguish because my conducts are only *possible*'[16] (BN/EN: 55/66). This example is in relation to future projects. In more general terms, human beings are necessarily an anguished freedom precisely because this freedom, which we have seen is the very spontaneous fibre of our conscious being, renders a world in which any resolution we may take, any decision or action, state of mind or opinion, towards past, present or future, is only supported by ourselves in that fleeting, already-gone moment, and there is absolutely nothing – precisely nothing – preventing it from being otherwise. Sartre's examples of someone walking near a precipice (BN/EN: 54–6/65–7) and of a gambler breaking his resolution not to gamble (BN/EN: 56–7/67–8) do indeed show that this basic affective recognition of our freedom possibilizes so many more specific emotions – fear and horror in front of the precipice, regret and giddiness at the gambling table – because there is nothing but oneself preventing one from falling off the edge, both literally and metaphorically. Indeed, whether this falling is instantiated in a cliff or a roulette table, it is in both cases a more specific concretization of a more general, ontological anguish that we are.

Anguish is thus just as much an integral part of our human existence as is our freedom. In fact, this once-again technical notion is nothing other than the immediate and pure 'reflective apprehension of freedom by itself' (BN/EN: 63/74). In this manner, our whole existence is a perpetual battle with anguish, for even the morning ring of the alarm clock, something so apparently trivial and mundane, instantly shows us the utterly anguished nature of our being; it is 'me and me alone'[17] (BN/EN: 62/73) that confers a demand on the alarm clock in that there is precisely nothing preventing me from smashing it against the wall and returning to sleep (cf. BN/EN: 61–2/72–3).

The scenario is the same across the board, for even the values we hold most dear are nothing but so many more alarm clocks; 'My freedom is the unique foundation of values and … *nothing*, absolutely nothing, justifies me in adopting … this or that particular scale of values' (BN/EN: 62/73). Nevertheless, although we are hereby 'without justification' (BN/EN: 63/74), we are also absolutely 'without excuse' (ibid.); although we may be or choose anything, we still must be and choose something, and be responsible for such choice. The anguishing thing about our freedom is that we are at one and the same time unjustified in selecting such and such, as well as totally responsible. Thus, one creates one's essences by figuring out how to cope with such anguishing affectivity at the root of our relation to self, and one thereby assumes one's responsibility for one's choices and values, although it is also common to try and escape this through bad faith.

Such is the ontological instantiation of anguish, how being-for-itself recognizes itself. Second, regarding the for-itself's primordial relation to being-in-itself, this is one of nausea (*nausée*). Nausea is our immediate and basic affective recognition of the utter contingency of the in-itself, that is, of nature stripped of any real significance, human or otherwise. Such basic ontological recognition makes a whole host of more specific, emotive nauseas and disgusts possible as such – precisely through an intensification of this more general affective background.

This dynamic is corroborated in Sartre's well-known novel; that which nauseates can be almost anything, from the famous tree-root example (N: 182–93/181–92) to existence in general (for instance, N: 200/199). Importantly, there is also reference to *the* nausea, as if it were some kind of entity (cf. N: 33/37). Here 'the' nausea is experienced, by Roquentin, as a kind of unavoidable, existential illness. If it is not directly upon him, if it is not actuated in a particular disgust or nausea, *the* nausea is never far away – and when it does hit, it is an enveloping feeling of disturbance. In this manner, nausea can take on many particular forms, but it also seems to have an underlying current that runs much deeper.

What, more specifically, does this deeper current entail? The answer to this is found in a crucial passage of *Being and Nothingness*: 'Far from having to understand the term *nausea* as a metaphor drawn from our physiological disgusts, it is, on the contrary, on its foundation that all concrete and empirical nauseas are produced (nausea from rotten meat, fresh blood, excrement, etc.)'[18] (BN/EN: 362/378). This passage highlights Sartre's ultimate view on a kind of ontological nausea, as well as its relation to more particular and empirical nauseas and disgusts. We see, in fact, that ontological nausea is an existential condition of our being. Like before, this does not mean that we experience this condition at every turn in an empirical manner, because we can engage and take flight in various activities and distractions through a whole host of desires, pleasures and pains. It does however mean that this – again technical – term argues that our existence is conditioned by yet another ontological element. Here, just like anguish refers to a very basic recognition of our perpetual freedom, nausea is the automatic, ontological recognition of our and the world's utter, brute contingency (and often, by extension, absurdity – cf. N: 185–6/183–4). This is because all of us simply are, ultimately without any higher rhyme or reason, and it is up to no one but us to deal with this brutally contingent fact.

Nausea, for Sartre, is therefore the recognition of an all-pervasive contingency that is always already *de trop*; it can surge upon us at any given moment, and when it does this through a particular phenomenon it can become a more concrete and empirical disgust or nausea with concrete emotive qualities as well as specific objects. Underlying all this, however, is a more pervasive, ontological form. This is why Roquentin can be nauseated by almost anything, and this is why he also refers to 'the' nausea as if it were an inescapable condition of his existence. Indeed, all of the more particular nauseas and disgusts are only possible because the world and our lives are contingent in their very essence; there is no real necessity or intrinsic value to any of it; the *goût fade* (cf. EN: 378) of nausea is precisely that automatic recognition which gives us this existential taste that everything, ultimately, will fade away. And before it does, it is always already *de trop*. It is, once again, our most immediate affective taste of the in-itself, that simple stuff which founds all more particular contingencies (our bodies, our pasts and the like). Although we would like things to have a more enduring meaning, purpose and value, ultimately Sartre's existential analyses, both in novel form and in his ontological system, show that at the end of the day all our desires and wishes will be gobbled up by things that simply are.

Lastly, with regard to our relation with others, shame (*honte*) is our most original recognition of ourselves as objects in front of others. This we have already seen in the preceding subsection. Of course, shame can have the normal, everyday meaning of a negative, often moral emotion that is focused upon (an aspect of) oneself. However, shame has, once again, deeper ontological roots in Sartre, and in its essence 'refers to my loss of transcendence' (Visker 1999: 335–6). In fact, as already explained shame in its most basic sense is nothing other than the ontological recognition of the look itself – one is aware of the permanent possibility of being looked at, and of thereby being transfigured into an object. Thus everyday emotions of shame, where a negative emotional reaction to aspects of one's objectivity predominates, as well as feelings like pride and vanity that affirm aspects of our objectivity in a bad faith manner (cf. BN/EN: 314/330), are all once again only possible because – and are indeed intensifications of – a more primary and basic form. In short, Sartre's technical usage of shame in his ontological system refers to our most basic and immediate recognition of our being as an object for another subject.

In this manner, shame makes us foundationally aware that we are not at the centre of the world. It is Sartre's term that underpins all of his subsequent thoughts on our more 'concrete relations' (cf. BN/EN: 383–433/401–71) with others, just like anguish underpins all more specific episodes of choice, and nausea all of our more manifest, explicit grapplings with contingency. Crucially, these three ontological forms show why consciousness is always already affective. They make certain types of affectivity belong to our very ontological structure, specifically the basic awareness of our free subjectivity (anguish), the objectivity and contingency of the world (nausea), as well as our own objectivity in front of others (shame). Such basic types of affectivity can and do crystallize and intensify into more specific, stronger emotions in our daily interactions and engagements. Precisely how each and every emotion arises from these basic ontological interrelations is quite infinite. Suffice it here to say that affectivity is always already at work in our experiences precisely thanks to its three most basic, ontological forms.

Affectivity therefore grounds, ontologically, our emotions. It shows how consciousness interacts with itself and the other categories of being on a most basic level. Furthermore, because our emotions are inherently magical, it also grounds emotive magic as well. Indeed, our emotions grab and have sway over us precisely, once again, because of a more basic and pervasive structure of affectivity that makes the crystallization process into emotion possible as such.

In Sartre therefore, the three privileged forms of ontological affectivity make all other more empirical emotions possible, precisely because they are responsible at bottom for linking up the three categories of being. In other terms, they provide the tonalities for some of the most basic interrelations between the three different forms of being that make up Sartre's ontological system. On top of this, we then have a plethora of emotive, evaluative experiences that are also only made possible through various qualities for which affectivity is once again that basic experiential bridge in and between self, world and others. Actually, affectivity is precisely the phenomenal reason why these three elements – self, world and others – are always already fused into a lived dynamic. This ultimately means that our existence is one that has many powers to captivate, ranging from our own immediate reflections and feelings, to the captivation of the world, its things and images, as well as to the wonderful but also frequently difficult draw of others.

These dynamics may now be spelled out a bit more concretely through other key themes of *Being and Nothingness*, themes which will finally bring magic to the fore. I am speaking of value, possession and quality and language.

## The impossible synthesis: Facticity, value and magic

Being-for-itself, as freedom, as bad faith, always highlights the same fundamental truth: consciousness is what it is not and is not what it is. This sounds like a rather fantastic, if not completely magical, formulation. And indeed it is, for this is the whole point; the definition of magic as an irrational synthesis between spontaneity and passivity in the *Sketch* finally finds its ontological foundation in *Being and Nothingness*, for what is the nihilative dynamic between for-itself (viz. spontaneity, freedom) and in-itself (viz. brute stuff, facts) if not an 'irrational' – which is to say conflictual – synthesis between two diametrically opposed forms of being that, in their very synthesis, remain in a relation of a perpetual schism?

In order to elaborate this main point more concretely, I will highlight the three main structures where magic is at its most prevalent in *Being and Nothingness*, namely, the issue of value, that of possession and quality, and finally that of language and the other. I believe that the significance of these elements in Sartre's system has been underemphasized, especially in connection with the earlier works, not least emotion and yes, affectivity. I will address the first in this section, the second two in the next two.

Beginning with the issue of value, the key for understanding it comes with an analysis of two of the five[19] 'immediate structures' (BN/EN: 97/109) of the for-itself: facticity and contingency, and desire and value.

Glancing back on the in-itself, Sartre notes once again that 'no more total plenitude can be imagined' (BN/EN: 98/110). Consciousness, on the other hand, is a total 'decompression of being' (ibid.) whereby 'it is impossible to define it as a coincidence with itself' (ibid.). The for-itself nevertheless is. It is in the manner that we have already pointed to, namely, as a 'being which is not what it is and which is what it is not' (ibid.). On the level of facticity, this formula must also be applicable. Here, being-for-itself exists as facticity both as presence in and to the world (is what it is not, namely the things of the world), as well as having a body and a past (is not what it is, namely, its body and past) (cf. ibid.). Facticity is thus the for-itself's dual inherent link to being-in-itself. It is the aspects of the latter that are preserved through the nihilative act. Put more simply, facticity means I necessarily am part of the world, and I necessarily have a body and past so long as I live. However, I am none of these things in an in-itself manner; I always must relate to the world, as well as my body and past, in various concrete, transitive ways.

Additionally, although facticity allows the for-itself to be, precisely because of this it is always felt as utterly contingent, as 'an unjustifiable fact' (BN/EN: 104/116). Here we need to remember that being-in-itself was also labelled contingent, and if facticity is simply the for-itself's necessarily nihilative link to the in-itself, then it must follow that this link is experienced as one of contingency too (cf. BN/EN: 105–6/117–8).

The inherent nihilative nature of consciousness excludes, by definition, it giving a necessary ground to itself – or, for that matter, of receiving it from elsewhere. However, facticity does constitute, as the for-itself's 'original contingency' (BN/EN: 106/118) of its own upsurge into the world, a 'nihilated in-itself' (ibid.) that can be seen, at least to some extent, as a kind of nihilated foundation. Moreover, because being-in-itself gives itself no such thing (it just is), we see that 'foundation appears for the first time' (ibid.) within the nihilative act of being-for-itself. Such a foundation is a strange one, however, for although facticity is the 'factual necessity' (BN/EN: 108/120) of our existence (as present in a world with a body and a past), precisely because we are always separated from – and yet still inextricably bound to – our facticity by a perpetual nihilative process, this latter ultimately amounts to the rather unsettling idea where the 'perpetually evanescent contingency of the in-itself, which, without ever allowing itself to be apprehended, haunts the for-itself and reattaches it to being-in-itself' (BN/EN: 107/119). Such reattachment always 'has the feeling of its complete gratuity' (BN/EN: 108/120), 'as being there *for nothing*, as being *de trop*' (ibid.). Facticity therefore assures us that we exist, that we are and that we are even responsible for such existence. However, beyond this – concerning the whys and wherefores – it remains utterly silent.

Hence the for-itself's need for immediate structures of desire and value. Indeed, the for-itself as value can be seen as the polar opposite of facticity; 'The in-itself of facticity' (BN/EN: 113/121) is experienced as 'pure presence in the world of the for-itself' (ibid.), whereas value, as the ultimate ideal(s) towards which we strive, is 'the missing in-itself' (ibid.), 'pure absence' (ibid.). This means that, precisely because being-for-itself is, in its structure, a nihilation of being-in-itself, the former cannot help but determine itself as *'a lack of being'* (BN/EN: 109/121).

This is the ontological origin of all desire for Sartre. This lack is the deepest of all our 'internal negations' (BN/EN: 110/122) and constitutes being-for-itself as essentially missing being-in-itself in the manner of an aching and troublesome hole that we incessantly yearn to fill (cf. BN/EN: 110–11/122–3). Such a constitution, moreover, is also the primordial origin of all transcendence in that being-for-itself as consciousness (of) its own inherent lack necessarily seeks to found itself in numerous ways by going beyond itself into the world, as well as into the three 'ekstases' – taken in the literal sense of consciousness 'standing out from' itself (cf. BN: 651) – through temporality, reflection and being-for-others. Desire and value are the immediate, immanent structures of such movements. With the former the for-itself seeks that which it lacks concretely – and it does this, crucially, because it is always already constituted as a valuing being. In other words, although what we value might be up for grabs, that we value at all certainly is not.

In this manner, Sartrean desire can be seen as a concrete instantiation of the valuing being that we are. Thus these two, desire and value, always condition each other, whether positively (desires in line with one's values) or not (desires in conflict with one's values).

Focusing further on value, it is very broad here. Indeed, if morality in a widest sense is just all the values we might have, this is not yet an ethics. For me this latter is more of a prescriptive and formalized system of norms. In Sartre's thought it occurs in other works (Sartre [1939–40] 1995 and [1945] 1983). Indeed, in *Being and Nothingness* authenticity is only mentioned once

(BN/EN: 94/106), with its details more or less postponed for another place. Nonetheless, because ethics systematizes a broader category of valuing and desiring in general, it completely depends on this more basic conception, which is my focus here due to its ultimately magical nature as well.

On this level then, value is any ideal, in-itself absence that the for-itself may strive towards to try and give itself meaning and foundation. At a very mundane level it could be almost anything; for example, 'I will start getting up earlier in the morning, work harder, eat better'. However, such an example already shows one is heading towards, and even presupposes, something more abstract and general. Perhaps in this instance that 'it is good to be healthy in body and mind'. This in its own turn presupposes something higher, Sartre says, thus showing that the for-itself always 'surpasses itself' (BN/EN: 114/126) towards an ever-higher value, ultimately culminating in an absolute 'value' that was always already implied, and has always already meant that the for-itself as lack has had the final project to ground its own self absolutely through a permanent synthesis with the in-itself. Such a synthesis Sartre calls a being-in-itself-for-itself, a consciousness that would be its own sturdy foundation; in theological terms, God.

Such an accomplishment *would* make consciousness its own necessary reason for being and would thereby fill one's lack and obliterate one's contingency, once and for all. But alas, it is an 'impossible synthesis' (ibid.) due to the inherently nihilative nature of being-for-itself and the utterly simplistic being of the in-itself. In short, the two can never merge into a harmonious union because they are diametrically opposed to each other in their ontological nature. However, notwithstanding – or precisely because of – the impossibility of actually being a for-itself that founds its own being, our ontological lack must hold such a wish as an ultimate ideal, as 'Value'.

In this manner, 'Value' is ultimately the unconditional being that also is not – namely, is ideal, a nothingness, a self (cf. BN/EN: 117/129). Moreover, value more generally is 'consubstantial' (BN/EN: 118/131) with the immediate structure of being-for-itself and its desires. Since we lack being ontologically, and since we try to supplement this lack through desires and values – with the former never being fully satisfactory and the latter never possessing anything with sufficient concreteness or endurance – our desires and values perpetually haunt us and our freedom like so many concrete (desires) and invisible (values) ghosts.

Going even further, Sartre states that value is nothing less than 'the being of the self' (BN/EN: 117/129). Moreover, precisely because it is borne out of a lack that we are, a fixed value as such is completely unattainable. We are thus doomed to strive without ever attaining to anything other than just more lacks attached to yet more values. It is, unfortunately, the perennial reason why the grass is always greener on the other side (cf. also Johnston 2005: xxviii).

The main question in this context must now be this: What can such theory contribute to Sartre's conception of magic? Well, as already hinted, I contend this exposition of being-in-itself, being-for-itself and its essential nihilative process, as well as the resulting interminable interplay between facticity and value, ontologically grounds Sartre's concept of magic. With the ego, magic showed how we instil personal reflections with powers of their own that then seep into pre-reflection; with emotion, magic showed how we can always transform a causal, determined world through our own psychophysiological incantations; and with the imaginary, magic showed how we have the spontaneous capacity to evoke absent and irreal things that, like with the ego and objects of emotion, can take on pseudo powers of their own and thereby captivate and transfix us. The common thread to all of this is a strange synthesis at work between consciousness and objective aspects, between pure activity and passivity. In other terms, through this strange synthesis objects come to imbue powers that seem to belong to them originally and essentially. To give examples, I become a bad person through my reflections upon past acts and qualities; a bus becomes hateful through my shaking fist and cursing mouth; and that image becomes mesmerizing thanks to the affectivity my spontaneity imparts to it.

In all these cases, each and every time, activity is given over into passivity; spontaneous conscious life instils power into originally inert and passive objects. Such consciousness, ontologically defined, is nothing other than being-for-itself; and the inert, passive objects are nothing other than instantiations of that most primordial form of being, being-in-itself. Indeed, human being always has the capacity for magic because it is always, at bottom, a strange synthesis between categories of being that logically speaking does not make much sense. It is precisely because such a synthesis is an illogical and thus an ultimately impossible one that it is also a constantly frustrated one. The dynamic between facts on the one hand and desires and values on the other – in short between facticity and freedom, between in-itself and for-itself – is nothing but the ontologization of these insights. *Being and Nothingness* is thus the culmination of preoccupations Sartre had for years; magic is ontologized here because Sartre provides the ontological conditions for all the spontaneity and creativity that human beings have, as well as all their contingency and absurdity.

With facticity and valuing, this magical ontological dynamic is filled out even more. As that 'being of the self' that drives (cf. Bernet 2002; O'Shiel 2013) all of our desires, value further emphasizes that we are a perpetual flight towards a synthesis that can never actually be completed – ultimately a *passion inutile*. However, even if ultimately futile, such valuing being is, nevertheless, the necessary structure that we are, giving rise to an infinite amount of desires, ranging from the sublime to the ridiculous. This is indeed the magical being of Sartre's ontology; all conceptions of personality, all emotion and all imagination are all ultimately rooted in this dynamic, made possible by the nihilative activity of consciousness that at once separates us off from, as well as binds us inextricably to, so many facts, desires and values that can come to take on lives of their own. In this manner, we are never fully solid nor completely fluid but an admixture of facts and freedoms that dance around each other in an interminable movement of choice, desire, creation and despair.

By finishing on values more pointedly, through these and the evaluative qualities they give rise to, objects come to imbue powers that seem to belong to them essentially, even though they do not (e.g. a beautiful car and a stupid computer). Here, each and every time we have pure, spontaneous consciousness instilling life and power into things that cannot have such values in themselves, on their own – and even, moreover, to the point that these things come to have sway over us and not the other way around. Values are thus lived through a general affective valuing that spikes into explicit evaluative qualities in our emotions. In this way, emotion is nothing other than lived, bodily value.

A recent article by Hartmann has pointed out that many interpretations of Sartre are overly cerebral and reflective; there is a 'rationalistic reading of appropriateness that dominates much recent literature on emotion' (2016: 145), Sartre included, where the focus is on how our emotions somehow match up with 'emotion-independent facts about the world' (id.: 162). The fact is, however, that 'emotions create their own evaluative standards' (ibid.); emotions are how values are lived out most immediately, in a psychophysiological manner. Reflection upon them would show, more explicitly, what we hold dear and not, including perhaps levels of appropriateness. However, these latter issues are decidedly not there in Sartre's most primary, pre-reflective account.

We have already seen that emotion opens up a realm, a veritable new dimension beyond the purely pragmatic. Indeed, we are neither Vulcans nor robots because of this world of emotion. Such a world, crucially, would not be possible were it not for a general valuing affectivity. In this manner, I think concrete emotions are only possible thanks to a more basic and automatic affectivity that can of course reveal actual, matter-of-fact qualities of objects. However, such affectivity, when fused with value, also harbours a capacity to instil objects with strong and personal evaluative qualities (beautiful, hateful, disgusting and the like) that can thereby crescendo into explicit emotions and all their transformative capacities. In this manner, Sartrean affectivity is at the root of both more straightforward *Wahrnehmungen* (perceptions) like a yellow lemon, and more emotive *Wertnehmungen* ('value-ceptions' – cf. Scheler [1913–16] 2009/2007: 197–8/200–1) like a hateful scene. In this latter, one instils the hatefulness into the phenomenon precisely through one's spontaneous anger, repugnance and the like. This can reach such a pitch that we can actually become possessed by – and even subsequently dispossessed – our very own evaluative incantations.

## Possession, quality and magic

Possession is yet another fundamental structural dynamic that is constantly enacted between for-itself and in-itself, consciousness and things of the world. After briefly reiterating his theory of value (BN/EN: 596/621), Sartre transitions to an incredibly similar discourse on possession, which has value as a vital conditioning factor throughout. Indeed, for Sartre, possession, whether physical (ownership, property), playful (a sport), artistic (a work of art) or serious (scientific knowledge of something) (cf. BN/EN: 606/631), 'is a magical relation' (BN/EN: 612/637) where there is yet again an 'impossible synthesis' (BN/EN: 600/625) 'of self and not-self' (BN/EN: 599/624). Here, although these two poles vary in significance depending upon the type of possession under consideration (artistic creation emphasizes the self for Sartre; scientific knowledge emphasizes the facts, i.e. the non-self), 'there is within the same syncretism a self becoming not-self and a not-self becoming self' (BN/EN: 610/635). Hereby there is always a dual movement in this dynamic, or what Sartre calls a 'dyad' (BN/EN: 613/638). Firstly possession, which is always governed by concrete desiring and ideal valuing, contains 'in the vast majority of cases' (BN/EN: 606/632) reference to 'a contingent and concrete in-itself' (ibid.), in short a thing of the world. However, it also contains, secondly, reference to an ideal '*in-itself-for-itself*' (ibid.), for which consciousness once again tries to found itself through that which it possesses.

Basically the items of possession are nothing other than the concrete and symbolic manifestations of our ideal valuing being (cf. 613/638); we desire and possess things, people and ideas because we are always ultimately driven by values that we live desirously, emotively and reflectively. Additionally, such values are ultimately grounded in the inalienable as well as impossible desire to be a consciousness – namely, a non-coincidence – that would nevertheless coincide with itself absolutely through the items we possess. In this manner, our values are spontaneously incanted (cf. BN/EN: 613/638) into the objects we desire and possess. Here, 'as the object rises up in my world, it must simultaneously be wholly me and wholly independent of me' (BN/EN: 612/637). This is indeed another strange culmination of magical logic in Sartre's system; being-for-itself and -in-itself try to coalesce through the values of the former being spontaneously incanted and thereby inhering as qualities in the latter.

This logic is pushed further when one again hones in on the magical theme of originally inert, passive objects accruing a borrowed spontaneity from consciousness. Indeed, the dynamic can go so far that things we own can, in a manner of speaking, come to *dis*possess us. Think of someone who takes a significant loan, or has spent his family's life savings, to buy a sports car, and then spends every spare minute caring for it. Here the possession, the car, can come to have such a power on one's desires, values and emotions that it can even become the centre of one's life, moreover damaging or even destroying one's relations. It is in this manner that possessions can come to dispossess the person because, in fact, they take advantage of the fact that one is always already 'decentred' (cf. Visker [2004] 2008: 79–82). In Sartrean language, this involves a 'continuous degradation' (BN/EN: 611/636) of value into inert things of the world that thereby become animated, thereby seem to contain a centre and power of their own, whereby you depend on them and not vice versa. This is precisely because they imbue aspects of our most cherished – as well as ultimately our most unattainable – desires and values. 'Unattainable' because the latter are insatiable in Sartre's system; once quenched there might be momentary satisfaction, but it will not last long for most.

There is also a deeper structural issue. On the one hand, the possessed object is created 'as independent of me' (BN/EN: 612/637); 'In the relation of possession the dominant term is the object possessed; without it I am nothing save a nothingness which possesses, nothing other than pure and simple possession, an incompleteness, an insufficiency, whose sufficiency and completion are there in that object. In possession, I am my own foundation in so far as I exist in an in-itself' (BN/EN: 612/637–8). However, on the other hand, and at the very same time, 'this object is reabsorbed in me, it is only myself' (BN/EN: 612/638); without me to sustain my possession, it would not be significant, of value. Indeed, a car does not possess anything in itself – it just is.

Thus we see, once again, an irrational synthesis between an inert object that nevertheless holds sway over me. Such sway, as felt in the object itself, is only possible because of my inherent magical capacity to incant my desires and values into items I want, own and strive for. This is the 'crystallizing synthesis' (BN/EN: 617/642) of possession whereby a 'concrete quality … has been spread over' (ibid.) the thing – and even the world – indelibly.

To further corroborate this, it is Sartre's subsequent discourse on quality, where a strange admixture of objects possessing qualities that are nevertheless only made possible because of the advent of consciousness witnessing such qualities, that comes to the fore in its full import. Here, the tricky issue is that a certain quality (e.g. the yellow of a lemon) 'really belongs' (BN/EN: 621/646) to the thing, and yet it does 'not belong to the in-itself' (ibid.) because one needs the advent of consciousness for qualities to be experienced and thereby arise at all. Let us look a little bit closer.

For Sartre, qualities have to do with the various meanings (cf. ibid.) of things of the world. One subcategory are '*material* meanings' (ibid.), such as in the yellow of a lemon. Here, although they only have meaning for us – or at least only for a conscious being with some kind of vision – they are nevertheless 'as real as the world' (ibid.). In this manner, these meanings of things, which nevertheless presuppose (cf. BN/EN: 622/648) a conscious subject, are still objective thanks to the inherently and automatic transcendent nature of consciousness; 'Man, being transcendence, establishes the meaningful by his very coming into the world, and the meaningful because of the very structure of transcendence is a reference to other transcendents which can be interpreted without recourse to the subjectivity which has established it' (ibid.). In short, consciousness establishes meanings that go beyond it; because consciousness is always already out in the world, always already conscious of things and qualities it is not, these material things, essentially supported by the transphenomenal nature of the in-itself, accrue a qualitative autonomy of their own that can actually be explicated without reference to this most fundamental upsurge of consciousness. In fact, Sartre goes as far to say that quality 'is nothing other' (BN/EN: 624/649) than the object's being; 'The yellow of the lemon … is not a subjective mode of apprehending the lemon; it *is the lemon*' (ibid.). The yellow of the lemon is in the lemon through and through; to take it away would prove impossible precisely because it belongs to the lemon, even though, at the same time, such yellowness appears only to a conscious being.

Of course, one can now account for the colour yellow in a scientific, in-itself manner (i.e. wavelengths and the like). However, from the immediate phenomenological perspective one has to enter into a discourse on how phenomenal qualities are both in the object as such and yet still – at least partially – constituted and witnessed by us. From such a perspective, material qualities are only made possible because of a dynamic between consciousness and the objects it is conscious of. These things have, thanks to their support in the material realm of the in-itself, a nature and autonomy of their own that we nevertheless witness as material qualities.

What about less material qualities? How about a personal, sentimental feeling imbued in a particular thing, like a St. Christopher's medal? Here Sartre's idea of magic enters the fray. Indeed, here such qualities are more personal and more singular in the sense that not everyone would have sentiments and memories triggered by the sight of the particular object. Nevertheless, the main dynamic is still there, for any particular for-itself will always already experience qualities out in the world of things, even though the particulars will often differ massively depending on one's bodily constitution, culture, past, tastes and values.

Actually, opposed to material qualities we are here looking at evaluative qualities. These latter, precisely because they are more personally determined in that they essentially harbour particular values based on one's own life, past and situation, are thereby more singular and prone to magic as well. All lemons will have a colour; not all objects will however imbue the same values for different people, and not all objects will even imbue the same values for the same person over time. In this manner, evaluative qualities like beautiful, hateful, disgusting and the like are where Sartrean magic raises its head properly; it is here that consciousness once again incants strong evaluative qualities into objects which do not originally contain such properties, to the extent that they come to have extra powers and can thereby hold great sway over us.

It is thus through values and their qualities that 'psychic meanings' are always already incanted into the materiality of the world: 'All this occurs as if we surge into a universe where feelings and acts are all charged with materiality, have a substantial stuff, are *really* soft, flat, slimy, low, elevated, etc., and where material substances originally have a psychic meaning that renders them repugnant, horrifying, attractive, etc.'[20] (BN/EN: 626/651–2). Here we witness another dimension of the strange synthesis running throughout much of *Being and Nothingness* – not only is it as if material substances are invested with psychic meanings in the form of evaluative qualities; quality also signifies the opposite movement, namely, that all our feelings and engagements are materially charged with stuff from the world too. The variations and gradations here are infinite; I am particularly interested in phenomena that highlight our magical being, namely, when the syntheses carried out accrue a character of emotion, as well as pointing to the values imbued in such emotions.

On this note, of course, perceiving a lemon is usually an unemotive experience. In other words, a basic perception is quite unmagical because it is not transformative. However, there are also many experiences that can highlight, very well, the magical syntheses that Sartre has been at pains to express in his investigations into our personal reflections (ego), our emotive being, our imaginations, as well as into our basic nature as valuing and possessive beings. Indeed, although *Being and Nothingness* provides the general ontological foundations of our magical being, it also provides a useful main example on the slimy (*visqueux*). Here, although many qualities, usually material ones (e.g. yellow), are quite straightforward and non-magical, disgust at something slimy highlights an experience where consciousness's project of possession backfires with full ferocity; 'the slimy reverses the terms, the for-itself is suddenly *compromised*'[21] (BN/EN: 629/655) by inert qualities that nonetheless seem to be 'animated by a sort of life' (BN/EN: 630/656) which turns 'against me' (ibid.). Sartre alludes to this as 'a symbol of an antivalue' (BN/EN: 631/657) whereby a challenge of materiality can become so strong and crude that our values are besmirched and violated through strong, visceral emotions like disgust (cf. also O'Shiel 2015b). In this manner, evaluative qualities are instilled into objects through our inherently valuing affectivity, thereby facilitating magical transformations in the form of a certain emotion.

Indeed, the mixture of self and things other than self is precisely the basic affectivity I have been trying to articulate. Affectivity is that automatic lived bridge between our subjectivity and its objects. It is responsible for both material qualities like colours and evaluative ones that give rise to a whole world of feeling, emotion, passion and upheaval. These latter are the ones that often lead to captivation and (dis)possession. This means that the items of possession are nothing other than the concrete and symbolic manifestations of our ideal valuing being. Moreover, it can now be reiterated that emotions are the various, dynamic and complex crescendos of a more basic and ontological Sartrean affectivity.

In other terms, emotions are more pointed and crystallized versions of the broader, more diffuse feelings we have.

It should now be clear how emotion is a magical transformation of the world, from determinism to non-determinism. It should also now be clear that affectivity pervades all modes of consciousness – it lies at and with the root of our conscious lives; it is how we feel on the most basic, psychophysiological level, as well as how we sense and make sense of the world and its beings. Now, although emotion is only facilitated because of a more primordial affectivity, it is ambiguous whether this more basic structure is itself magical, or merely facilitates magic in its various manifestations. I have mentioned that perceiving a lemon, for instance, is not magical – usually it is straightforward perception. Disgust or anger at something is, however, magical precisely because such evaluative qualities (1) do not belong to the object itself, and yet (2) it – the evaluative quality (or set of qualities) – nevertheless inheres in the object in the experience to an intensity and extent that (3) one is emotively and psychically dominated by this quality (or qualities). It seems, then, that magic arises precisely when a more general affectivity is transformed into a pointed emotion whereby one or a few evaluative qualities come to dominate and captivate in a kind of reverse intentionality. In other words, it is precisely when an evaluative quality takes over one's more normal and balanced perceptual experiences to the point where one cannot but be fixated and possessed by a certain quality that consciousness has nevertheless put there itself. In the concrete world evaluative qualities hereby get added onto or into something material. This can range infinitely, from an artist being mesmerized by a particularly beautiful shade of yellow, to someone being thoroughly revolted by something slimy.

In short, magic is characterized as a curious synthesis between activity and passivity because it is precisely when passivity takes on a pseudo activity of its own. Thus affectivity facilitates Sartrean magic without being magic itself; this latter occurs in emotion when transformation and captivation occur, even reaching a point where one becomes completely dispossessed by the object. In this manner, affectivity is a necessary but not a sufficient condition for Sartrean magic. Material qualities depend on basic affectivity but remain mundane and uncaptivating in a whole host of circumstances. When strong evaluative qualities are instilled, however, this is when emotion proper is evoked, with objects accruing characteristics and powers they do not originally contain, thereby leading to magical transformations in their fullest sense.

More generally, one can also say there is no need for a strict either-or distinction between mere affectivity and full-blown emotion; it can also be conceived as a scale with various degrees. Here our lives would be on a continuum stemming from a rather indifferent or pragmatic affective mood on one extreme, to complete emotional upheaval and bewitchment on the other (cf. O'Shiel [2016] 2017). This whole axis is pervaded by affectivity, which can be very mundane and material on the one end and captivating and powerfully evaluative on the other. Thus the difference still holds, although the two poles can be conceived in a more fluid lived dynamic.

Nonetheless, there is a nagging issue: the line is not so clear when asking where strong affectivity (e.g. a rotten mood) might end and weak emotion (e.g. a quiet sadness) might begin, as well as the fact that in certain cases emotional upheavals might crystallize into enduring magical moods and states (e.g. mourning – cf. Didion [2005] 2012). Here I can only suggest that strong and enduring moods would usually produce even stronger emotions, weak moods weak ones, so one could say that even here the dynamic might still remain generally sound. Nevertheless, there is so much variation here that I am not sure a full account for all eventualities is ever possible; it does us well to at least have grasped a very important structural dynamic, with further elaboration of the limitless particular instantiations coming in the second half of this work.

All in all, Sartrean magic is multifaceted with various manifestations and yet also has a fundamental ontological structure of consciousness instilling objects with powers they do not originally contain in themselves. This, I have argued, is a key but overlooked theme in *Being and Nothingness*, not least in dynamics like affectivity and emotion, desire and value, and possession and quality – combinations of which allow for the most mundane, basic and non-magical experiences on the one hand and the most cataclysmic upheavals on the other.

## Language and the magic of the other

We are not quite done there, either. Although Sartre's explicit remarks on the magic of the other are rather scant in *Being and Nothingness*, it is still necessary to dwell on it a bit in order to complete the picture, as well as relate these insights to ones from the previous chapters.

The main explicit point regarding Sartrean magic and the other in *Being and Nothingness* is a remark on language in his chapter on concrete relations. Here, language is one of seven – along with love, masochism, indifference, desire, hate and sadism – fundamental 'attitudes' (cf. BN/EN: 386, 401/404, 419) that we often take up with others concretely. They are indeed concrete, but once again these seven attitudes are analysed in order to highlight the extremes of being looked at and looking; they are the concrete manifestations and instances of the ontological rules and dynamics that have been under study. In this context, language (along with love and masochism) is on the side of being looked at because it is primarily through these attitudes that we make ourselves objects in various ways – a linguistic object, a fascinating object and an embarrassing object respectively. Through these the other can 'possess' (cf. BN/EN: 386/404) us through their own subjectivity – but we can also of course respond. Indeed, the other four attitudes start more initially from our own looking, from us affirming elements of our own subjectivity over others, to which they in their own turn can also of course respond. These two extremes, once again, always end up inverting onto the other side of the seesaw, and I believe there is, once again, plenty of room for more anthropological and ontical considerations and dynamics in between the extremes when considering our everyday lives.

I must focus on language and its magic here. Sartre says it is 'sacred' for the agent and 'magical' for the patient (cf. BN/EN: 396/414). Sacred means when I speak or do something, what I say or do is picked up by others in a way that transcends my grasp; how the other may interpret my words, gestures or movements, what precise influence they might have on the other is beyond me, at least in part. In Sartre's terms, 'the "meaning" of my expressions always escapes me' (BN/EN: 395/413). This means language always has a transcendent element to it, something that goes beyond my own immanent intentions and awareness of others precisely because it is always possible to be taken up and (mis)understood by the other in ways that I can only try to approximate and comprehend through yet more language. In Sartre's terms, 'language reveals to me the freedom of the one who listens to me in silence, that is, their transcendence'[22] (BN/EN: 396/414). In this manner, the other has a transcendent position on my expressions that I cannot possibly have or experience as they do; they are precisely other because they can see us and our expressions in a way that we, from our own position, cannot. Put simply, 'I cannot hear myself speak nor see myself smile' (ibid.).

Such is the transcendent sacredness of language for Sartre. On the other side of this, Sartre calls the other's language when I am listening magical. This is the inverse of sacred, because for me as a listener I can never with certainty predict what will be said or done by the other at any given moment; others are always completely free to surprise me in what they do or say (and vice versa of course). Naturally, one can get to know specific people and their habits of expression, but the fact remains that language, and engagement with others through it, is ultimately inherently unpredictable, and can thereby be enchanting and surprising precisely due to its spontaneous and inaccessible origins.

Generally, this basic structure is so because the other as other has to remain so; we gain access to the other through language, but we never experience the other from their own particular standpoint. If we did they would not be other. This is actually what makes a speaker a 'magical object' (ibid.) for a listener; 'Attitudes, expressions and words can only ever indicate … other attitudes, other expressions and other words'[23] (ibid.). Language is thus the one and only bridge between subjectivities whereby one can nevertheless never fully traverse to the other side. Indeed, it is precisely because each subjectivity – each side – is ultimately unobtainable in this manner that others can remain an eternal source of captivation. In short, the magic of language is, for Sartre, 'an action at a distance of which the other [i.e. the listener] exactly knows the effect' (ibid.) – knows the effect once something has been expressed, but never grasps, for their part, the wellspring or cause in all of its immediacy and spontaneity. This source remains transcendent and magical for a listener, just as the effect remains transcendent and sacred for the speaker, thus resulting in a permanent possibility to surprise, enchant and shock.

Of course there are factual structures to language, like rules of grammar. Here, the dynamic is once again *between* freedom and facticity. It is a fact that every human being has language instilled in them through a particular upbringing and education. Yet again, though, it is how one relates to one's language and manners of expression and behaviour that demonstrates freedom and choice are also involved. Freedom and facticity here again necessarily interact through one of our most basic being-for-others.

Actually, language is nothing other than our being-for-others; it is the only way we can communicate. Indeed, Sartre states simply that language 'is originally being-for-others'[24] (BN/EN: 394/412). Here it is important to note that language goes way beyond the merely verbal – it extends to 'all the phenomena of expression' (BN/EN: 395/413). What, how and which language one speaks are all of course vital elements. Nonetheless, language for Sartre is again much broader and must include all other forms of communication, from gestures and personal mannerisms to body language and how one even dresses and presents oneself. Such a fundamental, varied and ubiquitous structure is why language always has the capacity to fascinate on very many levels (cf. BN/EN: 396/414).

Such are the main elements to Sartre's rather short analyses on the ontological structure of language, its magic included. Once again, here I am at pains to emphasize that this is another instance of ontologizing phenomenological analyses that Sartre was preoccupied with from the very beginning of his philosophy. Indeed, the trend with the other and its magic is no different. Firstly, we already saw the 'public' (cf. O'Shiel 2015a) and interpersonal nature of the ego in Chapter 1, and how our personal reflections make us 'sorcerers for ourselves' (TE: 35/119) but also for others. This motif is extended even further in the *Sketch*, where Sartre even goes as far to say that 'man is always a sorcerer to man and the social world is primarily magical' (STE/ETE: 56/108). Then, regarding the next main philosophical work, *The Imaginary*, one may think that others and sociality are not main points of interest. There are passages that are relevant however, for instance, how our interpersonal relations have most force when played out within the inexhaustibility of perception (cf., for instance, IM: 144/277), as well as the quite clear and more general idea that for empathy, that is, when we think of others 'in their shoes', we must use our imagination. In fact, a very incisive article, already cited, by Van der Wielen (2014) has linked Sartre's earlier insights here to strands in *Being and Nothingness*. She shows that the other and its look is always experienced through an emotion (i.e. the *Sketch*), which then gives rise to images (i.e. *The Imaginary*) of the other's subjectivity. This latter can only occur as an image – as an irreal object (cf. id.: 70) – precisely because perceiving the other's subjectivity as a subjectivity is off limits by its very nature.

In this manner, the other and its magic already runs through Sartre's early philosophy – and again it gets ontologized in *Being and Nothingness*. Indeed, the structure of being-for-others in all its complexity, with the look as its main principle, its necessary concrete instantiation in language, as well as its necessarily magical, captivating components, ontologically grounds phenomenological structures and dynamics of interpersonal sorcery that Sartre was, once again, preoccupied with from the very beginning.

Hereby I have shown that significant, basic and pervasive elements of *Being and Nothingness* provide the ontological apparatus and roots for various phenomena that all have Sartre's intriguing, technical and multifaceted concept of magic at their heart.

# Interlude

As a kind of intellectual pit stop, let me shortly summarize some of the main issues traversed so far, as well as where we will be heading.

We have just seen the general ontological architectonics of Sartrean magic and how these ultimately ground the more particular phenomenological manifestations of the first three chapters. Regarding these latter, the ego is magical because personal reflection gets planted onto the pre-reflective level, emotion is magical because evaluative qualities are incanted into objects through psychophysiological stirrings and the imaginary is magical because images can come to take on a life of their own, even to the extent of (dis)possessing us. All of this points to a general underlying structure to Sartrean magic as pure spontaneous consciousness instilling life and powers into originally passive phenomena. In very short, activity gives itself over into passivity – it is a reversal of power where purple can be pink, and up sideways.

I have then argued that these basic dynamics, as well as their underlying structure, are significant motivating factors for Sartre's ontological system of 1943. Indeed, through ontological affectivity and emotion, facticity and value, (dis)possession and quality, as well as language, I have shown that there is always an interplay in this work inspired by Sartre's preoccupation with magical experiences and phenomena from the 1930s. In fact, I even contend that such preoccupations greatly contributed to the construction and justification of the ontological system as a whole, not least the for-itself, chiefly through affective evaluative qualities, giving over elements and aspects of itself to the in-itself, as well as to others, thereby allowing it to be captivated and enchanted therethrough.

In various nutshells, this is the road basically travelled so far. Where now? Well a lot of the preceding has been rather theoretical and technical, ultimately a phenomenological ontology in the vein of Sartre, as is fitting in a detailed exegesis. Now, though, it is time to show how such theory and technics are actually significant and of worth to a number of rather pressing contemporary issues. Indeed, the imminent second part, 'Sartrean magic in operation', applies the theoretical insights gained to a number of issues that are of no small import in today's world. The first (Chapter 5) will be largely positive, showing how Sartrean magic from 1936 to 1943 can give quite a constructive and intriguing account of the arts and artistic creation. The next three cases then take on progressively darker tones. This is because Sartrean magic, so often opposed to reason, logic, nature and the like, is often of the black variety. Indeed, the second case (Chapter 6) will show the power and captivation of advertising, including its more sinister side. The third (Chapter 7) will enter into certain social pathologies like racism and sexism in order to show, even further, that pernicious instantiations of magical thinking can take hold to quite chronic and societally dangerous degrees. Finally, the last (Chapter 8) case will look to when magic can take over the mind quite completely, specifically in a certain clinical instance of psychopathology (Schreber).

Such analyses will show the significance of these Sartrean insights, as well as what avenues might be of importance to consider for the future. Indeed, I will show that our magical being, although it can be divinely inspiring and creative, is also, sadly, often bone-crushingly ridiculous and destructive. I actually fear the latter is more prevalent nowadays, and perhaps always has been within human reality. On this note, just how we might consider this issue more, and how we might aim to make changes and rectifications therefrom when possible, is a chief goal of these illuminating but often disturbing cases. Indeed, a more explicit knowledge of our own magical being can only help to encourage the fantastic, as well as minimize the ridiculous and pernicious when and where possible.

What should nevertheless be clear by the end is that the two – creative and pernicious magic – are possible within human reality to quite amazing degrees. This is precisely because all magic stems, as the first part has shown, from our personalities (egos), emotions, images and values – nay, even from our very ontological fibre. In this manner, understanding our magical being is to provide a theoretically grounded philosophical anthropology that also presents various live cases which simultaneously give the theory more actual substance, application and relevance, as well as educate us as to the benefits of productive and enjoyable forms of Sartrean magic, as well as to the pitfalls to try and avoid when considering more dangerous instantiations.

# Part Two

# Sartrean Magic in Operation

## 5

# Magic and the Arts

Obviously neither I nor anyone can cover the arts as such, it being such a gargantuan human domain. I do however wish to extract a general theory of artistic creation from Sartrean points revolving around magic, which then can be applied, or at least seen as relevant, to numerous forms of art and entertainment. This will be the first section and is thus obviously not exhaustive by any long stretch of the imagination. I do it because there are applications and parts of Sartre's early philosophy – not least his concept of play, as well as the role of the imaginary and magic in art and artistic creation – that are more or less not covered in the literature. And they should be, because such analyses could go on to develop an interesting aesthetics based on these early insights. Indeed, the complexity, subtlety and richness of *The Imaginary* in particular have been overlooked for too long on this matter.

With regard to Sartre's own art as a writer, there is already a good deal of scholarship (for instance, Barnes 1973; Daigle 2010), including the various phases he went through. Yet again, though, I find a relative dearth when it comes to considering his earliest phase of writing, both philosophical and in novel form, and especially how the two interrelate. This is before the 'engaged' (cf. Barnes 1973: 25) or 'committed' (cf. Daigle 2010: 98–110) phase stemming from the seminal work *Qu'est-ce que c'est la littérature?* ([1948] 1985). Sartre's stance here is quite well known. Moreover his last phase, when literature was ultimately denounced as any kind of salvation (cf. Barnes 1973: 25), has also been quite well documented. For me, then, Sartre's earliest period strikes me as interesting to dwell upon because it is here where literature and philosophy – as well as the use of magical tactics in both – coalesce together the most and to the greatest effect. This will therefore be the second section of this chapter, finishing on a note for philosophy today.

## Play, artistic creation and magic

To get to the inherent magic throughout artistic creation and the arts, I will need to proceed here quite methodically. First I will articulate Sartre's two main 'spirits', of seriousness and of play, and how art may be considered as a type of serious play. This will open the door to art and creativity. Here I will analyse Sartre's explicit comments on art as found at the end of *The Imaginary* and also provide some of my own input. Such input will bring in key issues and themes we have seen in the first part to this work, as well as some other considerations.

I have already briefly mentioned Sartre's spirit of seriousness towards the beginning of Chapter 2. What I did not there mention is that it is set in opposition to another spirit, play. This opposition, like so many Sartrean oppositions, is bound together in a dynamic. Further, this pairing mirrors other pairings that we are already quite familiar with, not least facticity and freedom. Indeed, if the spirit of seriousness is best encapsulated by the scientific preoccupation with empirical facts, the fascination we have for play in its own turn entails a predominantly imaginative and frivolous engagement with the world, one's thoughts and others (cf. BN/EN: 63, 601/74–5, 626). In the former, idle and self-indulgent thoughts are barred for a focus on what is really observable and the case in a real, factual and causal manner; in the latter reality, its fact and causes can be transcended and even stripped of any real concern, often with a preference to be simply entertained. Considering this, the spirit of seriousness is predominantly on the side of the real, perception and the in-itself, whereas the spirit of play is more on the side of the irrealized, the imaginary and the pure spontaneity of the for-itself.

If either extreme is overindulged in for a sustained and disproportionate amount of time, Sartre suggests (cf. ibid.) that they can also mirror the two kinds of bad faith I have already explained in Chapter 4 in the subsection 'Being-for-itself'. Indeed, a brute and inflexible adherence to just the facts, like Dickens's Gradgrind (Dickens [1854] 1995: 9), reeks of bad faith because it tries to deny any freedom and frivolity to the human world. On the other end, a passion for just pure untethered freedom without any concrete and factual concern is an extreme spirit of play that tries to escape various facticities and all their inevitable influences and consequences. Once again, then, a dynamic balance seems required whereby sustained periods in either extreme are to be avoided through one's own openness for, and engagement in, both ends of the spectrum.

Within this spectrum, one could assume that there must be room for both playful seriousness and serious play. A science museum for young people might be an example of the former; professional sports would be an instantiation of the latter. Regarding this latter, I also believe this captures art and artistic creation quite well. In short, I view art and artistic creation as a form of serious play.

Let me explain. If seriousness is on the side of measuring and documenting facts of the world, play is on the freer side of creation, inspiration and entertainment. Now, one need only to look at Fink's ([1957–75] 2016/2010) recently translated works on play to know that it is a massive topic in itself; I am here merely interested in Sartre's brief and technical conception within his system and how it relates to art. Regarding this, it does indeed seem that art and artistic creation requires an interactive and dedicated combination of elements from both play and seriousness. Indeed, facts without creation would be science, and creation without actual factual instantiations would remain mere wisps of the imaginary, already disappeared. Of course the imaginary, more playful side to artistic creation is of vital importance. However, for it to actually come to fruition it actually has to be produced in some material form and thereby also depends upon some rather basic causal, physical principles.

As a literal matter of fact, every art form has materials with which one must work in certain ways through learning, obeying and manipulating certain mechanical laws – of vision, of sound, of movement and the like. Painters must work with paint and canvas and know how to capture and portray various visual forms. Musicians must use instruments and know the rules of musicality and sound, even if they are to bend them. Dancers must instantiate their artform through their own bodies' movements, often including collaborative efforts. Even writers must indeed write and know how to use at least one language in a readable, accessible and interesting manner.

Of course one's style is precisely how one engages with these various mechanics; one freely adopts to paint, play, dance, write in certain ways, indeed to the extent that the pioneers and forerunners in each field usually do this in a rather singular and captivating manner, not simply regurgitating themes that have been around forever and thereby have grown tired, redundant and nauseating. In this manner, veritable creation questions and often breaks the bounds of the status quo. This, however, also never happens in a vacuum; there is a melting pot for every artist, and some basic principles must have been learned and followed, as well as endlessly perfected and pushed. Hereby, play and seriousness are another instance of the interminable human dynamic between freedom and facticity.

This is briefly what I understand by art as a form of serious play, where one's free creative proclivities engage with a particular medium which necessarily has certain basic structures and laws that one must learn and develop for one's own ultimate aims. What, however, does Sartre say about art himself? His explicit analyses and arguments come right at the end of *The Imaginary*, in the second and last section to his conclusion no less, entitled 'The Work of Art' (IM: 188–94/361–73). Most of Sartre's analyses there concentrate on how one experiences a work of art, as well as what it is and is not. There are, however, a few crucial pointers regarding the creative process that will ultimately allow me to broaden it into a more general and encompassing idea, including the necessary role of magic in its various guises. I will first go through Sartre's main foci before expanding upon the passage directly addressing the creative process itself.

Sartre starts the section with the understandable disclaimer that he does not want 'tackle … the work of art as a whole' (IM: 188/361). Rather, he wants to capture 'the existential type of the work of art' (IM: 188/362), which he then immediately claims is 'an irreality' (ibid.). Irrealities are irreal objects, the objects available to us through the mode of the imaginary, as we have already seen at length. Moreover, we have also already seen that they are necessarily opposed to perceptions in that the latter's corresponding objects are always experienced as real. By calling the existential type of the work of art an irreality Sartre is placing the arts firmly in the realm of the imaginary.

Sartre's first example is a portrait of Charles VIII. A main point here is it is almost impossible to perceive the painting as a mere perceptual configuration of pure colours and shapes; we automatically see an image *of* Charles VIII – or barring such knowledge of him, a royal personage – in and through the portrait. This is what Sartre means by an 'aesthetic object' (IM: 189/362), which can moreover be grasped as so precisely because it is not just an immanent assemblage of colours and shapes but a depiction *of* something or someone that is transcendent. In Sartre's terms, our vision of Charles VIII 'is an *irreality* in so far as he is grasped *on* the canvas' (IM: 189/363). To use more of Sartre's terminology with which we are already familiar, the vision of Charles VIII is of an irreal, transcendent object that does not ultimately exist as the canvas and paint do, and yet it is made present on or through the canvas to us precisely through these external and physical analogical materials, plus my knowledge (or ignorance) of whom it is. It is in this manner that '*real* tones … enable this irreality to be manifested' (IM: 189/364); Charles VIII as an irreal, imaginary object must by its very nature remain 'entirely outside the real' (IM: 192/370) and yet the only way we have access to such irreality is because the physical painting 'functions as an *analogon*' (IM: 190/366) for him.

Even in more abstract painting Sartre notes that 'it is … in the irreal that the relations of colours and forms take on their true sense' (IM: 190/365); analogical materials as basic as colours and shapes can, in the aesthetic attitude, open up a transcendent space for feelings, significances and meanings that go beyond the mere physical qualities of such colours and shapes. Indeed, once again it is usually the automatic reaction to view portraits and other paintings in an aesthetic – which for Sartre is to say an inherently imaginary – attitude, whereby not only the external physical materials but also psychophysiological materials of knowledge, affectivity and kinaesthetic movements go into constituting the aesthetic object and experience (cf. IM: 190/364).

The same basic structure of analogons providing access to transcendent irreal objects runs throughout the whole of art for Sartre:

> What we have just shown regarding painting can also be easily shown with regard to the arts of fiction, poetry and drama. It goes without saying that the novelist, the poet, the dramatist constitute irreal objects through verbal analogons; it also goes without saying that the actor who plays Hamlet makes himself, his whole body, serve as an analogon for that imaginary person. (IM: 191/367)

Thus in every instance of an artwork there is external, physical analogical material that moreover gets invested with various psychophysiological elements and evokes aesthetic objects and experiences therethrough. Actually, Sartre goes even as far to say that 'the real is never beautiful' (IM: 193/371); to view something, even a person or a landscape, in an aesthetic manner is to make an image of it and thereby enter the realm of the imaginary. The materials, such as physical items like paintings and psychophysiological elements like feelings, are all of course real when considered in themselves. However, the crucial point here is that they are always already irrealized in aesthetic experiences. Thus, this mode of the imaginary, in its very noetic structure, automatically allows these materials to feed into, stand in for and thereby constitute a transcendent irreality that actually ends up structuring and governing the whole experience.

Considering these points, to have an aesthetic experience is to enter this main spirit of serious play, both on the side of the patron and on the side of the artist. For example, with an actor 'a transformation is made here similar to that which I indicated in the dream: the actor is gripped, entirely inspired by the irreal'[1] (IM: 191/367-8) – in this instance the character of Hamlet. This can be said of the patron too; the more familiar one is with the play and the more impassioned one is by the actor's rendition it, then the more one is likely to be immersed in and captivated by that particular performance precisely because it gives one good and interesting access to the ultimate transcendent objects of the whole experience. Such objects can be the play *Hamlet*, for instance, but the arts more generally evoke all kinds of emotions, images, ideas and concepts that often swirl in and around the aesthetic objects as well.

The same holds for music for Sartre too. Here one might think this is just about the perception of an arrangement of sounds, but yet again Sartre maintains the structure is once again analogical materials evoking a transcendent object that is, in a certain sense, outside of time and reality. Of course particular sounds have been recorded at particular places, and there are also countless live performances. The transcendent lynchpin holding all of this together, however, is ultimately the irreal song itself (e.g. 'Yellow Submarine'). This can – actually must – be instantiated in certain places and times in certain particular analogical materials to better and worse degrees, and yet it never, Sartre maintains, ever fully collapses into such real materials. Sartre's own example is Beethoven's Seventh Symphony:

> Let us first consider that I am listening to *the Seventh Symphony*. For me, this 'Seventh Symphony' does not exist in time, I do not grasp it as a dated event, as an artistic manifestation that unfurls in the Châtelet auditorium on 17 November 1938. If tomorrow or a week later I hear Furtwändler conduct another orchestra interpreting this symphony, I am once more in the presence of *the same symphony*. It is simply being played better or worse. (IM: 192/369)

It is the Seventh Symphony as such that holds all of this together. Of course the symphony can be written down precisely as it was originally penned, but this is not, Sartre says, what we are aiming at when playing or listening to it. Indeed, what we access through the actual playing and listening is this irreal object that is ultimately not 'in time' because it is never fully instantiated in one particular concrete version at any one moment. Sartre does of course allow that such irreality depends on the real; 'That the conductor does not faint, that a fire breaking out in the hall does not put a sudden stop to the performance' (IM: 192–3/370). This is to say that some kind of actual analogon must be there to evoke the irreal object – and yet the ultimate object, the symphony as such, must escape the real by its very nature (cf. IM: 192/370).

This interaction between transcendent object and the actual analogical material is also the crux for a Sartrean understanding of creative processes in general, as well as how they captivate and entertain us. Indeed, in a crucial passage Sartre explains that artistic creation should not be understood, as he says it often is, as a realization of something irreal, but rather as attaining something irreal (or even ideal) *through* real analogical materials:

> It is often heard said, in fact, that an artist first has an idea as imaged and then *realizes* it on canvas. The error made here is the idea that the artist can, in fact, start from a mental image that is, as such, incommunicable and at the end of the work deliver to the public an object that anyone can contemplate. It is then thought that there was a passage from the imaginary to the real. But this is in no way true. What is real, we must not tire of affirming, are the results of the brush strokes, the impasto of the canvas, its grain, the varnish spread over the colours. But, precisely, all this is not the object of aesthetic appreciation. What is 'beautiful', on the contrary, is a being that cannot be given to perception and that, in its very nature, is isolated from the universe. ... In fact the painter in no way *realized* a mental image, but simply constituted a material analogon such that anyone can grasp that image if only one considers the analogon. But the image thus provided with an external analogon remains an image. There is no realization of the imaginary.[2] (IM: 189/3634)

This is quite a claim; in artistic creation there is no passage from irreality to reality, from the imaginary to perception – the two remain as mutually exclusive experientially here as they do more generally. Indeed, the insight here is that in artistic creation one is *already* in the realm of the imaginary precisely when one is engaged in the creative, aesthetic process. This is where art would differ from playing or watching a sport live, for instance, because there one remains – at least primarily – in the perceptual realm. In artistic creation and engagement, to the contrary, one uses very real pieces of knowledge (e.g. a painting technique, a language), feelings (certain affectivities) and movements (e.g. brush strokes, typing) – as well as all kinds of external materials (e.g. paint, a computer) – all to constitute, attain and represent something else that is ultimately transcendent and irreal (e.g. a certain painting, a specific novel) by definition. It is the irreal, imaginary object that is the apex guiding the whole project, and thus no brush stroke or typed letter is ever put down merely for itself at any moment.

Ultimately, through this process the external analogon becomes the instantiation of the piece of art. Here, even in one-of-a-kind pieces like certain paintings, the transcendent element ('Oh That's Kandinsky's *Yellow-Red-Blue*') is what holds it all together and is what, moreover, makes the analogon an analogon rather than a mere perception. Actually, the idea here is that in the arts it is impossible to perceive images; so long as one sees Charles VIII in the painting, it is precisely an image *of* this person. And even if you do not see Charles VIII, you will still see 'some guy'.

To expand upon this, reading a novel, hearing a song and other forms of aesthetic engagement all have the same basic structure for Sartre. Here the claim is that it takes almost an impossible effort to try and merely perceive an image – to see just the colour and form and not the face of someone, for instance. In fact, if one perceives a mere colour then the 'image' precisely ceases to stand for something and thereby precisely ceases to be an image. Likewise, it is almost impossible not to see a word as a word (as well as its meaning if it is in a language one knows). The same would go for a sound coming from a violin – one automatically, through the imaginary, experiences it as a note, as a sound usually within a larger transcendent whole, a specific song or piece of music. This is the power of the imaginary; wherever images, signs, symbols, sounds and the like are, we automatically view them, treat them and interact with them in an aesthetic – which is to say imaginary – way.

Such interactions are highly engrossing and entertaining. Indeed, merging with the materials and attaining transcendence therethrough happen precisely when artists and patrons enter the aesthetic powers of the imaginary to their full force. We have seen that for Sartre, just as patrons of art have already entered the imaginary when looking at a painting, reading a book or listening to a piece of music, so too do artists in their creative processes; they use materials both physical and psychophysiological in order to evoke something that will never be fully there. Actually, at an earlier point in *The Imaginary* (cf. IM: 146–8/282–5), Sartre says there are people that have more or less wholly entered imaginary life. Artists are one such type of people, leading primarily imaginary lives, devoted to a type of serious play where an aesthetic enrapture with all kinds of phenomena and thoughts facilitates a predominantly creative attitude towards life.

Of course an artist goes through their life having perceptions. However, a great deal of the time such individuals seem to seek an inner kind of resonance and meaning to such basic experiences – even a greater, more transcendent kind of significance. In this manner, from things one has learned to feelings one has had, in the creative process such materials, if significant, are not really dwelt upon purely for themselves but precisely often used as materials to produce something else. Such materials must combine and interact with external physical materials, as well as often with other people's ideas. It is precisely this wholesale interaction between various elements that sows the seeds for any kind of creation as an engrossing aesthetic endeavour and activity.

Of course, one can have a specific idea or image one wishes to attain, and it can indeed only be attained through physical (e.g. a painting) or psychophysiological (e.g. a dance) materials. Here again, though, it is not that ideas cannot guide and inspire artistic creations; it is rather that all of this already happens within the adoption of the imaginary, aesthetic attitude that uses and plays with things beyond their simple perceptual and pragmatic possibilities. One may even say that the aesthetic process is precisely when everyday feelings, pieces of knowledge and all sorts of other materials and ideas are given free but serious rein, whereby new forms and significances are created through a dialogue with so many irreal and irrealized possibilities. This is what Sartre must mean when he says the ultimate objects of art are irrealities; the irreal is that realm where art not only can flourish but also can exist in the first place.

And it is of course a magical realm. We have already seen the inherently magical power of the imaginary, and art and artistic creation are doubtless some of the most significant powerful instances. First of all, it should be clear that although all artworks need to obey at least some basic physical laws to be instantiated in the real through analogons, through their inherently transcendent and imaginary nature they also necessarily harbour the capacity for representing and evoking non- and otherworldly phenomena, thus often leaving the shackles of deterministic nature far, far behind. A fantasy novel is one such clear instance.

Second, it should also be clear that both the creative process and the aesthetic appreciation thereof are exceedingly captivating, if not wholly enrapturing, emotional and (de)possessing experiences. Indeed, the whole fascination with art and entertainment more generally is that one becomes utterly immersed in producing or experiencing the works to the extent that they can come to hold great emotional and intellectual power over us. A simple example here is a particular song or other artwork that greatly moves you, 'speaks to you' (think reverse intentionality) and generally instantiates certain values and emotions you might hold dear. Such experiences can of course be instantiated in many forms, where the imaginary structure allows one's feelings and thoughts to be taken up into a transcendent world of wonder, enchantment and inspiration, even to the extent that returning to the real from such climes can often be quite brutal:

> Aesthetic contemplation is an induced dream and the passage to the real is an authentic awakening. We often speak of the 'disappointment' that accompanies the return to reality. ... In fact the discomfort is simply that of the sleeper on awakening: a fascinated consciousness, stuck in the imaginary is suddenly freed

by the abrupt ending of the play, of the symphony, and suddenly regains contact with existence. Nothing more is needed to provoke the nauseous disgust that characterizes the realizing consciousness. (IM: 193/371)

Aesthetic experience is a realm in its own right, with its own captivating, magical laws. We get emotionally and intellectually invested in this realm even to the extent that a return to the everyday and merely perceptual can feel quite crushing and despairing. Indeed, art and its creations can create long-lasting resonances in its creators and patrons. What is more, many artists need such primal resonance to even produce in the first place. Such resonance can, it seems, be (a mixture of) intellectual, emotional and bodily elements, which correspond to Sartre's three main internal analogical materials (knowledge, affectivity and kinaesthetic movement). For short, we may say so many psychophysiological affectivities, from rather naked conceptual thoughts on the one hand, to rather physical forces and movements on the other.

Third and finally, it is also a realm where others and their creations can be expressed to their fullest transcending and captivating potential. Indeed, if the other is primarily language, with the constant potential to surprise and enchant, as well as shock and appal, then art is one of its most powerful and exquisite domains. One need to only think of great works and moments of art down the years in order to see how one of the main captivating aspects is that artists pour quite literally their lives into their works, which then go on to inspire and enrapture whole groups and generations of people. It is thus one of the most productive and intriguing types of sociality, where mesmerization and influence can be at its strongest, not only in one's emotions and thoughts but also as one goes on to build oneself as a character (ego) with one's own interests, values and goals. All in all the arts, its productions and the experiences they induce is a main domain of Sartrean magic that involves all of the latter's dynamics in various intricate ways, and that moreover greatly utilizes and emphasizes many of the most positive, playful and creative aspects of our humanity. Such magic is, in quite short, at the root of much of the rapture we take in various forms of creation, entertainment and beauty.

## Sartre, literature and philosophy

Of course Sartre himself was an artist. He wrote many plays and novels. As I have already mentioned, this has been quite well documented. I do however think it is useful to dwell further on his earliest mature years as a writer. Indeed, I am interested in this early period because I believe his prowess as a writer, both in literary and philosophical forms, uses tactics of magic that often blur the lines between the two. This, moreover, could be said to continue, at least to some extent, throughout his intellectual and artistic life.

*Nausea* may be seen as a philosophical novel. Less evident however might be the idea that *Being and Nothingness* and other early philosophical works are indebted to a kind of literary philosophy. To explain this in more detail, I will first make a brief claim as to the potential difference between philosophy and literature. I will then show how Sartre often blends these categories and thereby makes his literature philosophical, as well as significant parts of his philosophy literary. A few examples of examples will help my points here, as figures often traverse his works, both literary and philosophical, embodying more than just themselves. This is where magical elements, not least the captivation of his presentations, hold serious sway. Finally, I will finish on a note that, as appealing and as captivating as Sartre's style and writing can be, one must also embrace the more laborious technical side of his philosophy if one is to understand and utilize it to its full potential. This is precisely what this present work is doing, finding the right blend between his captivations and technics. Indeed, I believe Sartre's blend still has much to offer in contemporary philosophy (and perhaps even philosophical literature) because it strikes a careful and powerful balance between images and concepts.

Regarding this latter point, broadly speaking one can claim literature primarily evokes images and imagery through a narrative of some kind, whereas philosophy primarily makes, studies and employs concepts. Cut and dried like this, it is in line with the basic differences between the imaginary and concepts as I have explained in Chapter 3 in the section 'Situating Sartre's imaginary: Between perception and concept'. In short, there is a difference between the image of a character like Roquentin on the one hand and the concept of, say, freedom on the other – even though the former can embody the latter and the latter be a condition for the former. Indeed, literary images are normally described and developed through various literary techniques and storylines; philosophical concepts are rather explained and developed through more concepts, reasons, arguments and examples.

Sartre often blurs these lines, however, notably through the last category, examples. For example, on the side of fiction Roquentin lives and embodies and interacts with many ideas, themes and people in ways that Sartre was also at pains to express philosophically, which is to say conceptually. This is why *Nausea* can be considered a great philosophical novel; its characters and themes embody concepts in a manner that is open to the imaginary. On the other side of this, Sartre's early philosophy is replete with examples, examples that, due to his literary talent, make the concepts under study quite accessible and even captivating.

I will look at *Nausea* first. As a literary piece, it should be clear how one's affective and intellectual materials feed into, and thereby help constitute, the narrative and imagery provided through Sartre's particular words, characters and style. In this manner one gets emotionally and intellectually invested in the work, whereby one can also reflect on the characters and other elements in reference to one's own feelings, character (ego) and values. This is why literature not only is aesthetically engaging but also has the potential to be emotionally, intellectually and morally enriching; it taps into various elements of affectivity and knowledge, blending these with enchantments and storylines of fictional others that all go into an imaginary medium which can have real effects on one's everyday (inter)personal reflections, emotions, thoughts and values. Thus literature teaches various sensitivities through an imaginary, irreal form that precisely through such a form can have intrigues and powers enough to influence one's everyday feelings and thoughts.

Concerning *Nausea* more specifically, it is backed up by, or actually instantiates, Sartre's whole early philosophy. First of all, Roquentin is reflectively obsessed with his own dull person and existence and yearns for special, one-of-a-kind 'adventures' that have now largely passed (cf., for instance, N: 39/43) – things like this employ theory from *The Transcendence of the Ego*. Second of all, he and other characters also show how emotion and desire take hold of one and can lead one to uncontrollable and even socially unacceptable acts, like the case of the Autodidact molesting a boy in the library and then getting assaulted by someone for it (cf. N: 234–8/232–6) – things like this employ theory from *Sketch for a Theory of the Emotions*. Third of all, Roquentin is also often alone daydreaming and brooding, captivated by various images and memories that he inevitably weakens through overuse (cf. N: 53/56) – things like this employ theory from what would become *The Imaginary*. Fourth of all Roquentin, as I have already analysed, frequently suffers from an ontological nausea that comes upon him and besmirches all of his desires, values and relations – things like this, finally, employ theory from what would become *Being and Nothingness*. All of these are the magical dynamics and structures I have been at pains to express throughout this work, and that come out quite exquisitely in this literary form. Actually, given the fact that the novel is in and around the earlier shorter philosophical works, and actually predates *The Imaginary* and *Being and Nothingness*, one may reasonably think that Sartre was often able to get at images of basic phenomena and experiences before he was able to articulate them in a more conceptual, technical and philosophical manner. This would be in keeping with what we have seen in Chapter 2, namely, that concepts are frequently reached through images and are, if reached at all, generally more difficult to attain.

Such is a piece of philosophical literature; powerful and captivating imagery that is also underlain with conceptual dynamics and categories. However, when Sartre turns to more philosophical works, literary images do not disappear but actually greatly help elaborate and even explicate the concepts under discussion. Thus if *Nausea* is imagery with underlying conceptual issues, his early philosophy is concepts supported by literary descriptions and imagery.

This is done primarily through examples and figures which, I might say, function as 'particular universals' in the sense that they instantiate, through precise description and detail, a general concept or idea. Sartre's early philosophy is replete with such instances, none more so than the recurring figure of Pierre. We have mentioned him already quite a bit, for he is indeed Sartre's go-to figure in his early philosophy. Indeed, whether he is a friend that needs to be aided in *The Transcendence of the Ego* (TE: 18/105), someone I hate with passion also in *The Transcendence of the Ego* (TE: 22/108–9), the person we are trying to capture through images in *The Imaginary* (IM: 18/41–2) or the friend we are looking for in a café in *Being and Nothingness* (BN/EN: 33–4/44–5), Pierre takes on an almost mystical status within Sartre's early philosophy in that he is able to imbue pretty much any principle or concept that is under discussion.

A lesser-known example, but one that can help highlight this, comes from *The Imaginary*. The conceptual point Sartre wishes to make is that perception is inherently more powerful and inexhaustible than the imaginary, and this is why something like a long-distance relationship, for instance, often fails. To support the argument Sartre uses an example described with phenomenological, as well as literary, elements. It is an example of a beloved having left and the lover left behind tries to battle with the impoverishment that the now-necessary imaginary attitude towards the beloved has in contrast to the previously richer perceptual one. The main figure here, unsurprisingly when we think of *Nausea*, is Annie:

> Little by little the feeling will be schematized and will congeal into rigid forms and correlatively the images that we have of Annie will become banal. The normal evolution of knowledge and of feeling require that at the end of a certain time this love loses its own *nuance*: it becomes *love* in general and somewhat rationalized: it is now that all-purpose feeling that the psychologist and the

novelist describe: it has become typical; this is because Annie is no longer there
to confer on it that individuality that made it an irreducible consciousness. And
even when, at this time, I would continue to conduct myself as if I loved Annie,
remaining faithful to her, writing to her every day, dedicating all my thought to
her, suffering being alone, something has disappeared, my love has undergone a
radical impoverishment. Dry, scholastic, abstract, tended towards an irreal object
that has itself lost its individuality, it evolves slowly towards absolute emptiness.
It is around this moment that one writes: 'I no longer feel close to you, I have lost
your image, I am more separated from you than ever.' (IM: 144–5/278–9)

This is clearly not a case of straight-up literature. What it is, though, is using
an accessible and thus powerful example that also has some narrative (this
segment is only a piece of a much longer description) in order to explicate and
reinforce the conceptual point the author is trying to make. I dare say that Sartre
was talented at this more than most. Indeed, this should come as no surprise
seeing as his mind seems to have straddled the imaginary and the conceptual,
the literary and the philosophical, all at once. It is this blend of literature and
philosophy that makes, in my opinion, his early work so captivating. Considering
this, it is not only the theme and contents of his early work that often concerns
magic; here the point is Sartre's style is also imbued with magical methods and
tactics through the use of both philosophical literature and literary philosophy.
In short, Sartre adds enchantment and imagery to concepts, as well as gives
more conceptual underpinnings to fictional works such as *Nausea*. It is thus a
two-way street; Sartre utilizes mechanisms of captivation in order to stimulate
one's images and concepts into a dialogue, whereby emotional, imaginary and
intellectual investments are created and sustained through stirring and accessible
descriptions and imagery that also engage with conceptual issues, both in novel
and philosophical forms. All of this contributes to display his conceptual points
in a multifaceted and colourful manner, as well as to their utmost force.

In fact, the resonance that Sartre's examples establish can often be so
enchanting that one loses sight of the drier, more difficult and technical aspects
of his philosophy. Indeed, Sartre often uses such descriptive examples because
he, much like many other phenomenologists in and around his time, had such
a technical vocabulary that it would remain rather inaccessible without some
more particular description and imagery. The problem here, though, is that the
captivating and detailed particular descriptions and imagery, as well as the literal
everyday meanings of terms (e.g. 'freedom', 'shame'), often cloud out the more
technical conceptual points that Sartre is trying to make. In this work I have been
at pains to show that it is important to strike the right balance between accessible

and colourful examples, as well as the willingness to get one's hands dirty with the conceptual technics of this systematic and surprisingly consistent thinker. Images and examples may indeed strike up easy and powerful resonances with readers, but the laborious technical terms also need to be grappled with and understood in their fundamentals. If considered well, these two sides always ultimately match up and in fact complement and reinforce each other greatly. Without this balance, however, between how examples always instantiate and colour the underlying conceptual points, the examples on their own remain mere particulars, while the concepts without the flourish of examples often remain aloof and inaccessible.

I think these points can also be considered a note for contemporary philosophy. For me, too often are thought experiments spewed out without really considering the more ultimate significance of the point in question; and on the other side, pure conceptual arguments have also now, in certain circles at least, forgotten the power and appeal of being relevant, accessible and colourful. I believe Sartre, when read attentively, manages to escape the extremes of particularism and universalism – as well as rather haphazard jumps between the two – by always seeking for a blend between the concrete and conceptual. This, in fact, is what his phenomenological ontology is all about, which can be expressed as philosophy with a literary touch, as well as literature with a major philosophical intrigue. In short, Sartre's employment of both literary enticement and conceptual rigour is ultimately bound together in a lived dynamic that always has a little touch of captivating magic to it. This is, I believe, something all intriguing philosophy and literature – as well as their blends – may aspire to.

# 6

# Advertising

Captivation does not stop with literature and philosophy of course. If literature is mainly about captivation through imagery and narrative, and philosophy through concepts, one may say that this new instance – advertising – taps primarily into our desires and values. Advertising is of no small importance in today's world, and it often has a rather sinister side. To articulate this, first I will describe advertising and show how it is thoroughly magical in the Sartrean sense. I will then consider how the increasing predominance of capitalism and concomitant rising technologies are only giving advertising increasing force and reach, and certainly not always for the better.

## Advertising and its magic

I am sure everyone is aware, whether they like it or not, of all kinds of products through all kinds of media which nowadays barrage us quite relentlessly. The sheer fact that many of today's richest companies make most of their revenue from advertising already shows the quite flabbergasting power this capitalistic method has on human desire and value. Of course there is a wide range of advertising, from quite artistic and delicate to downright idiotic and deceitful. Moreover, although whole styles of advertising can tap into our sensibilities and rationality, even in these forms one of its most basic magical capacities often remains to turn general wants into specific needs. Even further, on the dark side of sensibility and rationality, advertising is very often nothing more than pure magic, from anything from zany images and messages that make a product stick in one's head just for the sheer bizarreness of it, to quite wild associations between a product and something else that, when looked at more objectively, have absolutely nothing to do with each other.

Some pieces of advertising are so well known to a general Western population that they do not even need to be reproduced. For me, one such notable example is Uncle Sam's 'I WANT *YOU* FOR THE U.S. ARMY', with a look and finger both pointing directly at its viewer. These posters, from 1917, encapsulate much of what Sartre has said about the imaginary and its captivating powers. Originally a British recruitment idea (cf. Pincas and Loiseau 2008: 30–1), it was quickly adopted by all major battling forces of the First World War period (cf. ibid.) to great success. Why was it so successful? In short, it is hard to look at it without already being under the power of *its* intention: Uncle Sam wants *you* to fight for *him*; it is a quintessential case of Sartrean magic whereby the supposed object (the image) is already suffused with a power that puts you, the supposed active subject, under its sway. It is a case of reverse intentionality where the thing holds the subjective power, and you are the object of this power; we get bewitched and made a passenger by a mesmerizing, strangely active object. One can of course deny the claim, the intention, simply reject the idea of joining the army. However, the claim is already there, imposing its power and request upon you.

Advertising, whether political or not, essentially utilizes the imaginary and its array of magnetic fantastical powers. No matter the medium, advertising always utilizes technology in order to present analogical material that tries to sell an audience its product, often with complete disregard for the laws of nature and reason. Advertisements are, in short, the universe of Sartrean analogons and their magic par excellence. The actual product, whether it be joining the army, buying a can of Coke, or seeking out one's favourite brand of jeans, is always evoked through the advertisement. This means the product is never the actual advertisement itself; advertising is essentially medial, and thus squarely in the transcending realm of the imaginary.

Magritte, who worked in advertising (see: Hoffman 2003: 94), understood this basic insight very well already in 1928 and played with it. In his world-famous piece of what I would call 'anti-advertising', *La trahison des images*, there is an image of a pipe with the sentence *Ceci n'est pas une pipe* ('This is not a pipe'). Magritte was indeed playing here with the difference between an image of something on the one hand and the thing itself on the other. I find this 'playful' because a lot of advertising entices one in and then the actual product often does not live up to its billing – for example, a lot of fast food. In this manner, Magritte's piece is anti-advertising because it uses the principles of advertising – namely, analogical material that includes an image and a message – that nevertheless do not try to sell or offer you anything. There is a picture of a pipe, and then the claim that this, in fact, is not a pipe. And certainly it is not; it is an image of – or in Sartrean terms an analogon for – an actual pipe. Here Magritte already recognized the difference – and treachery – of images over against what they actually stand in for.

It should be clear that such images, like all images under this conception, are not real; they are irreal. However, they can represent realities (actual products) which forcefully move our desires, wishes and values in very real ways. It is in this essential interplay between what advertisements represent and promise, and what they actually make us feel and deliver, where their whole drama – and magic – plays out.

To engage in a rather brief historical summary, advertising can be recognized as incorporating, to various degrees and emphases, two main schools or stances: 'hard sell' or 'reasons why' advertising and a more creative and artistically focused pole (cf. Fox [1984] 1997: 226; Tungate [2007] 2013: 43). To phrase in Tungate's words (ibid.), 'If the history of advertising has one overriding theme, it is this constant tug of war between two schools: the creative, who believe art inspires consumers to buy; and the pragmatists, who sell based on facts and come armed with reams of research.' This seems to once again mirror Sartre's two spirits, of play and of seriousness respectively. Indeed, the history of advertising is a history of balancing between, or preferring, the actual, reasonable qualities and values of the product, over against more creative and frivolous types. Further, the technique that dominates in any period is normally conditioned by the economic and social climate of the time, with recessions and depressions usually reflected in no-nonsense, hard-fact advertisements (or perhaps in extreme cases little or no advertisement at all), whereas times of plenty usually give space for more colourful campaigns that play more on the emotions and whimsies of the largely prospering public. Indeed, Fox's book may be summarized as a detailed exposition of this basic to and fro.

In this sense, the history of advertising has deep links to the history of any given society or culture, not least the economics. Of even more significance for us here, however, is the role technology plays in the every-burgeoning amount of products and their advertisements. I mean technology in a twofold sense here: not only did the industrial and technological revolution create exponential growth in the range of products produced and made available; additionally and concomitantly, the media necessary for advertising such products, from newspapers to smartphones, grew rapidly and inordinately as well. In this manner, advertising was an inevitable concomitant of the industrial revolution (cf. Pincas and Loiseau 2008: 25; Tungate [2007] 2013: 8) where the births of newspapers, magazines, radio, TV, computers, the internet and now smartphones and tablets were all essential media required to harbour all the analogical material vital for the advertising platform as such. Indeed, such physical materials are and will always remain an essential component for the imaginary process that advertising utilizes; one needs such real platforms in order to represent irreal dreams and wishes that can be satisfied if one goes and actually purchases the product. Here then, real and irreal are once again mutually implicated to the extent that they condition, influence and depend on each other.

Also fundamentally at work are desire and possession. For example, seeing an advertisement of a car while driving in that car would have a rather different feeling – perhaps 'Ha! I've already got it!' – than seeing it while driving in your old banger – 'Oh! I wish I had *that one!*' This small example already shows that advertising can constantly play on one's desires, emotions and values, not least those of betterment and the possession thereof. The basic message is very frequently such: if you buy this product, you will be happy. Nowhere is this more apparent than in the rather recent (2009) Coca-Cola campaign of 'Open Happiness'. Here Coca-Cola is actually equated with happiness; the two are the same, interchangeable, Coca-Cola and happiness, so if you drink this drink, you will be happy. Of course, on the one hand this is a bald-faced lie; Coca-Cola is not, and can never be, happiness (it being merely a drink). On the other hand, drinking an ice-cold Coke on hot summer's day can produce a real feeling of pleasure which, rather stretchily speaking, could be considered as at least contributing to a happy moment. In this manner, even a soft drink reaches a level of representation where all of one's problems could be resolved, at least momentarily, if you partake in it.

Another point here is that nowadays advertising is inescapable. New ad-blocking technologies notwithstanding, it is still everywhere, and this is no coincidence. Already in 1923, Ernest Woodruff, then president of Coca-Cola, wanted 'a Coke to be "within arm's reach of desire" of people worldwide' (Pincas and Loiseau 2008: 59). He more or less got his wish. Why, however, is this significant? First of all, it demonstrates Sartre's basic claim that reality and irreality always run in tandem for human beings; not only are a society's desires expressed in its advertisements, but advertisements can actually come to infiltrate many cultural elements themselves. The red and white of Santa Claus, for instance, is heavily appropriated by Coca-Cola at Christmas time; beer bottles are brown and green because of a 1961 campaign for a certain beer that emphasized the taste-improving qualities of such a light-blocking colour (cf. id.: 148), and there are a whole host of words ('Hoover' instead of vacuum cleaner; 'Q-tip' instead of cotton bud; *un bic* instead of *un stylo*), as well as sayings ('Diamonds are forever'; 'Because you're worth it'; 'Just do it') that are all just so many small instances of how advertising and its barrage of images and messages can come to infiltrate our lives and thoughts at every turn.

Taking such insights more generally, advertising is a perfect example of how reality and the irrealities spawned in and around them come to enmesh us in a world where our hopes, dreams and tastes are already out there in the world calling to us, wanting us to choose a particular product or brand. In short, in the land of advertising and its desires, everyone wants *you* to the extent that a perfect advertising campaign is when supposedly free individuals each want the very same product and still feel utterly free and individual about it. The demand for Apple's various products is currently a very good example of this. In Hoffman's words, 'Advertising … is an engine that works to have it both ways – making you feel like you are exercising your freedom as an individual while encouraging you to make the same choice as everyone else' (2003: 75). It is hereby a strange, magical mix of thinking one is in control, choosing just for one's self – and yet one is just doing as the next person is.

Indeed, even the choices we have are conditioned and limited by what is out there, by the companies' and producers' supply. In this manner, they enact a sly and clever magic trick of making consumers think that they are in power when actually it is they. It is another reversal, another inversion whereby our 'own' choices ultimately depend on, and are in fact often wholly subservient to, the mesmerizing draw that certain products hold over us. Thus, as a handmaiden and mirror of reality (cf. Fox [1984] 1997: 217), advertising already shows us that the consumer world of products is always already suffused with our desires and values to the extent that we become quite bewitched, and often quite powerless, in front of them. This, more technically, is exactly Sartre's concept of magic as a strange synthesis, where consciousness instils a power in objects to the extent that it becomes captivated by the borrowed power of such objects, even to the point where one goes out and procures these things with frenzied excitation.

Here, it will not be necessary to go into much detail of how annoying and stupid many advertisements are – for example, TV ads of women in bikinis partying with beer, where it is magically insinuated that 'if you drink this beer, you'll get these women'. Nor will I spend much time on how the market is often so flooded that we have a kind of mechanism (and now the technology – ad-blocking applications for online; recordable and fast-forward TV) to ignore most of them (or so we at least like to believe). No indeed; to see the fantastical absurdity of many advertisements one need to tune in to any sporting event – the

FIFA World Cup sponsored by MacDonald's and Budweiser, for example – where if the athletes performing were to actually consume these products they would be unable to compete. Indeed, here it should be clear that such advertisements are for the people watching the sports rather than for any real link with the event under sponsorship. Instead of focusing on such targets, then, I will focus on a number of subtler advertisements, wherein a quite powerful idea has been reached with regard to the product and its own standout context. In marketing lingo, this is the supposed USP, the 'unique selling point'. Indeed, by making the product stand out from the rest in a more intelligent manner, I believe one can see the real magic and captivating qualities good advertising inherently has, which is then watered down in the more everyday, banal barrages.

One of the most celebrated series of all time (cf. Fox [1984] 1997: 256–8; Hoffman 2003: 29, 32; Tungate [2007] 2013: 49–52) has to be for the Volkswagen (VW) Beetle, not least the 'Think Small' (1959) and 'Lemon' (1960) advertisements one would find in magazines of the period. Given the historical context, it was a piece of daring and artistic creation that not only boosted VW's sales enormously but also made the advertising agency (DDB) one of the most dominant of the 1960s, as well as revolutionizing the way advertising was carried out in general. The context is this: 'They wanted us to sell a Nazi car in a Jewish town' (Lois in: Tungate [2007] 2013: 49). In fact, the original Beetle design was commissioned and fervently supported by a Ford-inspired Hitler, as well as designed by Ferdinand Porsche (cf. Rieger 2013). Here, although the Second World War obviously derailed the Nazis' plan to implement the *Volkswagen* as its signature car, various permutations (cf. ibid.) led it to enormous success in West Germany and Europe in the 1950s, followed by the United States and other countries. With regard to the latter, the VW campaign seemed daring to say the least; not only did the German company want to push its product in post-war USA, but it also wanted to sell a particularly odd-looking and small car in a land where the big and powerful reigned supreme. This advertising series managed, however, to captivate enough Americans that it was a wild success.

Similar to Magritte's piece, the advertisement has an image and a message, but with a crucial difference; the image (the car) and the message ('Lemon') do not seem to correlate, and yet they ultimately do in an intriguing and compelling fashion. The apparent incongruity is already ingenious because it piques the curiosity of the reader; 'Why is this car a "lemon"?' one might ask on seeing it. As one begins to read the text underneath one starts to learn that the image is actually an image of a particular, single VW Beetle that 'missed the boat'. Why did it miss the boat? Because it had a tiny scratch on the 'chrome strip of the glove compartment'. This was enough, according the meticulousness of the German checking system, for it to be rejected for sale and to be classified as a lemon, a reject. This story therefore, by intriguing the reader and highlighting a rejected model, in fact leads to a discourse on what sets VW cars apart – precisely because of such (German) meticulousness the consumer gets only the very best (the 'plums'), thus ending with the catchy and memorable punchline: 'We pluck the lemons; you get the plums.'

With the recent ongoing VW scandal over emissions, this line now strikes us as highly ironic; there now seem to be more lemons than plums. Be this as it may, at the time it was a runaway success. Indeed, if the image of a VW Beetle popped into your head when next thinking (small!) of a car to buy, then the advertisement's work had been done. What creates such power is, generally, the advertisement's capacity to captivate the audience, laying its seed often quite subliminally.

Of course there are advertising methods that simply beat the viewer, through sheer repetition, into remembering their product. Subtler advertisements endure, however, because they play enough on reasonable values (rigorous safety checks), emotions (humour) and intelligent reversals and messages (small and efficient is better) that all end up setting the product apart from the mass of other options. Indeed, along with novelty (cf. Tungate [2007] 2013: 192) and resonance (cf. Reichert 2003: 213) this tactic of 'making virtues of … apparent deficiencies' (Fox [1984] 1997: 256) is a great and hugely successful ploy in advertising.

This is very evident in Guinness's long-running and highly successful idea of 'Good things come to those who wait'. Here, an apparent deficiency of a pint of Guinness would be that 'it takes 119.5 seconds to pour the perfect pint', meaning you have to wait longer than other pints. Many Guinness advertisements turned this slightly irksome practical issue on its head however, thereby transforming the longer pouring time into a virtue for product and consumer alike, in that if you are patient you will receive a superior beer (and by corollary superior things in general). Personally speaking, I have never seen so many people want to like a product when they actually do not. I put this down to the power and endurance that Guinness's branding, through its advertisements, has reached over the decades.

One final example, again a TV commercial, is the 'Cog' (2003) advertisement by Honda. This is a world-renowned advertisement where an almost two-minute process of car parts, which underwent almost no computerized manipulation, roll and click and knock into each other in an ingenious technological puzzle. The process ends up triggering a funk song accompanying a brand-new Honda

Accord gliding to a halt with the punchline – 'Isn't it nice, when things just work?', whereupon a small sign 'Accord' (meaning to agree in French) drops down. The hidden irony here is that it took months for the conveyer-belt maze of bumping parts from another disassembled Accord to work. Nevertheless, the implication is that if you buy the Accord, it will just work. The message here is simple, and yet the advertisement will very likely remain in the memory for its technological ingenuity and wit.

We have seen advertising essentially utilizes our capacity for the imaginary by captivating us to the extent that we remember the product and are thus more likely to buy it. To continue, we must still see why all of this relates to Sartre's concept of magic in a more systematic fashion. In order to do this, I need to go through the fourfold, but interrelated, theoretical distinction that I made in the first part of this work.

We have already seen the magic of the imaginary. Advertisements are irreal items that can be imbued with pseudo powers to the extent that you want to buy the actual product. In other words, images motivate our desires by enacting a borrowed spontaneity from these very same desires and their accompanying values. It is, once again, an experience that necessarily involves a curious synthesis of original non-conscious passivities (pictures, sounds and the like) that nevertheless get spontaneously imbued with some of our very own conscious activities (desires and values).

Often essential to this is affectivity and emotion as well. Of course, in hard sell or reasons why advertising things are bought purportedly because it makes complete rational sense to do so. Such a case can still however be seen as involving affectivity; an affective pull of a product because it is the 'sensible' or 'reasonable' product to choose. In such a case, these latter qualities are precisely the affective ones assigned to the product and are why one wants and values it.

Going further, often there is an additional magic trick. We are very often induced to buying things we do not actually need, even if such purchases are (the more) sensible ones. Indeed, if one takes 'need' in the strict sense of water, food, shelter, healthcare, sociality and the like – namely, things strictly necessary for survival and basic wellbeing – then a great deal of what we buy are either elaborate wants that do satisfy needs as well as go way beyond them (e.g. a mansion) or just pure wants unrelated to any real need at all (e.g. the latest and greatest smartphone when your current one still works perfectly). Indeed, our desires and the emotions they give rise to are, we have seen, quite insatiable and often extremely inordinate; advertising exploits this to often quite staggering degrees. Actually, two of advertising's most powerful tricks are to precisely transform mere wants into felt needs, as well as create other wants out of seemingly nothing. Emotionally here, one 'simply has to have it' because 'everyone else does' – even though, strictly speaking, one does not.

It is in this manner that the magic of advertising taps into our emotions quite relentlessly. Indeed, there are many instances where reasons cannot distinguish between the different options; a lot of products are fundamentally the same in their basic ingredients (e.g. jeans, medications, perfumes), meaning it is often *only* the marketing and the personal emotions it triggers that differentiates them. Here we normally come to prefer one choice to another because it 'pleases us' more somehow; it has a certain 'I don't know what' superiority to it.

Think of Levi's jeans perhaps. People (myself included) often pay much more for this particular brand because we emotionally delude ourselves into thinking they are somehow special. All denim jeans are, however, made in pretty much the same way with pretty much the same materials. Perhaps Levi's pays more attention to detail somehow? But then why can jeans half the price last the same amount of time, or even longer? Here, just like in normal emotions, we assign magical, evaluative qualities ('superior', 'longer-lasting' and the like) to items that do not originally or objectively inhere in the items themselves. In this manner, advertising manipulates our emotive capacity to transform and augment objects by giving them extra powerful evaluative qualities, thereby making us see 'actual' differences where often there are only negligible ones, or even none at all.

An even stronger example here is certain painkillers, such as paracetamol. In many countries (e.g. the UK) different brands must legally contain the exact same ingredients, and yet we can – and often do – pay double for an identical product through a kind of 'illogical loyalty' (Packard [1957] 2007: 66) merely because the packaging is branded in a certain familiar, comforting and supposedly superior way. This again shows how advertisement unlocks and manipulates the transformative and magical potentials of emotive consciousness, as well as the projective capacities of the imaginary, in order to transform basic, objective things into the same things with 'that little something extra'.

An even stronger claim here would be an actual placebo effect where a certain product will make the consumer feel better even though the product is not specially designed for what it claims. This came up in a Neurofen scandal a few years ago where 'targeted reliefs' for headaches, back pains and other 'different' types of pain were all actually the same product, just with different packaging and prices. This would be magic right down to the psychophysiological level, where only apparent psychological differences actually seem to influence the person in their physiological wellbeing. Thus magic here is when objects of the world, especially when personally and alluringly presented, have the power to hold values and qualities for us that they do not actually or necessarily contain themselves, but that can still nevertheless very much affect – and even effect – us on various emotional, psychological and even physiological levels.

With regard to the ego – our (inter)personalities – advertising is yet again a perfect example to show how what we buy and which brands we use can come to define us as a person within various social groups. Indeed, one's self-image is constantly mediated not only through our own reflections and others but also through what the market has to offer and what we choose to partake in (and not). Here, just as 'We are what we eat' (Feuerbach) we are also what we wear, drink, live, do and so on. Owning an Apple computer, for example, is not just because of explanations why it might be a better product; it is a fashion statement through which one identifies as a person to oneself and to others. Indeed, most people who own an Apple computer do not even think about, much less use, the extra advantages that this device has over its competitors; it is often merely a public ego bewitchment of *das Man* whereby the individual does as everyone else in order to be like – and get along with – them. Coupled with such commonalities could indeed be some rather idiosyncratic tastes, projects, procurements and buys that may set one apart. Nonetheless, even here – unless one is extremely independent and creative – one can only move largely in and against what the market provides.

We have seen that actions, qualities and states of the ego make up the person. In the ego's magic, moreover, such originally reflective and object-like elements can come to be hypostatized onto the subjective level. Thus, even if the products one buys go against the grain slightly, they are still often related to in a manner where there is a magical hypostatization of material and other possessions into character traits and activities that come to 'really' define who you are. Thus an originally immaterial aspect of ourselves (consciousness) comes to be solidified, both materially and psychologically, in and through the products we own and the activities we engage in – in short, what we spend money on. In this manner, advertising goes a long way in defining how and in what manner we live out our lives, because it conditions our choices, activities and even our (inter)personalities often to quite sly and large extents.

Finally, we come to value and possession. Here, values are nothing other than the reasons why we buy something, from the most logical to the most outlandish. So, whether it be cheap, exclusive, beautiful, enjoyable or whatever, these are so many values that we hold and want to have in concrete instantiations – in our possessions and activities. It is advertising that acts as the main trigger for our values to be incanted into actual products through our (inter)personal reflections, emotions and images, wherethrough we then go out and try to make sure we possess the desired item(s). Once owned, we are content, at least for a while, until new products and new advertisements raise countervalues (e.g. 'too old') that begin the cycle all over again. Thus, also – or even particularly – in consumerism does the ceaseless interplay of value, desire and possession play itself out, where we try to secure relatively lasting enjoyments through objects we value, want and possess, thereby attempting once again to fix our flighty freedom onto and into sturdy, synthesized grounds that never, however, actually stop moving.

It is in these ways that advertising is a very powerful case of Sartrean magic. Indeed, if an advertisement works for you, it has, through stirring one's personal reflections, emotions, fantasies, image of self or values, made you spellbound and desirous for a specific product that you simply must have, sometimes even at all literal costs.

## Advertising, the market and rising technology

As technology continues to advance advertising's captivating powers will continue to advance as well. It is, and will continue to be, so successful and influential because, as we have just seen, it taps into and harnesses many of the magical aspects of our being. While admitting such power, it would also be fruitful to be aware of the more serious pitfalls to this captivation. Indeed, the structures and mechanisms of advertising in today's capitalistic societies go way beyond our decisions to buy, or not buy, a certain soft drink; today there are many political and ideological campaigns that come to shape not only how certain individuals but also how whole societies and even whole nations feel and think.

Advertising is key in such a process. In fact, nowadays the importance of advertising's central influence on our buying habits – from cans of Coke to whole political ideologies – has spawned a whole new scientific discipline known as consumer behaviour (cf., for instance, Szmigin and Piacentini 2015). Here, psychological systems and explanations of consumer's past and present buying habits and cultures are scrupulously analysed in order to understand future trends – as well as, of course, future possible manipulations. Missing from such an account, however, has been the more deep-rooted discourse of how and why advertising orchestrates and manipulates many of our (inter)personalities, emotions, fantasies and values. This study has, till here, made a modest movement in this direction. Now, it would indeed also be well to comment briefly on the broader issues of how a combination of today's high capitalism with high technology is giving advertising unprecedented force and reach.

It should be abundantly clear that advertising is one of the main engines of today's capitalist societies. Actually, beyond material goods it is also a predominant force in non-material – which is to say psychological and virtual – goods as well. Such advertising thus also shapes many people's online behaviour, as well as even one's everyday political and moral beliefs. One need only look at the colossal advertising outlays for all kinds of referendums, elections and moral stances; no massive budget for advertising will basically mean no chance of victory in these campaigns. What is more, here increasingly less of the content has to be empirically accurate nowadays, or even empirical at all; a lot of advertising on this level often flouts laws of nature, reality and reason, where online images and messages can often be completely fantastical and fake, as well as moral and political messages often utterly skewed or baseless when compared to the facts. Indeed, all that matters here, in textbook capitalistic fashion, is that the product or idea sells – that people buy or buy into it.

One can thus see how Sartre's tectonics for the arts of magical persuasion are relevant here too. Indeed the basic structure remains. Of course one needs the products of all kinds, from physical to virtual to ideological. However, one also needs consumers to be aware of them. Here again, it is precisely advertising that provides the visible and audible bridges for this vast and complex system often known as the market. Such a market now sells anything with relentlessness and vigour, from a cheeseburger to a staunch political stance. It also looks like this will only increase as technologies develop in tandem with such economic and political forces for the foreseeable future.

Capitalistic markets depend quite obviously on having capital that can then generate goods for its consumers and profits for its operators. Indeed, capital has an inherent power to generate resources, products and yet further capital, as opposed to the power mere money has to more or less just consume. To work, the generating process must meet some demand in the market in a purportedly special or unique way, for there is fierce competition to grab consumers' attention. It is around these two crucial terms, demand and competition, where advertising's whole being gravitates. Quite obviously, if your product is not known, it will not be demanded and thereby sell. Secondly, even if it is known, a competitor might do a better job of making their own product more appealing. And thirdly, capitalism by its nature encourages ever-increasing renewal and competition of products which, when successful, yield massive financial rewards for the instigators to continue the trend on and on.

One of the key magic tricks involved in this, which I have already alluded to and which is one of advertising's key special tasks, is to transform vague 'wants' into acutely felt supposed 'needs'. Here again, strictly speaking there are not so many needs absolutely necessary for mere survival – water, food, shelter, basic healthcare and the like. This is an admittedly strict and logical definition of need. Capitalism and the magic of its advertising have to combat this strict notion because it could not possibly flourish in such a limited and modest environment. This is because capitalism and its markets essentially rely on consumers being given, and then wanting, evermore. Indeed way more than any strict conception of need. In a good deal of the West's privileged, daily life most of us are always already beyond what is actually required for mere survival, if not in category then at least in magnitude and variety. Such massive and permanent stretches beyond what is actually needed for life – including many products that are actually damaging to said life – are part of what makes us human and are due, at bottom, to a combination of relative comfort with regard to basic needs on the one hand and insatiable drives and desires (cf. O'Shiel 2013) for a plethora of non-needs on the other hand. In such a mixture, survival and modesty is never enough for the vast majority. Our bottomless desire is actually, we have seen, a deep ontological nerve within us, and it is this nerve that the market and its advertising strike its mesmerizing pokers into with full force.

Indeed, advertising's mission, more often than not, is to sell one things that go beyond the call for mere need: a meal in a lovely restaurant, tickets to your favourite sports event, a trip halfway across the world to lie on a beach. Human desire is so broad, multifarious, endless and insatiable that it cannot rest still with the bare minimum; we all *strongly* want – that is, 'need' in the broader sense – that which we like, enjoy, desire. And if we have the means (and often even if we do not) we are going to take what we want. The pull here is strong, the magic enchanting, and reason is often left by the wayside utterly.

Once need is broadened in this way, and is coupled with all kinds of other people also trying to make livings and lives in hierarchical and competitive economic structures where not all – or actually only a tiny tiny minority – can actually buy, do and have all that they want, then the market and its advertisements become this gargantuan screen for human need, desire, play and competition, from the most basic and cheap to the most crazily expensive and elite. Within this massive system, once one thinks about it, one is merely a pawn to socio-economic forces and facticities. However – and this is the market's second main magic trick – when you have some money in your pocket it is *you* that feels empowered, to spend on whatever you want, so long as it is more or less in your price range or line of credit. In such a mechanism advertising's seeds have already been sown, its powers are already working. Indeed, once coming into money one quite often already knows where it is going, or one even saves because of the particular draw of a particular product one has seen, noted and secreted away. Advertising's subtlety here, as the perennial smiley face to much deeper and more invisible forces, is to precisely hook one into its webs of desire while still making the consumer feel like it is *they* that are in charge, that it was *their* idea to like, want and need such and such. It is a quite dazzling trick, works enormously well – if not completely in all facets of one's life then certainly in a good number. It is once again a paradigmatic case of Sartrean magic in operation, a reversal of power that largely goes unnoticed; one is actually under the sway of invisible market forces and all of their advertising's dazzling colours and messages, and yet one still feels totally in control so long as one has enough money in one's pocket for what one wants to do or buy next.

Such magic – transforming wants into needs and giving consumers the illusion of control and power – is why advertising has a sinister side, for it can often convince you to buy and subscribe to something or someone you often would be better off without, as well make you an ignorant commercial slave to a brutal, relentless system which seems to necessarily come with a seedy, exploitative underbelly that leaves a majority poor and destitute. Reason would teach wariness here, reason would teach minimalism and scepticism, reason would teach activism against the more egregious and pernicious travesties of the mechanism. Indeed, ideally reason would allow one to only partake in that which you can truly and healthily enjoy and which does no or minimal harm to the wider whole. But alas, it is increasingly hard to see how reason can live in such a cutthroat and impassioned environment, where quick, immediate and over-the-top gratifications seem to thrive. By plugging into our more unreasonable proclivities, reason is often quite powerless in front of the bright lights and passions advertising enchants us with, and it is thereby blocked out and tricked by personal reflections, emotions, images and values that simply want to enjoy and possess and to hell with the consequences.

It looks like this predicament will only augment as technology augments too. Indeed, I think it should be clear to everyone how abundant and influential advertising is online. What such technologies are also starting to bring, however, are new genres of products, namely, irreal, virtual ones.

In classical advertising, it is a structure of the imaginary that still nevertheless leads you to something physical and concrete – a can of Coke, a car, a meal at a restaurant, a holiday in Spain. With the internet, coupled with rapidly increasing capacities for virtual technologies – not least virtual reality – more and more products are now of an irreal, imaginary nature, where one does not go out and buy anything, but partakes in the product right from where one sits. Companies like Netflix have already prospered massively here, where one owns a laptop and an online membership rather than thousands of physical films. One step further will be when the content itself is no longer as anchored in the real and perceptual. Virtual porn, eSports and online gaming industries are products that are getting to such a point, where the product is wholly (or at least primarily or partially) digital.

Where such markets start surfacing, advertising will inevitably extend its tentacles. What is more, one can envisage not-so-distant technologies where the actual roots in reality and perception might be superseded by totally manufactured, irreal things and characters that then, in full-circle fashion, come to advertise actual products from their virtual vantage points. On this note there are already virtual models and celebrities (e.g. Shudu) that (or who?) already garner quite significant followings online, followings who then go out and buy whatever this digital supermodel is 'wearing'. This trend towards the importance of the irreal and virtual – in short what comes at one through one's various screens – looks set to augment as younger generations now grow up in an environment where distinctions between real and irreal, perceivable and imaginary, genuine and artificial are all becoming less clear and might even be said to be inverted in the order of significance and time spent. The market and its advertising is once again a main driving force in such developments, which now provide digital and virtual enchantments and escapes that are unsurprisingly coming at the same time lines between true and false, genuine and fake and the like are being blurred and manipulated more widely.

Is there anything to be done? Shut down advertising for its sinister antics? Were this even possible (which it is not), it would not even be desirable. We are well within our rights to enjoy various things should we have the means to do so and should these activities not be hugely damaging and exploitative to others. There is no escape from the magical beings that we are; we will always be captivated, moved by and give ourselves over to various phenomena. Better then would be to understand how advertising pulls one in and how one should react when one being sucked in by something that one could simply do without, or that is seriously damaging. At present, the economic and political market is so that suffering seems to be winning. What advertising does need then is more education on its own sinister aspects, as well as more ethical varieties that warn and disseminate with regard to its most pernicious and damaging elements. The market and its advertisements are not going anywhere – in fact with technology they will augment – so better to harness the power through organizations, websites, movements and the like, so that all the more positive potentials of advertising and its magic are utilized for combatting the more exploitative and gargantuanly greedy operators and manipulators. Good starts have been made, but more needs to develop if we are to further think and act upon what we actually need and not, as well as what such supposed needs do to our ourselves, others and our environments.

# Racism and Other Figures of
# Magical Non-Thinking

If advertising is an instance of Sartrean magic that has some rather sinister elements, the focus here now shows how magic can get to the point of denigrating, abusing and even dehumanizing whole classes of people. To get to this I will first show how Sartre presents racism as purported thinking that is ultimately not thinking at all. Then, secondly, I will discuss how this extends to other figures of non-thought, which can be so societally pervasive and ingrained that it is hard to see past them, even for some of the targets.

## Not thinking, like a stone: Sartre on racism and stupidity

Racism is stupid. Just why this is so was a major preoccupation for Sartre throughout numerous periods of his life. Here I intend to show that this issue highlights how magic can become societally chronic, where purported thinking only masquerades as such.

In order to do this, I will give an account of Sartre's account of racism, focusing primarily on some of the main conceptual points made in *Réflexions sur la question juive* (1946). In a second step, I will link these main points to some points regarding stupidity, here focusing on certain comments made in the first volume of *L'idiot de la famille* (1971), as well as certain passages of the first volume of the *Critique de la raison dialectique* (1960).

Sartre begins his *Réflexions sur la question juive* with a short but dense discourse on opinion. Opinions are slippery customers for him; because of their inherent malleability they are all seemingly 'permitted' (ASJ/RQJ: 7/9) in a democratic and tolerant society. In such societies, moreover, very different opinions and character traits can live together in one group or individual without any real clash. The same therefore applies for specifically anti-Semitic opinions, where they appear 'to us to be a molecule that can enter into combination with other molecules of any origin whatsoever without undergoing any alteration' (ASJ/RQJ: 8/10). In this manner, a 'man may be a good father and a good husband, a conscientious citizen, highly cultivated, philanthropic, *and* in addition an anti-Semite' (ibid.). If one questions why he holds such a latter stance, Sartre says that he will, if comfortable around you, simply enumerate so many experiences, facts and statistics that have led him to come to this, his opinion (cf. ibid.).

This has the already-curious result that 'anti-Semitism appears to be at once a subjective taste that enters into combination with other tastes to form a personality, and an impersonal and social phenomenon which can be expressed by figures and averages, one which is conditioned by economic, historical, and political constants' (ASJ/RQJ: 9/11). Such is the general nature and structure of opinion for Sartre; it is a curious blend of subjective stances backed up by – albeit cherry-picked – 'objective' facts. In this manner, the opinions of anti-Semitism take advantage of such a structure like any other stance might; 'It's just *my* opinion, but if you look to the facts (that I have chosen), then' and so on. Under this guise, if one is to deny the anti-Semite's opinion as wrong, then one might also be led to deny other opinions that seem more valid.

Sartre quickly turns against such a potential pitfall, however. Indeed, he flatly states that 'anti-Semitism does not fall within the category of thoughts protected by the Right of free opinion'[1] (ASJ/RQJ: 10/12). Why? Because the opinions of anti-Semitism are, in fact, not thoughts (*pensées*) at all but are passions (cf. ibid.). Sartre proceeds to elaborate upon this latter concept in great detail. First of all, ordinary passions (which I will name emotions for the sake of clarity) are, as we have seen, triggered and maintained by an object; 'I hate someone who has made me suffer, someone who contemns or insults me' (ASJ/RQJ: 17/19). The passion of an anti-Semite, however, acts in a different way, even to the extent that it transforms normal emotions into pathological ones. Here it is Sartre's claim that ordinary emotions 'love the *objects* of passion: women, glory, power, money' (ASJ/RQJ: 18/20), to name but a few examples. The anti-Semite, to the contrary, has chosen the passion of hatred *itself*, meaning 'we are forced to conclude that it is the *state* of passion that he loves' (ibid.). In this manner, the hated object (or class of objects) is an almost incidental consequence of such an all-consuming commitment to anger and hostility.

This 'life of passion' (ibid.) stems from 'an original fear of oneself and a fear of truth'[2] (ASJ/RQJ: 19/21) for Sartre. On this note, we have already seen plenty regarding the flighty, unstable and angst-ridden nature of original consciousness; on truth and reason however, we have seen relatively little. Regarding these latter, Sartre explicates the basic thrust in an illuminating passage:

> The sensible man groans as he gropes for the truth; he knows that his reasonings are no more than probable, that other considerations will come to cast doubt on them; he never knows very well where he is going; he is 'open'; he may appear to be hesitant. But there are people who are attracted by the permanence of a stone. They wish to be massive and impenetrable, they wish not to change: where, indeed, would the change take them?[3] (ASJ/RQJ: 18–9/21)

Contrary to what one may have thought, then, proper thinking and reasoning for Sartre does not have the character of inviolable, sturdy grounds that never change. Actually, proper thought is open and adaptable. Counterposed to this, it is the passion of the anti-Semite – and indeed the passion of racists in general – that seeks and establishes the immovability and permanence of a rock-like structure. Anti-Semitism is thus a perverse 'faith' (cf. ASJ/RQJ: 19/22) that 'has originally chosen to devaluate words and reasons'[4] (ibid.). In this manner, 'only a strong sentimental prejudice can give a lightninglike certainty'[5] (ASJ/RQJ: 19/21) where one will not be moved from one's opinion, where all the reasons and arguments in the world will simply not convince you that someone who is Jewish is just another person like you, me or anyone else.

Anti-Semitism – and by extension racist thought in general (cf. ASJ/RQJ: 57/54) – is, hereby, not real thought at all, because thinking like a stone is, in fact, not thinking at all. This, however, is not to say that racism as stupidity is a mere privation of some kind of true thought or knowledge. Indeed, Breeur's recent work (2015) has comprehensively shown that there is more to the mechanisms of stupidity, foolishness and the like than a mere privation of proper judgement. We are all guilty of acts of stupidity – though of course not necessarily of racism – precisely because it is a transcendental human structure (cf., for instance, id.: 80–1). Concerning racism, this is a particularly pernicious form of stupidity because it is an impassioned commitment to a sturdy stance that simply will not budge, stubbornly holding on to its perspective like a piece of granite does, come rain, wind or shine. One may thus say it is a chronic case of stupidity due to its highly inviolable, irrational and impassioned position. Moreover, it is especially damaging because it seeks to demonize and dehumanize whole groups of people on the basis of a property (e.g. black skin) alone, propped up and continually reinforced by utterly magical non-thoughts.

Just like racism invokes an all-too-perverse use of chronic emotion (i.e. passion), so too is it a perversion of our values. Indeed, in another important passage Sartre highlights how the anti-Semitic attitude petrifies one's values just like it petrifies one's emotions:

> The anti-Semite does not really wish to have values. Value has to be sought like truth; it is discovered with difficulty, one must deserve it and, once acquired, it is perpetually in question; a false step, an error: it flies away; in this manner we are without respite, from the beginning of our lives to the end, responsible for what we value. The anti-Semite flees responsibility as he flees his own consciousness; and, choosing for his personality a mineral permanence, he chooses for his morality a scale of petrified values. Whatever he does, he knows that he will remain at the top of the ladder; whatever the Jew does, he will never get any higher than the first rung.[6] (ASJ/RQJ: 27/30)

Value, just like truth, needs to be open to change. The 'values' of the anti-Semite, on the contrary, are in fact anti-values, which is to say values that have accrued the massivity of rock in order to dominate, a massivity that weighs down thoughts to the extent that they no longer think at all – 'thoughts' that, precisely because of such contamination and perversion, come to accrue a rock-like fecundity that can ceaselessly generate yet more stubborn and stupid non-thoughts. In Sartre's technical vocabulary, the solid nature of the in-itself has come to take over the originally fluid nature of the for-itself. Thus it is a chronic and utterly deluded form of bad faith, when often the route back to a more sane fluidity and openness can be very difficult indeed. Such chronic flight is done in order to escape the uncertainty and responsibility that a more open, flexible way of living would necessarily entail. Racism thus creates a highly rigid scale, based on aggressive passions, that magically asserts one type or quality of being over another.

This is why racism is utterly stupid. Indeed, turning to crucial section of the first volume of *L'idiot de la famille*, we further see that this structure of solidified 'thinking' is not, in fact, proper (i.e. reasonable) thought at all. This is indeed nothing other than Sartre's concept of stupidity (*bêtise*[7]), of which racism is a particularly pernicious instance; 'Stupidity is inert and opaque since it imposes itself by its weight and since its laws cannot be modified, it is a *thing*, finally, because it possesses the impassability and impenetrability of the facts of Nature. The mechanical flattens the living, generality suppresses the originality of singular experience, the prefabricated reaction replaces the adapted praxis'[8] (Sartre [1971] 1981/2010: 596/615). Stupidity then is the universal human mechanism whereby rigid aspects of 'nature' (i.e. the in-itself) come to contaminate and solidify one's thoughts into so many opaque passions, habits and anti-values, all of which starve the subject of singularity and of the need to think for oneself.

Further, if racism is an instance of stupidity, stupidity is a 'species' (id.: 597/616) of what Sartre calls the 'pratico-inert' (ibid.). Here, 'praxis' is Sartre's updated term for consciousness or being-for-itself; the inert for being-in-itself. The pratico-inert is hereby a hybrid of the two where the former, praxis, instantiates itself through habits and social mechanisms in structures to the extent that it loses any real spontaneity. However, such structures, precisely because of praxis, are also fed with a pseudo life that keeps them from being fully dead or passive (i.e. inert). Bureaucracy as well as its institutions is one such example, where people, 'absorbed by materiality and things, bewitched by the action that seals them, are interchangeable'[9] (ibid.) – it is humans mechanized to the extent that one's thoughts become mechanized as well, where societal structures govern and condition the supposed individual quite completely.

In this regard, racism is also a case of the pratico-inert, this time a more chronic, damaging one, where individual freedom of thought and spontaneity is gobbled up by a corrosive, abusive pratico-inert which mechanizes thought and actions through equally mechanized social practices, structures and rituals that keep on feeding the machine to the detriment and abuse of a certain despised group.

Such a discourse also shows why this is another case in point of Sartrean magic; racist behaviour and its 'pseudo-thoughts' (cf. id.: 598/618) are phenomena where original spontaneities are degraded through so many mechanized and petrified emotions (i.e. passions) and 'values' (i.e. anti-values) that transform the world in a magical, unreasonable manner, even to the extent that it can pollute one's own, as well as other people's, entire lives. Such a way of being, which harbours 'the secret hope that thought is a stone' (Sartre [1960] 1976/1985: 300/406), is thus a magical form of non-thinking that actually gobbles up and alienates the individual into a system 'entirely governed by alterity' (id.: 720/800). In other words, racism thinks you and not the other way around; it is another magical reversal, a victory of a kind of 'counter-man' (cf. id.: 227/336) that not only denigrates and devalues a certain group but also saps the life and freedom out of the one who hates with so much intransigent and stupid venom.

Such is my summary of Sartre's account of racism and its inherent link to the mechanism of magical non-thinking as a chronic form of stupidity. What still remains to be shown here is how this phenomenon is also explained in the fourfold motif of magic more explicitly, as well as the important role of disgust in this pernicious mechanism.

Racism is clearly a case of magical thinking because, as has been shown, it is not really thinking at all, but only an imposter and corrupter of correct thought. More specifically, racism can be explained in more detail according to the fourfold concept of Sartrean magic. Beginning with the ego, it is clear that racism not only rigidly solidifies and hypostatizes one type of person over another; it also does this in a thoroughly magical manner whereby certain qualities (e.g. black and white) take on charges which cannot possibly come from the objects themselves, but which nevertheless come to take on an absurd weight that can actually dominate one's whole way of acting in the world and of viewing its people. Indeed, the high absurdity of letting a colour colour all of one's personal reflections and judgements of others is a clear case of magical thought whereby a given quality, passionately and irrationally conceived, contaminates and corrupts a great deal. Thus someone who hates 'all black people' because they are black also simultaneously asserts their own, utterly contingent quality (e.g. white skin) over all else in some kind of fantastical move for supremacy. Here a few basic perceptual distinctions ('he's black; I'm white') take on highly charged magical significances way past what they merit, coming to corrupt whole systems of thought with ludicrous stories and pseudo facts and reasons cherry-picked, constructed and manipulated in order to pervert, set up and charge the basic distinction with highly irrational prejudice. In this manner, the ego – the personality – of a white supremacist, for instance, invokes a difference in colour to create a whole world view that denigrates his detested group as filthy, inferior, subhuman and the like. This simultaneously promotes his or her own characteristics as higher, purer, better and the like. In Visker's (1999) terminology, the racist recentres himself *and* his despised group by fixing each with equally nonsensical, highly charged qualities.

It should be obvious how this person no longer has to think; they have figured it out, once and for all, white equalling good and the rest equalling bad – a kind of idiotic, magical non-logic that solidifies the person into a pseudo-thinking being where the stupidity has become a psychological disease, degrading the detested objects into pseudo things, as well as heightening one's own person into rigid and static delusions of superiority. In both respects, the complex public ego dynamic between consciousness and its and other personalities has been starved and decapitated, bastardized into a bad faith extreme where all has become magically clear.

This is the crux of the issue regarding the magical thinking involved in racism: original thoughts (spontaneities) get solidified and bastardized into impassioned pseudo thoughts which see and make value distinctions and judgements that are simply unfounded. Here one may see how the other three aspects of Sartrean magic, namely, emotion, images and value also all play important roles. With emotion, we have already seen that it takes on a radical, impassioned form that no longer considers the object properly, but in fact focuses and feeds off the emotion itself, thereby perverting it into an irrational, magical passion that will not be swayed by any evidence to the contrary. Such radicality means a racist person has already transformed the world into a colour- or quality-coded scheme, suffused with anti-values (e.g. white = good; black = bad) that are not actually there. In this manner, it is a form of psychosis where the anti-values are, through passion, incanted into a world in a manner whereby one has taken leave of one's more basic senses; it is a transformation whereby groups of people are already preformatted and categorized into a hierarchical and value-laden structure that has no room for any sense of flexibility, measure, openness or reason.

On top of this, many images, symbols and myths – in short the magic of the imaginary – are always free to take up such ceaseless anger and turn it into pseudo systems that try to rationalize the stances, forming cults and tribes where like-minded people come to share in their views (e.g. the KKK). Here, a personal sorcery becomes a social one that can feed and sustain itself, thereby further immunizing itself from a more balanced and open appraisal of the world and its people.

In all of this, disgust plays a major role. Indeed, the history of racial prejudice is also a history of disgust; the hated group has always been assigned the vocabulary of the disgusting – filthy, vermin-like contaminants. Moreover, because of such magical qualities they are also conceived as a constant threat to the supposed 'purity' of the favoured group. Such discourses, which have often utilized the magic of ideological propaganda, have led to many exterminations, of which many are unfortunately all too aware.

Disgust is not an exclusive weapon for racism, however; indeed an anti-racist may be just as disgusted by a racist as a racist is of his or her detested group. Thus the structure of disgust as violation of value (cf. O'Shiel 2015b) remains formally the same, meaning the content becomes of paramount importance. Regarding such content, it is quite simple for anyone who reasons properly: racist non-thoughts are precisely non-thoughts because they cannot be rationally founded; anti-racist thoughts can be because they use real arguments and openness for new ideas and progressions.

There is however, at times, a tendency to an opposite extreme, whereby promoting the universality of all human beings can make singularities fade away overmuch. Here one must also be careful, because the colour of one's skin, where one is from, the culture one grew up in and the like are all of course important characteristics – facticities – that one always has to relate to in various highly complex ways, just like one has to relate to any element of one's facticity. This means it is also a piece of magical thinking to suggest that the truism that 'we are all human' may solve all of these problems in one fell swoop. This is evidently not so. We are indeed all human, but we are also singular individuals with certain character traits and properties that do play major roles in our lives. Here, precisely how one can actually relate to such elements, whether general or particular, remains open to question and detail. Indeed, even though Sartre's thesis of consciousness necessarily implies facticity as a transitive phenomenon, perhaps a good number of elements and statistics we try to associate with ultimately remain intransitive due to the inherent blind spots in our existential makeup (cf. Visker 2007). All in all, the dynamic between our general and particular humanity is a lifelong, tricky balancing act where one does indeed seem to have to constantly navigate between the all too particular and the all too universal, where pitfalls of magical thinking lie on both sides of the road. This road is complex and endless, and we are moreover responsible for such an uncertain journey. Such is our freedom and the world's magic, of which racism is one extreme and chronic instance to steer well clear of.

## Magical non-thought, society and philosophy

We have just seen how racism is a strong form of chronic – and often permanent – stupidity. Going further, racism is of course just one instance of a larger structure of magical non-thinking, often chronic and pernicious but not always so. Here I would like to dwell a bit further on magical thinking in general, and also then briefly on some other dangerous instantiations that today's societies are grappling with. A message here will be that philosophy and education can help precisely because they try to minimize the more pernicious instantiations of magical non-thought through employing one's reason to think for oneself, as well as with others.

We are all guilty of magical thinking, wishful and wistful desires that spontaneously surge up even though we know, rationally speaking, they have no real possibility for fruition. Such fantasies remain rather innocuous if reason generally pervades.

In a further step, there are also pipe dreams, long-distance thoughts that, although highly unlikely, might turn out to be a dream come true for a few if enough time, effort and luck is poured into one's projects. Here, achieving one's wildest dreams can precisely feel unreal because they have been dreamt of and have seemed so distant and outlandish for so long.

There are then magical thoughts that try to deal with a set of real circumstances which we would rather not – or which we cannot – deal with in all of their brutality at the current time. Mourning is a prime example of this, with Didion's memoir ([2005] 2012) proving a detailed and well-presented testament. Here a reality, such as someone's death, is all too much for the personality, emotional sensitivities, images and values of the one left behind. Here more rational appraisals are hijacked in favour of a kind of defence mechanism; one must, for instance, hold onto your beloved's shoes in case he will come back (cf. id.: 37). In sounder mind and more benign circumstances one of course knows that holding onto a pair of shoes will not bring one's deceased husband back; magical thought however allows one to buck the limits and restrictions of reality and thereby enter a more emotionally charged imaginary situation where one's emotions and values are given precedence. Actually in cases like mourning one may say that it is a process of one's personality, emotions, images and values coming more gradually to terms with a new, shocking reality, a cataclysmic event that most often cannot be swallowed in one rational gulp.

Magical thought thus has its advantages at times, from frivolous ideas, to fuelling distant but not wholly impossible pipe dreams, to spontaneously reacting against and beginning to process a set of circumstances or series of events that are all too real and raw for our delicate and sensitive spontaneities. However, magical thought also has much darker and more damaging sides. Racism is of course one instance of this. There are also, unfortunately, many other instances, including other '-isms', not least sexism.

Sexism is still rife in our societies, and it is another instance of rather ingrained and chronic magical non-thought. A lot of these societal phenomena get their fuel from the generalities of crude stereotypes that are usually coupled with aggressive drives seeking release. Related to this, the phenomenon of jokes usually tries to find a balancing act between releasing enough pressure so as to evoke laughter, but not go too far so as to become offensive. More generally, stereotypes usually have basis in some reality because they are precisely generalities – some women, for instance, are homemakers – and indeed humour and jokes are constantly testing the taboos and generalities of societies, picking out various classes (e.g. a particular race, women, people of a certain nation) who can then become the butt of sublimated aggression in the form of a joke. What is permitted within any given society changes as the society itself changes. Indeed, nowadays a racist joke is no longer permitted for most, sexist jokes are on their way out for a good deal of people, while a joke about a certain nation (e.g. the Irish as heavy drinkers) are still more or less tolerable, still viewed as fairly innocuous. What is tricky in all of this is that the line between some supposedly harmless fun and something offensive is often very fine and is often highly variable depending on the people involved.

What is more clear cut, however, is a more solidified and pernicious instantiation of a racist, sexist or indeed even a strongly nationalist attitude. These are precisely solidified, chronic and pernicious when it is no longer merely about a misplaced joke but more about a life stance towards – and more pertinently against – certain groups or types of people. Indeed, just as a racist has decided that a certain group is inferior in a certain way, so too do sexists and nationalists decide in their own way against their despised objects, simultaneously inflating themselves. The structure here remains the same and is often backed up by various like-minded people, if not whole social, political and religious mechanisms and movements. Indeed, there are even whole political and religious systems, stances and cases that have such idiotic rigidity where to no longer be against a certain issue (e.g. abortion) would be to destroy at least part of the essence of what they 'stand for'.

The thing with pernicious and socially predominant magical mechanisms is that they have an extremely powerful ally, a basic structure to society that they utilize to maximum effect. Indeed, there is actually a structural societal law that helps promulgate – with the help of all kinds of advertising and propaganda – a dominant line of non-thought. This seems to be the case because, quite frankly, not thinking for oneself and just going along with what one is bombarded with is very often much easier than actually thinking and entering into proper, honest and open dialogues and debates. This structure I am thinking of is Heidegger's concept of *das Man* (cf. [1927] 2006: §27). *Das Man* is that necessary social structure where one (*man*) does as the next because that is simply what one (*man*) does. *Das Man*, often translated as 'the they', is a phenomenon of 'being-with' (*Mitsein*) and denotes everything about one's self that does *not* stand out. I dress and speak like pretty much everyone around me; I have similar thoughts and desires, structured and conditioned almost completely by my environment (in my case a privileged Western one) and what I take in from it. *Das Man* is hereby all those social forces and mechanisms where the 'individual' is rather a myth, a mirage on top of a much more sturdy and all-encompassing social organism that does not like too much difference. Standing out a bit in a good way, like in artistic creation, can get one praise and admiration from one's peers. However, there are many ways where standing out quite rapidly renders one a freak or pariah or weirdo. This can be extremely damaging for a person in all kinds of social, psychological and economic ways. Considering this, Heidegger's ingenious insight is we are first and foremost as others are; 'Everyone is the other and no one is himself'[10] ([1927] 2012/2006: 165/128). It is actually ourselves as singularities which is the covered-over element that is hard to get to, and that can remain submerged for most of our lives. In short, the 'I' in social life is primarily other.

*Das Man* is thus a very fundamental concept to explain how we *are* the social forces we live in and around. It is quite unavoidable for the most part, a deep, pervasive and powerful existential structure (cf. id.: 167/129). *Das Man* can, much like Sartre's look, be instantiated in many many things, from the clothes one wears and the language one uses, to the food one buys and the political and ethical opinions one has. It is even the audience laughter on one's favourite 1990s' sitcom.

In all of this, although the formal structure is a permanent and ineradicable fixture of any human society, its contents can and do change significantly over time. At any current moment, *das Man* is basically what any society condones as permissible – and impermissible. For instance, not so long ago in the United States and elsewhere it was permissible to own slaves. Even more recently (and still argued for in various places all over the world) it was permissible to believe that a woman's place is fundamentally in the home. And currently, all over the globe there are growing nationalistic movements, fuelled by populist parties, seeking to promote and protect a certain home group over and against supposedly invasive others who do not have the same qualities, and therefore should not have the same rights. Here, such cases show that *das Man* often makes use of magical thinking to create quite rigid divisions – white and black, male and female, native and alien – even though the reality is of course always much more complex, detailed and nuanced.

Indeed, it is this often quite literal black-and-white thinking which is the hallmark of rigid non-thoughts in social structures – in Sartre's terminology yet more cases of the pratico-inert – that are always already absorbed quite automatically into whole populations and belief systems. To put things rather bluntly, a black person must be a thief because she is black; a woman must live in the kitchen because she is a woman; a Mexican must be a drug smuggler because he is Mexican. Now of course there are black people who thieve, there are women who cook, and there are Mexicans who smuggle drugs. A main fallacy in magical thought here is one skips over complex particulars to a single universal – *all* of such and such must be like that because they are such and such. The circularity is of course nauseating, stupid, and yet it has great power on the social and political level, not only because it is simpler to insinuate and convey but also because one then no longer has to think further about it.

Thinking is hard, endless, and perpetually nuanced; current populist and other movements are having so much success because, along with other factors like insufficient education and false representation and dissemination of information, they simply tap into our desire to not overly think, to be a stone and just get along as the next idiot does, automata in a dance of biased and interested manipulation.

What is even more staggering is such magical social forces can be internalized not only for the '-ists' but also for the targets. Indeed, one of the most monumental achievements of de Beauvoir's *Le deuxième sexe* ([1949] 1986) was to not only show that various patriarchal cultural and economic forces have starved women of a proper and independent subjectivity for centuries and thereby made them objects; it was to also show that many women themselves did – and still do – have little choice but to continue to flee this more fundamental subjectivity, precisely because of such mechanisms and structures. This is another consequence of magical abuse; abused groups often end up with quite grave complexes and can even believe in their own supposed 'inferiority', not to mention the whole host of actual economic and social disadvantages that come with this.

What is to be done? Well strides are of course being made, although there are powerful and dangerous counter-movements as well. In some privileged societies women, for instance, are starting to gain parity on a least a few levels, although the situation remains dire for unimaginable amounts throughout the world. Generally speaking here – and I am indeed only able to point at the basic structure – one is fighting a powerful tendency to magical non-thought which allows one not to think too much, to release aggression, and to solidify one's stance so as to gain a delusive but comforting bed of certainty and conviction. Moreover, all of this can persist not only because one is often backed up by a plethora of like-minded others, but also crucially because of all the various economic, social, political and religious forces that simply do not want masses of people to think for and be themselves.

Thinking on the cusp of humanity's issues is difficult. It is always a fine balancing act between pushing the bounds of the status quo, but still remaining accessible – and thereby influential – to general populations. Science relentlessly proves the invalidity and absurdity of many magical non-thoughts, and yet these latter still prosper; art expresses a whole universe of ideas and images through beautiful, enchanting and provocative creations that nevertheless fall on blind eyes and deaf ears for many who simply do not care; philosophy and education more generally provide the thoughts, reasons, as well as the political and ethical arguments why such stances are impermissible and yet they continue to flourish. The power of the status quo seems to be only superseded by the powerful enticement not to think or bother too much, to find the easy way out and thereby return to the comfortable shell of delusion and prejudice.

All the same, a measured optimism and will to keep on challenging the pernicious elements of chronic societal magic needs to continue, for there are signs of improvement if only it is too slow. Regarding philosophy, it pretty much never has an instantaneous effect. Nevertheless, with the right amount of thought and the right ways of dissemination through all the abundant forms of technology, media and education we now have, the proper insights and reasons will eventually seep into the everyday structures of *das Man* (as history has already shown in various cases – for example, slavery), thereby dissolving the more pernicious current elements of social magic one trick at a time, all in the name of an interminable but hopeful progress.

8

Magic and Psychopathology

If racism and other '-isms' are societal, worldly pathologies, there are also more personal and otherworldly cases that have various forms of Sartrean magic in operation, not least the imaginary as a type of hypercaptivation. To show this, I will briefly analyse Sartre's main ideas on how extreme the magic of the imaginary can go, with dreaming and certain forms of psychopathology quite closely aligned on this score. On the back of this, I will provide a novel Sartrean reading of a very well-known case in psychopathology, that of Schreber. This will show how Sartre's insights on magic, not least his neglected pages on magic and psychopathology, are highly relevant for understanding various forms of mental trauma that still dominate many people's lives today.

## Hypercaptivation: Dreams and psychopathology

Sartre's analyses of 'Pathology of the Imagination' (IM: 148–59/285–308) and 'The Dream' (IM: 159–75/308–39) come in sections three and four respectively of Part IV, 'The Imaginary Life' (IM: 123/237). With artistic creation we have already seen that people often spontaneously opt for a predominantly imaginary attitude towards life; dreams and psychopathology are two other cases where the laws of the imaginary dominate for Sartre, actually in their most extreme form.

Dreams and psychopathology are however quite different experiences as well, not least in how we often enjoy dreaming but almost never mental illness. This begs the following question: Why does Sartre closely align them? Regarding this, he sees them as equally threatening to his thesis of a strict difference in kind between perception and imagination, and he is therefore at pains to show how they do not in fact blur the lines between perception and imagination, but actually push the logic of the latter to its limits.

Additionally interesting is that Sartre finishes the whole part on dreams, not psychopathology. This suggests that the former is in fact imaginary life pushed to its absolute limit. Indeed, if various kinds of psychopathologies – not least ones that involve hallucinations and obsessions, two of Sartre's foci – can be characterized as waking dreams (cf. IM: 152/294), dreaming is imaginary consciousness completely captive to itself (cf. IM: 164/317) precisely because perception has been minimized. In sleep perception cannot have been completely eradicated of course, otherwise one would never wake up. It is, however, put out of action (cf. de Warren 2010) to the extent that consciousness no longer has any point of reference as to what is real or not. Actually, for Sartre it is crucial to understand that in dreams it is not about taking things to be 'real'; in the moment itself it is more about a form of captivation, immersion and immanence so complete that one has 'lost the very notion of reality' (IM: 165/319). In other words, precisely because one is asleep one is 'isolated from the real world, enclosed in the imaginary' (ibid.). Dreams are so engrossing and captivating because they are the perfect example of a 'closed consciousness' (ibid.) for Sartre. If one were never to wake up one would never realize they were not real; it is after the fact – once perception resurfaces upon waking – that one realizes it *was* a dream (cf. IM: 162/312).

As we have seen in Chapter 3, the real and irreal need to be contrasted in order for us to know which is which. In sleep, the real is minimized so much that one forgets this very contrast. This makes the realm of dreams one that is 'sufficient unto itself' (IM: 169/326), where imaginary consciousness, pushed to its own limit, automatically 'grasps itself as spellbound spontaneity'[1] (ibid.).

This is why dreams are so magical, because they are the imaginary at its most spontaneous and self-sufficient best, where perceptual laws of causality and reason no longer apply. Dreams are precisely fantastical and enchanting because it is the utter spontaneity of imaginary consciousness unleashed unto itself. Indeed, Sartre finishes his analyses of the dream by characterizing it as a '"spellbinding" fiction' (IM: 175/338) where perceptual laws of causality, possibility and knowledge do not apply. Regarding causality, there is such immanent imaginary spontaneity and creation to dreams that the whole realm is divorced from realistic considerations. All kinds of things can happen that could not in a more solid spatiotemporal nexus. Not only are laws of causality flouted and transversed; there is not even time for possibility either. Indeed, regarding possibility Sartre insists dreams are 'fatal' (cf. 169/326) because the immersion and creation are so instantaneous that there is quite literally no space for if-then. As we have already seen, such deterministic conditionality cannot exist in a dream because of the utterly immediate and immanent character; there is no time or space for deliberation. Moreover, regarding knowledge it is in perception we know various things for Sartre, because the perceptual realm is first and foremost about evidence and presence (cf. IM: 163/315). By contrast, in dreams the mode of engagement is immersed belief. In perception we simply know things and are thus in no need of belief; 'Where evidence is given [in perception], belief is neither useful, nor even possible'[2] (ibid.). We do not need to believe in real things; we simply know they are real. With dreams, though, they are so irreal one does not even realize; because of the dream's utterly imaginary, flighty character, coupled with its strong captivation and enchantment, it is not about knowledge of various facts and events, but rather a doxastic immersion into one's own phantom creations that are only marked as 'only a dream' upon waking.

All in all, the experience of dreams is precisely a closed off, immanent one, where the magic of the imaginary self-captivates, and indeed the spell is only broken upon reawakening. Such a realm, being the imaginary pushed to the limit, is of course a fantastical one, where our (inter)personal issues (ego), emotions and all kinds of hidden desires and values are given free play and are additionally open to all kinds of interpretation after waking, remembering and reflecting. Here, although many dreams and nightmares can be unsettling, tormenting even, it is equally a realm where the mind is able to release much of the illogical and playful forces that are constantly swarming in and around our more measured, daily, pragmatic endeavours. Indeed, better to release such phenomena in the secret, quiet and downright forgetful solitude of sleep than out loud in everyday waking life. Dreams are hereby a realm where the magic of our minds finds some release, from deep unacknowledged wishes and urges, to frivolous and playful scenarios, to more serious anxieties, worries and nightmares.

Considering this, dreams are often not only innocuous but can actually be quite cathartic and helpful for releasing good portions of our magical tensions. In Freudian terms, wish fulfilment. There are other cases however, like in post-traumatic stress disorders, where dreams are so disturbing that one cannot or will not sleep. Then, things can be even further exacerbated when too many dream-like elements seep into waking life. For me, this is Sartre's main angle when speaking of at least certain forms of psychopathology.

Through his engagements with contemporary psychologists of his time, Sartre does indeed characterize psychopathology as waking dreams, from rather benign and infrequent to seriously chronic. This is because psychopathology is also a fundamentally extreme form of the imaginary for Sartre and can therefore be so consuming that it alters one's everyday beliefs and behaviour quite completely (cf. IM: 151/291). If we are all prone to psychopathology to various extents, for Sartre it generally occurs when various imaginary spontaneities – not a reflective will (cf. IM: 156/301) – start to let themselves go beyond the usual (cf. IM: 153/295). As the captivation of the irreal increases there is a concomitant increasing 'perceptual apathy' (ibid.); psychopathologies involving strong obsessions, hallucinations and the like occur because 'a radical alteration of all of consciousness and a change of attitude in the face of the irreal can appear only as the counterpart of a weakening of the sense of the real' (IM: 152/293). Therefore, much like in dreams the predominance and significance of the real – and with it its causal and logical rules – become weakened in favour of spontaneous creations from one's own mind, which can then even be misremembered and misreported as real and actual (cf. IM: 158–9/306–8). Contrary to what one might think here, such 'hallucinatory material' (IM: 153/295) is usually rather impoverished and repetitive, usually fixated on one or two key fantasies or desires, which actually makes this imaginary life more controllable, at least in the beginning. What is more, Sartre even claims that 'schizophrenics [for instance] know very well that the objects they surround themselves with are irreal; it is for this very reason that they make them appear' (IM: 148/285) because they have become self-captivated with their own creations to the point of an automatic preference for delirium. The primacy of the perceptual system can reinstate itself temporarily with doctors and other people, for patients usually do not hallucinate when someone else is present (cf. IM: 149/288). However, when chronic the significance of the irreal has already gained central place, where in solitude the captivation gets so strong that various visions and voices come to appear, speak and torment as if they were right there.

The problem here is of course how one loses touch with reality, increasingly tormented by one's own creations. Indeed, it is that main telltale sign of Sartrean magic where some of consciousness's own creations have been charged with such force and power that it is these objects, and no longer the conscious subject, that are in control. This is pushed to the limit in certain psychopathologies, not least psychoses. On this note, Sartre refers to 'spasms of consciousness' (IM: 154/298) that harbour a progressive 'disintegration' (IM: 155/299) and fragmentation (cf. also, Laing [1960] 2010). A very basic unity of conscious life usually remains, 'but this forms the indifferent ground upon which, in the case of a psychosis of hallucination, the rebellion of spontaneities breaks away. The higher forms of psychic integration have disappeared. This signifies that there is no longer a harmonious and continuous development of thought'[3] (IM: 155/299). 'Partial systems' (ibid.) develop where consciousness has lost control of its own freedom; the imaginary and its magical creations take on life and powers to extreme degrees, ultimately persecuting the very mind that spawned them.

Ultimately 'the distinction between subjective and objective ... [has] collapsed' (IM: 158/305) here, which is precisely when magic has become chronic. In both dreams and psychopathology there is an immanence to one's thoughts that gives one no space for other considerations. This is damaging in psychopathology because it occurs while awake, when usually perception and transcendence are supposed to rule. Here, then, one enters a kind of a 'twilight life' (IM: 157/303) with very little external and realistic attention paid to the perceptual world. Indeed it is a form of personal hypercaptivation by the imaginary, the consequences of which can be extremely disturbing and painful. Here, although the process is usually quite gradual, ultimately in serious psychoses 'a crystallization comes into effect and the patient will organize his life in accordance with his hallucinations, which is to say rethink them and explain them'[4] (IM: 159/307). This is a 'psychosis of influence' (ibid.) where imaginary magic has become radical and chronic, with 'spontaneities, wholly unforeseeable and fragmentary as they are, can be charged little by little with a certain ideo-affective material'[5] (ibid.). This, I believe, is precisely what happened in the case of Schreber.

## The case of Schreber: A Sartrean reading

Daniel Paul Schreber's illness took on an otherworldly character where the magic of his imagination ultimately led to a crushing and tragic collapse of his whole person. The case of Schreber is a Hydra; the more people try to make any comprehensive sense of it, the more heads it grows. From Freud's account ([1911] 2001/2012) that Schreber constructed a whole metaphysical-religious system in order to try and justify a basic sexual wish, to more recent accounts that emphasize the brutality of his upbringing leaving a damaged victim of a discipline-obsessed Germany (Schatzman 1972), to further accounts of Schreber's imaginative escape from – and defiance in front of – harsh psychiatric authorities of the late nineteenth and early twentieth centuries (Deleuze and Guattari [1972] 2008; Lothane 2003), to also, finally, interpersonal emphases that explicate how all his primary relations were failures leaving him so isolated that he wanted to become a woman in order to create a new human race (Dinnage 2000; Lothane 2003), the case of Schreber is as complicated as it is mysterious. Indeed, similar to how Schreber himself breaks up his God into 'anterior' and 'posterior' realms, 'upper' and 'lower' forms, benevolent and malevolent versions (cf. Schreber [1903] 2000/2003: 30/14), so too may one break up and emphasize these aforementioned themes that all seem to have contributed to his complex madness.

Although it may already be noted that all these aspects need to be borne in mind as I continue, I will be rather selective with regard to these various interpretations of Schreber's illness. As already mentioned, ultimately I will focus more on how the case of Schreber is an instance of our magical being, here pushed to such limits that a hypercaptivity of the imaginary results in the individual being unable to deal with reality in any proper sense.

Schreber's life seemed to go well enough until his first collapse in the mid-1880s, when he was in his early forties. He was a successful judge, married and respected. The 'seemed' is important here; when one looks closer, Schreber's life harboured torments and hardships from the very beginning, and thus, like so many psychotics, there were roots going back to very early traumas. This is brought to light in a number of accounts that, while incomplete (very little is known about his mother and sisters for instance), still provide good insight.

First of all to highlight on this count is Schreber's father, Daniel Gottlob Moritz Schreber. He was a celebrated physician who specialized in, and published copiously on, proper childrearing. The irony here could not be more acute: a celebrated expert of childrearing with two sons, one who killed himself (not before manifesting certain onset signs of psychosis – cf. Schatzman 1972: 50), the other then spending much of his later life in mental institutions, eventually dying in one in a completely crushed mental state (cf. Dinnage 2000: xiii). Is this just an unhappy coincidence? Were the father's supposedly sound methods simply wasted on his two sons? Not at all. In fact, one needs to only glance at Schatzman's article (1972) – and for more extensive treatment his book (1973) – to see that Gottlob Moritz's 'methods' should be viewed as sadistic torture; all kinds of straps and belts and braces and boards that all contributed towards physically conditioning and imprisoning the boys in bed, at their desks, at dinner and so on. Additionally, there were all kinds of mental habituations and torments that sought to 'suppress *everything* in the child' (Gottlob Moritz Schreber in: Schatzman 1972: 50), beginning even as young as 'five to six months' (Schatzman 1972: 50). This was indeed the goal: children, who were conceived as satanic creatures, had to be conditioned into proper, ethical beings through the most merciless disciplinary processes. Such 'household totalitarianism' (id.: 62) or 'poisonous pedagogy' (Miller [1980] 1997) meant young Schreber never developed the normal boundaries of a personality. Here is Schatzman on the matter:

> Many psychiatrists and psychoanalysts have said that the people they call schizophrenic suffer from an inability to distinguish 'I' from not-'I', that they lack 'ego boundaries'. I suggest that some of these people have been taught by their families they should not, or cannot, live with an 'I', as Schreber's father apparently taught him. Note that Dr. Schreber does not say children should not keep things from their parents; he says they should be 'permeated by the feeling of the *impossibility*' of it, i.e., they must feel that they *cannot*. (Schatzman 1972: 61)

Who is insane at this point, then? Certainly not the son. But he was to become so. Indeed, such exceedingly early and harsh maltreatment was to leave deep deep scars, creating monumental influences and materials for Schreber's later illnesses. Schatzman shows this convincingly, where many of the disciplinarian duties of the young boy are replicated – crucially in irrealized forms of 'miracles' – later in Schreber's psychotic behaviour. To give but one example (id.: 44), Gottlob Moritz constructed a mechanism to ensure children sat straight at their desk. It was called the '*Schrebersche Geradhalter* (Schreber's straight-holder)' (ibid.) and consisted of an 'iron cross-bar fastened to the table' (ibid.) that pressed against the collarbone and front of the shoulders of the child in order to ensure that he did not slouch. This was translated into Schreber's imaginary language as 'one of the most horrifying miracles' (Daniel Paul Schreber in Schatzman 1972: 44) where he still supposedly felt, all those years later, his '*whole chest wall being compressed*' (ibid.), thereby giving a feeling of suffocation that 'was transmitted' (ibid.) to his whole body.

This crazy mixture of torture by a nonetheless revered pedagogue most certainly also provided much of the crucial material for Schreber's inherently ambivalent relationship towards his God, to whom he was deeply and specially linked through 'nerves' and 'rays', but also mercilessly persecuted by. Because this all started at such a young age, it should be quite understandable how a very young Schreber was unable to process and understand such treatment, and it was never able to really do so. Indeed, such black and cruel magic at such an early age must permanently warp the mind under abuse. This had the result that Schreber automatically harboured away his feelings and memories to such an extent that they would never be able to break out in a direct form ('I hated my father; he tortured us.' – cf. Schatzman 1972: 58), but only in an irrealized, fantastical version, and only after the onset of illness.

Schreber's father entered a deep and long depression (cf. Dinnage 2000: xiii), dying quite young, when Daniel Paul was nineteen. From there not much is known (his brother killed himself when Schreber was thirty-five), except that he climbed the judicial ranks until his first, relatively short illness between 1884 and 1885. His second, much longer illness (1893–1902) started with commitment on a voluntary basis, but ended in a drawn-out legal battle, after which he was released and thereby free to publish his *Denkwürdigkeiten* in 1903, a work he viewed as morally crucial for the rescue of humanity. He then collapsed for the third and final time in 1907 after his wife had a bad but non-lethal stroke. He remained institutionalized and alone until his final demise in 1911, survived by his wife.

Schreber's wife is a vital but frustratingly enigmatic character in the whole story. Indeed, echoing Freud ([1911] 2001/2012: 37/271–2) it is now quite scandalous that nearly all of the third chapter of Schreber's work, specifically dealing with '*other members of my family*' (Schreber [1903] 2000/2003: 43/24), was suppressed and subsequently lost. Schreber rarely had a bad word to say about her (cf., for instance, id.: 165/131), except mentioning that they were both frustrated with regard to the repeated failures to have children (id.: 46/26). Nonetheless, there definitely was an unacknowledged tension working within him. This is evident when he himself acknowledges a major deterioration of his state in his second illness precisely when his wife went on holiday for a few days (cf. id.: 52–3/32). Additionally, and as has been noted, the onset of his final, all-consuming illness was when his wife had her stroke. In a footnote where he professes to 'retain [his] former love in full' (id.: 165/131) for his wife, he is also, in the main text, developing one of his main delusional ideas: the only way to save the human race is if he completes (according to Schreber it had already begun) his 'unmanning' (*Entmannung* – id.: 164/129). This is to say he had to become a woman for the survival and benefit of humankind, which had been – at least for a time – more or less destroyed, leaving only him, God and many transitory, ghost-like human forms (the 'fleetingly-improvised-men' (*flüchtig hingemachte Männer*)), his wife included (id.: 118–19/89). Of course from a Freudian perspective this 'had to' is actually a wish, a 'want to', and indeed Schreber did keep his transgender desires even after his release.

What did happen during and after Schreber's release is he reconnected with reality to the extent that he was able to somewhat defocus from his delusional system. Such defocusing simultaneously allowed him to focus more on the everyday endeavours needed to procure his release, publish his work and rejoin society (at least to some extent). Some believe such events and steps demonstrate a significant improvement; others believe it was more a 'sedimentation' of earlier, more acute psychotic episodes and hallucinations that tortured Schreber in his second lengthy illness:

> In the previous report it was detailed how President Schreber's acute insanity gradually passed into a chronic state, how out of the stormy tides of the hallucinatory insanity a sediment was, so to speak, deposited and fixed, and gave the illness the picture of paranoia. As the accompanying mighty affect gradually decreased and the hallucinatory experiences lost their confusing and directly overpowering influence, the patient was able to find his way back to a more orderly mental life. He did not, however, realize and recognize the actual products of his altered perceptions and the combinations built up on them as pathological, nor could he rise above the subjectiveness of his views and reach a more objective judgment of events. He could not achieve this, because the hallucinations persisted and delusions continued to be built on them; but as the accompanying effects became less strong, and common sense and orientation returned, there occurred a certain split in the totality of his ideas; the persisting pathologically altered field of his mental life became more sharply demarcated from the rest. (Dr. Weber in: id.: 341–2/283)

Before such a demarcation, Schreber seemed to have suffered greatly, constantly tormented by auditory and visual hallucinations that wreaked havoc with his thoughts and life. Indeed, bringing in Sartre at this point, the 'acute insanity' was precisely acute because the force of Schreber's visions were so strong that they seem to have 'coincide[d] with a sudden annihilation of perceived reality' (IM: 150/289). Sartre's point here means that hallucination is, as we have seen, not an image that is somehow perceived; on the contrary it remains an imaging act and in fact is an imaging act so forceful that the perceived is momentarily obliterated, only to return once the individual recounts their vision in an act of misremembering that then, in a secondary, reflective moment, supposedly fuses real (i.e. perceived) and irreal (i.e. imagined, hallucinated) together (cf. IM: 151/291–2). Once again, Sartre's strong thesis here is that such individuals know very well that their hallucinations are not real like other things are (cf. also: Merleau-Ponty [1945] 2014: 391–2), and yet they are imbued with a force so powerful that one can be transfixed to the point reality disappears to a great extent.

What imbues such imaginary sights and sounds with such power? Sartre's term was 'spasms of consciousness' (IM: 154/298; cf. also, Breeur 2005: 128); spontaneous acts of pre- or irreflective consciousness can often leave the reflecting subject confused and scared. In these cases, imaging consciousness liberates itself from consciousness's own reflective will to the extent that what I have termed hypercaptivation occurs, this often being very hard to extricate oneself from.

In front of such brute spontaneity there are numerous eventualities. One is what Schreber did. He systematized it, turned all the torments into a metaphysical-religious doctrine that placed an ambivalent God, rays and nerves, and a hapless but increasingly dutiful Schreber into an imaginary world view that he claimed to be the real order of things. Through such an imaginary system he became a sensual plaything who also had a very special, megalomaniac purpose: to rescue and repopulate the world through becoming a woman who would mate with God and His rays. Such is the main thrust of Schreber's *Denkwürdigkeiten*, where the opening pages do indeed read like any other metaphysical treatise. Nevertheless, Schreber's own person and his incessant imaginings come to take centre stage rather quickly, thereby making it a highly idiosyncratic system that cannot be verified by anyone else, and thus quite mad.

Such constant speculation over his system led Schreber to be ultimately convinced of a, for him, very important purpose, backed up by his own creation, to the extent that any former, more objective and interpersonal reality had lost much touch with him. On rejoining everyday life he had to confront reality again, a realm that had never been fully obliterated, but for all that had been largely covered over and forgotten, due primarily to his incessant reveries. Here, although he did re-engage with the world and some of its people during and after his release and although such re-engagement did bring about the aforementioned demarcation and crystallization of his system, his experiences and a subsequent devotion to a kind of 'hallucinatory conduct' (IM: 159/308) had left him very ill-equipped to actually deal with sudden and meaningful changes in this actual world. In this manner, his wife's stroke seems to have been the last straw, an event that was all too real for him. It was of such an actual jolt that he became totally crushed and silent, where even his system disintegrated into shell that would never recapture its former glory.

How may we understand such a process more systematically? I believe a few key psychoanalytic insights would be very helpful, plus a continuation of the Sartrean interpretation that has already begun.

For the psychoanalytic perspective, I will focus on aspects of Freud's account, as well as some points from Moyaert. Nowadays, Schreber is generally diagnosed as a paranoid schizophrenic. Freud has good insights especially with regard to the paranoiac aspects; Moyaert's article (2003) outlines schizophrenia in many of its most important facets, some of which may be applied very fittingly to aspects of Schreber's illness (which Moyaert also does himself at times).

We have already seen that after his childhood Schreber seemed to continue to develop in quite a normal manner. His crises only became manifest much later, in his early forties. How did this arise? One of the most notable triggers is Schreber's half dream where he thought that 'it must be really rather pleasant to be a woman who is subject to an act of sexual intercourse'[6] ([1903] 2000/2003: 46/26). Freud calls this the 'incubation period' ([1911] 2001/2012: 20/252–3) of Schreber's manifest illness, where the main motive for his whole subsequent delusional system had already been conceived. The centrality of this wish is further corroborated for Freud by the fact that the idea arose very early and was never relented upon even after his release (cf. id.: 21/253). Indeed, the complex system of persecution and then an eventual 'dutifulness' to being 'God's wife' (id.: 32/265) came out of this initial half thought. How so?

On this note, passages from Freud's account are indeed helpful, especially his section regarding the 'mechanism of paranoia' (id.: 59–79/295–316). In general, while Schreber was busy in everyday life the never-processed traumas of his infancy could remain unprocessed. Life took its toll however, and his dreams and private thoughts started to wander to the point that rather unsettling desires began to surface. Such wandering already signals the fact that Schreber had begun to be less invested in the world. In Freud's terms, Schreber's libido had been 'liberated' (id.: 72/309); it had started to withdraw from the world and its objects. This is also why his wife's little absence led to such deterioration; as Freud also notes, the presence of his wife acted as a kind of a 'protection' (cf. S: 46/281) against these secret wishes. This is why, during her short absence, Schreber's now semi-liberated energy exploded, where hallucinations signalled 'a struggle between repression and an attempt at recovery by bringing the libido back again on to its objects' (id.: 77/313). Here, as the battle became increasingly difficult, the perceptual world, its objects and their value all receded further and further in Schreber's isolation; the hallucinations gained such strength that they became the main occupation in his life. This is because, if libido withdraws, it has to go and be employed somewhere else. With Schreber it regressed onto his own ego (narcissism and megalomania), his own body (autoeroticism) and into systematizations of his tormenting voices and visions (hallucinations and projections), which often related back to some of his earliest experiences, but now in imaginary, irrealized forms.

Regarding these latter, they took on a decidedly paranoiac character precisely because what could not be personally or explicitly accepted meant that 'what was abolished internally returns from without' (id.: 71/308). To summarize in Schreberian terms, 'There is a God that is directly connected to me (through nerves and rays) and who is persecuting me – who wants me to be a woman and His sexual plaything, and I must submit if I am to save humanity and science.' Irreal starts to dominate for Schreber, only to become ever more deeply sedimented and systematized as the years passed. Such 'delusion-formation' (*Wahnbildungsarbeit* – id.: 38/273) is an attempt at a recovery, an imaginary 'reconstruction' (id.: 71/308) of real desires and traumas. As Schatzman notes (1972: 38), Schreber '*was persecuted*' in his early years. In this sense his later delusions do not come out of thin air; at least some of them are anchored in very – or even all too – real events and desires, not least his cruel upbringing and a strong desire to be a woman. Nevertheless, because he does not process or remember the real events as real, or properly and explicitly acknowledge his main desire, he is left with imaginary versions that come to consume and contaminate his whole life. Schreber then falls victim to one of the most basic category mistakes, misremembering and misreporting irreal hallucinations as real 'visions'. Once these are sedimented and systematized it is extremely difficult to fully recover from, and Schreber never really did.

These are the main paranoiac elements to Schreber's illness. Some schizophrenic elements should also be mentioned. Moyaert (2003: 43) begins by highlighting an element of schizophrenia that is similar to what has already been highlighted with regard to Freud's account; 'In schizophrenia, libidinal ties (connections) with reality fail in a radical and drastic manner: object cathexes are relinquished without this loss of interest making itself known by spectacular symptoms, such as heated arguments or histrionic behaviour'. This makes schizophrenia very hard to detect, until, perhaps, it is too late. Moreover, such withdrawal again means the drives 'amass … in the corporeal self' (id.: 44) from which there is no real exit (cf. ibid.). This also leads to a split where the individual's body is not really experienced as one's own; it is a plaything of forces and thereby has no real unifying principle. Indeed, because Schreber was never instilled with a coherent sense of self, it does indeed follow that when the illness breaks out there is, once again, a fragmentation that one has no real control over.

God is persecuting me, my body, my organs and the like, and there is little to be done about it. Such a process is known as 'a regression to an autoerotic stage'; 'The experience of the body falls apart into an amalgamation of partial drives which are not kept together and unified in a bodily incarnated unitary image of one's self' (id.: 45). In short, there is fragmentation throughout the self, both in mental and bodily form (cf. also IM: 155/299).

Such fragmentation is not the only factor, however. Indeed, a regression that focuses on a fragmented self also entails a regression to narcissism and often megalomania; 'In the return to auto-erotism a narcissistic libido remains active through which the subject attempts to surmount its disintegration' (Moyaert 2003: 46). How may it attempt such a reconstruction? By 'reconstruct[ing] the ties with the surrounding world, albeit through a world of fantasy' (ibid.). In this manner, such fragmentation gets dealt with and systematized on the imaginary level, a level that *tries* to recapture some connection to the actual, but precisely by doing so actually digs itself deeper and further away.

Moyaert is well aware of the stark difference between perception and imagination (cf. id.: 48). Schizophrenia however also changes the person's relation to their own imaginings; 'The schizophrenic clings so firmly to his/her body that even the images and perceptions that arise in it *are too close to the skin, and as it were break through it*' (ibid.); the imagination of the schizophrenic is 'without distance' (ibid.) and therefore 'oppressive' (ibid.). This is what I mean by hypercaptivation: the person's imaging acts have become so dominant and immanent that any real perspective is lost; even the body becomes the plaything of visions and forces that have a crushing result on the person, where an utter predominance of imaginary over real comes to (dis)possess the individual in a swirl of magical confusion. In short, *all* has become analogon for a rapacious and inverted imaging action that no longer takes any distance from its own creations.

Considering this perspective, we may also see why Schreber's ego came to be nowhere in the sense that his normal, everyday person lost its point of view because a fissure had been enacted between his consciousness and his ego. Actually, Schreber's ego was annihilated; his pathological, more spontaneous self came to dominate to the extent that realistic and measured personal reflection was more or less lost in place of insane imaginary incantations that, because they had lost any relation to the structuring coherence of the 'I', they also lost a structuring coherence with regard to the world – both of which, I and real world, Schreber felt as almost impossible to try and reclaim with any consistency or permanence. In this manner Schreber, overwhelmed by so many disturbing images and thoughts, comes to experience a more or less persistent anonymity that nonpathological cases do not have. We all have moments of anonymity of course. However, normally we are able to recuperate our person precisely through some personal reflections. Schreber's monstrous spontaneity of consciousness had cracked (cf. Fitzgerald [1936] 2009; also Laing [1960] 2010) this mechanism, whereby a constant foreboding, a continuous and suspicious threatening replaces any sense of security and integrity. Such insecurity then means consciousness creates other versions of self, ones which take on an imaginary, utterly captivating character that hypostatizes Schreber's delusions into false personal relations with God, nerves and the like.

On this note, we have already seen how a very young Schreber was not instilled with the normal interpersonal frontiers. Now, although he may have formed and lived by such a demarcation in his nonpathological moments, it is clear, in the years of his illness at least, that his conception of his own person is drastically affected because Schreber the man is almost nowhere to be seen. Sure enough he at times gives factual, historically accurate accounts of what he has done. However, these elements are really mere side issues within the broader context of his pathological system – for example, coherently and expertly arguing for his release *in order to* publish his *Denkwürdigkeiten*. Here, therefore, it is Schreber the redeemer that takes centre stage. A stage, moreover, that flouts the normal balance of reflective, personal consciousness. Indeed, Schreber the redeemer is not only at the centre of everything, he also has such a special place and mission that the rest of the world actually relies upon this one individual, this utmost focal point (along with God). If this is an ego at all, it is an imaginary one that has been inflated and hypostasized in a severe manner, enacting a kind of parody of Husserl's transcendental ego; there are no phenomena that do not somehow relate, through his concepts of nerves and nerve language, to this all-consuming point.

Such imaginary hypostatization is severe because it means the usual limits between I and world, I and God, I and other do not exist; Schreber's pathological 'I' has become an imaginary condition of possibility for the world, God and its beings to the extent that all of these are also irrealized through spontaneous captivations that nevertheless claim to be actual. In this sense, Schreber's pathological self has enchanted him so much that almost nothing can be considered apart from it. This starves and decapitates Schreber's normal conception of himself (ego); Schreber the man is nowhere because Schreber the redeemer (imaginary self) has come to be everywhere. Such a basic error also means that all states, qualities and actions of the ego, which are normally limited to the language of reflection, are perverted and intermingle into a new imaginary language, even to the extent that worldly and metaphysical phenomena directly and physically influence his person through repeated and incessant 'miracles'.

This is clearly a case of chronic magic, where very basic elements of the reflective language of the ego have been lost in place of more spontaneous irrealizations of the world in general. Everything is viewed and interpreted through mad glasses. This is only possible when we recognize that Schreber, in his illness, has always already irrealized the world so much that reality no longer has any significant influence upon him. His hallucinations, misrememberings and emotions all go into an increasingly complex imaginary system that is magical through and through. It bewitches him to such an extent that he supposes his own creations to have an actual force and power of their own, even claiming that this is the real state of affairs. Such a claim could not be maintained indefinitely however, as his final collapse suggests, where reality broke through once again, one last time.

One may say that a normal system of thought is based on reasons and arguments and is expressed in an accessible and comprehensible language. This allows for dialogue with our reason, dealing in concepts, with the imaginary reserved for illuminations through examples. Schreber's system has lost much of this; a highly idiosyncratic use of language, as well as a pseudo-logical chain of reasoning that has his own reveries as the main focus of everything, produces a caricature of systematic thinking where reference to any larger, realer state of affairs has been at best corrupted, and at worst completely lost. If normal systems predominantly use critical reflection, Schreber's is completely under the sway of imaginary objects and passions (cf. Breeur 2010) that have been magically charged to the extent that he thinks them to be all-powerful. In this manner, the irreal has bewitched him so much that he believes it to be the real metaphysical order of things. Even when he is released, he still harbours the idea that his so-called delusions are not delusions at all, but real states of affairs that no one else can see because he is special. Thus, in acute psychosis irreal predominates to the extent that real is obliterated; and in the sedimented paranoiac stance they are also inverted in their role and significance. It is a spontaneous and uncontrollable commitment to Sartre's imaginary attitude that constantly tries to pre-empt and stave off the shock of the real.

With such consuming imaginations one can see how Schreber fell victim to magical thinking and behaviour almost entirely. On this note, his emotions and values obviously did not escape. Indeed, his deep desire to become a woman always already transformed the world and its beings into a hierarchized realm which possessed emotional and evaluative qualities that simply are not there for other people. One notable strand here is his value distinction between masculine and feminine. For Schreber it was quite clear; the feminine is concerned wholly with 'voluptuousness' (*Wollust* – see, for instance, [1903] 2000/2003: 124–5/94), the masculine with all that is 'noble' (cf.: ibid.). This fundamental tension, where all that is sensual repulses his 'manly honor' (id.: 125/94), eventually becomes transformed into a magical synthesis whereby he discovers a duty (i.e. his manly honour) to be the object of sensuality (i.e. feminine voluptuousness). It is not as if Schreber desires or values this; he 'must' do it – it is his preordained duty.

Additionally, Schreber's mechanism of disgust operates between supposedly feminine desires, emotions and values on the one hand and supposedly masculine ones on the other. These two groups are, initially at least, opposed in his system, running parallel to the idea that in normal life 'pure' nerves are contaminated and thereby become depraved (cf. id.: 25/9). This means, moreover, that souls and their nerves must go through a series of 'tests' in order to purify the nerves, at least to some extent, ultimately resulting in a hierarchized '*state of Blessedness*' (*Seligkeit* – ibid.) where the masculine version is 'superior' (id.: 29/13) to the feminine, with this latter still consisting 'mainly in an uninterrupted feeling of voluptuousness' (ibid.).

Schreber's system ultimately legitimizes both of these opposed wishes. Indeed, much of his thought is a pendulum between experiencing sensuality while nevertheless remaining honourable; it is his duty to do so. In this manner, certain objects of his system are always already charged with his most basic affections and values. Although these are originally opposed, he ultimately finds a way to magically synthesize them into an ultimate state of affairs where he may have it both ways. Indeed, in Schreber's final synthesis value legitimizes previously repulsive desires.

Nonetheless, the inherent ambivalence and irreality of such a magical merger was never lost, and it seems to have had crushing consequences with the onset of Schreber's third and final illness, of which very little is known. This is because his distinctions and syntheses were wholly imaginary, meaning they had no ultimate effect on his actual person. In short he did not, in fact, become a woman. This is where the magic of the imaginary, when chronic, leads one down a rabbit hole from which there is no real return. Schreber's system was to never attain the reality to which it always claimed, it being created and sustained wholly in the irreal.

With so many individual and societal forms of chronic magic, humans are in a constant struggle to avoid damaging manifestations as well as maximize positive ones. Magic, by its very nature, instantiates itself in many different phenomena and in many different ways, from pieces of artistic genius to crushing psychological illnesses. Moreover, such extremes are not always mutually exclusive. In this manner, the magical being we are, from societal forms to more personal ones, shows that our existence constantly plays itself out on various tenuous knife edges, from sublime heights to desperate lows. Even the concept of normality itself – the status quo governed by *das Man* – can be seen to be an imaginary point trying to survive in and between so many magical phenomena and forces. Within all of this, there must be times for conscientious reflection and reason, as well as other times when one can go out and play. It thus seems clear ever since Aristotle that the aim remains to not be consumed too much or for too long in either of the overly rigid, overly bewildering, extremes.

# Final Remarks: Sartrean Magic, Philosophy and the Future

Magic flouts laws. Laws of nature, of logic, of reason. Magic exists in human reality because humans are not mere nature. Due to the free spontaneity of consciousness, we indeed have a *human* nature, a nature we have to relate to in many ways.

Human nature contains basic phenomenological experiences that are ultimately grounded in ontological structures. Within such a philosophical anthropology, we have seen with Sartre that magical being accounts for some very significant portions of our experience, as well as some very significant parts of our existential foundations. I have gone into Sartre's magical being in terms of (inter)personality (ego), emotion, imagination, as well as value, possession and language in extensive detail. I have also shown how such structures and dynamics are very significant for understanding some important contemporary issues, not least artistic creation, advertising, racism, as well as certain strands of psychopathology. What remains, now, is to very briefly highlight where such insights and analyses can and perhaps should go, as well as a note on philosophy's duty now and in the future.

I think one of the main issues to tackle in the coming years will be the rise of virtual technologies and how this is opening, almost literally, new planes for Sartrean magic. Our lives are now spent increasingly on screens, so many analogons for the imaginary, and our person is greatly influenced, captivated and indeed values whole worlds of virtual objects through our online personae, presences and interactions. Here, although the general structures of Sartrean magic I have delineated will remain sound, it is important to note that magic, through rising virtual technologies like social media, online gaming, as well as virtual reality, augmented reality and even mixed reality (cf. Boland and McGill 2015), could reach new terrains and forms and could start influencing and even changing these dynamics of magic in new and significant ways. Thus, although I am convinced that the magic of ego, emotion, the imaginary and value will always remain crucial in any philosophical anthropology, just how new online technologies are utilizing and even manipulating such dynamics and structures would be of interest and of import going forward. Indeed, it seems the precedence and preference for the irreal and virtual and all its captivations, as well as an increasing mechanization of human activity, both online and off, where borders between humans and machines are becoming less clear cut – these all seem to be issues becoming increasingly dominant in many people's lives, and not always for the better.

Such is, in my opinion, one important avenue for future ideas. Now it simply remains for a few words on the role of philosophy in today's current societies. As I have already mentioned, Sartre's 1943 work is one of the last great philosophical systems, and it still has, I have shown, much to contribute towards some contemporary live issues and problems our societies are still facing. The climate of – especially contemporary professional – philosophy has already changed greatly since Sartre's time, and indeed now it seems thoroughly audacious to have *a* system. There is simply too much out there. Nevertheless, an interest in basic ontological structures of human existence, plus a decidedly phenomenological method that applies theory to actually significant cases, seems to be a formula that can still yield great fruit and import, as I have shown here with Sartre and his magic. Long may it continue.

A rather commonplace notion of philosophy is that it is 'useless', that it has no real effect on the daily workings of people's lives. People who dally in it are just too scared to get a proper, 'real' and productive job, just have their heads in spurious clouds and do not serve society properly. I of course know nothing could be further from the truth, although with a caveat or two. First of all, although philosophy never really has immediate effects, it actually has some of the most profound ones over time. Results in political philosophy (e.g. Marx) and ethics (e.g. Aristotle) are the most obvious, but I equally convinced that even the more supposedly abstruse realms and branches of philosophy (e.g. metaphysics) all ultimately shape the way we feel, think and behave. All of us, not just philosophers.

For me philosophy is often quite literally a thankless task because its influence is often subliminal and slow. In any endeavour, most crucial findings and insights often break moulds and are the catalysts for real change and development, but they are also usually things that general populations are slow, reluctant or even dead against to take up. Such is why there is a necessary trickle-down effect for any groundbreaking work, whether this be in philosophy, science, art or otherwise. The key here is that it takes time – sometimes centuries. And it is almost never direct. Thus, as we strive to continually improve our educational systems, even if philosophy is not explicitly present from a relatively early age (although I of course believe it should be), it has still had – and will continue to have – quite a hand in a lot of basic ideas and concepts that shape and influence our populations.

I am not purporting that this present work is of such a groundbreaking nature. I do however firmly believe that this work has made important headway on a crucial concept in philosophical anthropology, one that is and will be relevant to a number of human phenomena and problems now and for the future. The key with this of course, now as ever, is that philosophy is and should primarily be a communal effort and engagement, and so I thank you for your time, and hope this work has captivated the minds of a few as we go forward to improve human reality – and irreality – together.

# Notes

## Chapter 1

1 Translation modified – « constitue … une totalité synthétique et individuelle entièrement isolée des autres totalités de même type et le Je ne peut être évidemment qu'une *expression* (et non une condition) de cette incommunicabilité et de cette intériorité des consciences. »

2 Translation modified – « l'Ego est un objet appréhendé mais aussi *constitué* par la conscience réflexive. C'est un foyer virtuel d'unité, et la conscience le constitue en *sens inverse* de celui que suit la production réelle: ce qui est premier *réellement*, ce sont les consciences, à travers lesquelles se constituent les états, puis, à travers ceux-ci, l'Ego. Mais, comme l'ordre est renversé par une conscience qui s'emprisonne dans le Monde pour se fuir, les consciences sont données comme émanant des états et les états comme produits par l'Ego. Il s'ensuit que la conscience projette sa propre spontanéité dans l'objet Ego pour lui conférer le pouvoir créateur qui lui est absolument nécessaire. Seulement cette spontanéité, *représentée* et *hypostasiée* dans un objet, devient une spontanéité bâtarde et dégradée, qui conserve magiquement sa puissance créatrice tout en devenant passive. D'où l'irrationalité profonde de la notion d'Ego. »

3 Translation modified – « entourés d'objets magiques qui gardent comme un souvenir de la spontanéité de la conscience, tout en étant des objets du monde ».

4 Translation modified – « spontanéité fantomale ».

## Chapter 2

1 Translation modified – « n'est pas un instinct, ni une habitude, ni un calcul raisonné. Elle est une solution brusque d'un conflit, une façon de trancher le nœud gordien. »

2 Translation modified – « Ne pouvant trouver, en état de haute tension, la solution délicate et précise d'un problème, nous agissons sur nous-mêmes, nous nous abaissons et nous nous transformons en un être tel que des solutions grossières et moins adaptées lui suffiront (par exemple déchirer la feuille qui porte l'énoncé du problème). Ainsi la colère apparaît ici comme une évasion: le sujet en colère

ressemble à un homme qui, faute de pouvoir défaire les nœuds des cordes qui l'attachent, se tord en tout sens dans ses liens. Et la conduite « colère » moins bien adaptée au problème que la conduite supérieure – et impossible – qui le résoudrait est cependant précisément et parfaitement adaptée au besoin de rompre la tension, de secouer cette chape de plomb qui pèse sur nos épaules. »

3   Translation modified – « le monde de nos désirs, de nos besoins et de nos actes apparaît comme sillonné de chemins étroits et rigoureux qui conduisent à tel ou tel but déterminé ».

4   Translation modified – « Lorsque les chemins tracés deviennent trop difficiles ou lorsque nous ne voyons pas de chemin, nous ne pouvons plus demeurer dans un monde si urgent et si difficile. Toutes les voies sont barrées, il faut pourtant agir. Alors nous essayons de changer le monde, c'est-à-dire de le vivre comme si les rapports des choses à leurs potentialités n'étaient pas réglés par des processus déterministes mais par la magie. Entendons bien qu'il ne s'agit pas d'un jeu : nous y sommes acculés et nous nous jetons dans cette nouvelle attitude avec toute la force dont nous disposons. Entendons aussi que cet essai n'est pas conscient en tant que tel, car il serait alors l'objet d'une réflexion. Il est avant tout la saisie de rapports nouveaux et d'exigences nouvelles. Simplement la saisie d'un objet étant impossible ou engendrant une tension insoutenable, la conscience le saisit ou tente de le saisir autrement, c'est-à-dire qu'elle se transforme précisément pour transformer l'objet. »

5   Translation modified – « la conduite émotive n'est pas sur le même plan que les autres conduites, elle n'est pas *effective*. Elle n'a pas pour fin d'agir réellement sur l'objet en tant que tel par l'entremise de moyens particuliers. Elle cherche à conférer à l'objet par elle-même, et sans le modifier dans sa structure réelle, une autre qualité, une moindre existence … En un mot dans l'émotion, c'est le corps qui, dirigé par la conscience, change ses rapports au monde pour que le monde change ses qualités. Si l'émotion est un jeu c'est un jeu auquel nous croyons. »

6   Translation modified – « il y a des émotions fausses qui ne sont que des conduites ».

7   Translation modified – « *pour croire* aux conduites magiques il faut être bouleversé ».

8   Translation modified – « saisies d'un caractère affectif léger sur la chose ».

9   Translation modified – « toutes reviennent à constituer un monde magique en utilisant notre corps comme moyen d'incantation. Dans chaque cas le problème est différent, les conduites sont différentes. Pour en saisir la signification et la finalité, il faudrait connaître et analyser chaque situation particulière ».

10  Translation modified – « une conduite magique qui tend à réaliser par incantation la possession de l'objet désiré comme totalité instantanée ».

11  Translation modified – « se détourne de la conduite prudente et difficile qu'il devrait tenir pour mériter cet amour et le faire grandir, … se détourne même de la femme qui représente, comme réalité vivante, précisément le pôle de toutes ces conduites délicates ».

12 Translation modified – « sont éphémères et sans équilibre … s'écroulent dès que l'aspect magique des visages, des gestes, des situations humaines est trop fort ».

13 Translation modified – « cette distinction entre deux grands types d'émotion n'est pas absolument rigoureuse : il y a souvent des mélanges des deux types et la plupart des émotions sont impures. »

# Chapter 3

1 Translation modified – « La conscience transcendante d'arbre en image pose l'arbre. Mais elle le pose *en image*, c'est-à-dire d'une certaine façon qui n'est pas celle de la conscience perceptive. »

2 Translation modified – « discontinuité au plus profond de sa nature, quelque chose de heurté, des qualités qui s'élancent vers l'existence et qui s'arrêtent à mi-chemin ».

3 Translation modified – « Chez toute personne qu'on aime, en raison même de sa richesse inépuisable, il y a quelque chose qui nous dépasse, une indépendance, une impénétrabilité qui exige des efforts toujours renouvelés ».

# Chapter 4

1 The English is rather awkward here, hence the French: « l'être d'un existant, c'est précisément ce qu'il *paraît*. »

2 Translation modified – « elle *n'est pas* moi ».

3 Translation modified – « nous … dévoilé ».

4 Translation modified – « l'être du phénomène ne pouvait se réduire au phénomène d'être. »

5 Translation modified – « doit échapper à la condition phénoménale ».

6 Translation modified – « L'être transphénoménal de la conscience ne saurait fonder l'être transphénoménal du phénomène. »

7 Translation modified – « il faut d'abord reconnaître que nous ne pouvons concéder au néant la propriété de « se néantiser ». »

8 Translation modified – « il faut avouer que seul *l'être* peut se néantiser, car, de quelque façon que ce soit, pour se néantiser il faut être. »

9 Translation modified – « *produire* le néant en demeurant indifférent à cette production ».

10 Translation modified – « L'être par qui le néant arrive dans le monde doit néantiser le néant dans son être ».

11 Translation modified – « Pour elle [la réalité humaine], mettre hors de circuit un existant particulier, c'est se mettre elle-même hors de circuit par rapport à cet existant. En ce cas elle lui échappe, elle est hors d'atteinte, il ne saurait agir sur elle, elle s'est retirée *par delà un néant.* »

12 Translation modified – « déduire ni de l'essence d'autrui-objet ni de mon être-sujet ».

13 Translation modified – « conscience irréfléchie ne pouvait être habitée par un moi ».

14 Translation modified – « hanter la conscience irréfléchie ».

15 Translation modified – « autrui est le médiateur indispensable entre moi et moi-même ».

16 Translation modified – « je m'angoisse parce que mes conduites ne sont que *possibles* ».

17 Translation modified – « moi et moi seul ».

18 Translation modified – « Loin que nous devions comprendre ce terme de *nausée* comme une métaphore tirée de nos écœurements physiologiques, c'est, au contraire, sur son fondement que se produisent toutes les nausées concrètes et empiriques (nausées devant la viande pourrie, le sang frais, les excréments, etc.) ».

19 The other three are the following: the 'presence (to) self' of the pre-reflective *cogito* (cf. BN/EN: 97–103/109–15); being-for-itself as possibility (cf. BN/EN: 119–26/132–9); and as 'the circuit of selfness' (cf. BN/EN: 127–9/139–41).

20 Translation modified – « Tout se passe comme si nous surgissions dans un univers où les sentiments et les actes sont tout chargés de matérialité, ont une étoffe substantielle, sont *vraiment* mous, plats, visqueux, bas, élevés, etc., et où les substances matérielles ont originellement une signification psychique qui les rend répugnantes, horrifiantes, attirantes, etc. »

21 Translation modified – « le visqueux renverse les termes : le pour-soi est soudain *compromis* ».

22 Translation modified – « Le langage me révèle la liberté de celui qui m'écoute en silence, c'est-à-dire sa transcendance. »

23 Translation modified – « Les attitudes, les expressions et les mots ne peuvent jamais ... indiquer que d'autres attitudes, d'autres expressions et d'autres mots. »

24 Translation modified – « est originellement l'être-pour-autrui ».

# Chapter 5

1 Translation modified – « Il se fait ici une transformation semblable à celle que nous indiquions dans le rêve : l'acteur est happé, inspiré tout entier par l'irréel. »

2 Translation modified – « Il est fréquent en effet d'entendre dire que l'artiste a d'abord une idée en image qu'il *réalise* ensuite sur la toile. L'erreur vient ici de

ce que le peintre peut, en effet, partir d'une image mentale qui est, comme telle, incommunicable et de ce que, à la fin de son travail, il livre au public un objet que chacun peut contempler. On pense alors qu'il y a eu passage de l'imaginaire au réel. Mais cela n'est point vrai. Ce qui est réel, il ne faut pas se lasser de l'affirmer, ce sont les résultats des coups de pinceau, l'empâtement de la toile, son grain, le vernis qu'on a passé sur les couleurs. Mais précisément tout cela ne fait point l'objet d'appréciations esthétiques. Ce qui est « beau », au contraire, c'est un être qui ne saurait se donner à la perception et qui, dans sa nature même, est isolé de l'univers. … En fait le peintre n'a point *réalisé* son image mentale : il a simplement constitué un analogon matériel tel que chacun puisse saisir cette image si seulement on considère l'analogon. Mais l'image ainsi pourvue d'un analogon extérieur demeure image. Il n'y a pas réalisation de l'imaginaire ».

# Chapter 7

1  Translation modified – « L'antisémitisme ne rentre pas dans la catégorie de pensées que protège le Droit de libre opinion. »
2  Translation modified – « une peur de soi originelle et … une peur de la vérité ».
3  Translation modified – « L'homme sensé cherche en gémissant, il sait que ses raisonnements ne sont que probables, que d'autres considérations viendront les révoquer en doute ; il ne sait jamais très bien où il va ; il est « ouvert », il peut passer pour hésitant. Mais il y a des gens qui sont attirés par la permanence de la pierre. Ils veulent être massifs et impénétrables, ils ne veulent pas changer : où donc le changement les mènerait-il ? »
4  Translation modified – « a choisi originellement de dévaloriser les mots et les raisons ».
5  Translation modified – « Seule une forte prévention sentimentale peut donner une certitude fulgurante ».
6  Translation modified – « L'antisémite n'a pas tellement envie de la valeur. La valeur se cherche tout comme la vérité, elle se découvre difficilement, il faut la mériter et, une fois qu'on l'a acquise, elle est perpétuellement en question ; un faux pas, une erreur : elle s'envole ; ainsi sommes-nous sans répit, d'un bout à l'autre de notre vire, responsables de ce que nous valons. L'antisémite fuit la responsabilité comme il fuit sa propre conscience ; et, choisissant pour sa personne la permanence minérale, il choisit pour sa morale une échelle de valeurs pétrifiées. Quoi qu'il fasse, il sait qu'il demeurera au sommet de l'échelle ; quoi que fasse le Juif, il ne montera jamais plus haut que le premier échelon. »
7  I will not broach the issue whether there is a difference between two types of stupidity (*bêtise* and *stupidité*) in French. For more cf. Breeur 2015.

8  Translation modified – « elle est inerte et opaque puisqu'elle s'impose par sa pesanteur et puisqu'il n'est pas possible d'en modifier les lois, elle est *chose*, enfin, puisqu'elle possède l'impassibilité et l'impénétrabilité des faits de la Nature. La mécanique se plaque sur le vivant, la généralité supprime l'originalité de l'expérience singulière, la réaction préfabriquée se substitue à la praxis adaptée. »

9  Translation modified – « absorbés par la matérialité et les choses, ensorcelées par l'action qui les scelle, sont interchangeables ».

10  Translation modified – 'Jeder ist der Andere und Keiner er selbst'.

# Chapter 8

1  Translation modified – « se saisit elle-même comme spontanéité envoûtée. »

2  Translation modified – « où l'évidence est donnée, la croyance n'est ni utile, ni même possible. »

3  Translation modified – « Mais elle forme le fond indifférent sur lequel se détache, dans le cas d'une psychose d'hallucination, la rébellion des spontanéités. Les formes supérieures d'intégration psychique ont disparu. Cela signifie qu'il n'y a plus de développement harmonieux et continu de la pensée ».

4  Translation modified – « une cristallisation s'opère et le malade va organiser sa vie par rapport aux hallucinations, c'est-à-dire les repenser et les expliquer. »

5  Translation modified – « spontanéités, tout imprévisibles et fragmentaires qu'elles soient, puissent se charger peu à peu d'un certain matériel idéo-affectif. »

6  Translation modified – 'es doch eigentlich recht schön müsse, ein Weib zu sein, das dem Beischlaf unterliege'.

# References

Alain [1928] (2007), *Propos sur le Bonheur*, Paris: Folioplus.

Barnes, H. E. (1973), *Sartre*, Philadelphia and New York: J. B. Lippincott Company.

Barnes, H. E. [1984] (1997), 'Sartre on the Emotions', in W. L. McBride (ed.), *Sartre and Existentialism. Philosophy, Politics, Ethics, The Psyche, Literature, and Aesthetics. 4. Existentialist Ontology and Human Consciousness*, 135–65, New York and London: Garland Publishing, Inc.

Bergson, H. [1907] (1912), *L'évolution créatrice*, Paris: Librairies Félix Alcan et Guillaumin Réunies.

Bergson, H. [1932] (2012), *Les deux sources de la morale et de la religion*, Paris: Quadridge/PUF.

Bernet, R. (2002), 'Sartre's "Consciousness" as Drive and Desire', *Journal of the British Society for Phenomenology*, 33 (1): 4–21.

Boland, D. and McGill, M. (2015), 'Lost in the Right: Engaging with Mixed Reality', *XRDS*, 22 (1): 40–5.

Bollnow, O. F. [1941] (2009), *Das Wesen der Stimmungen*, Würzburg: Königshausen & Neumann.

Bonnemann, J. (2007), *Der Spielraum des Imaginären. Sartres Theorie der Imagination und ihre Bedeutung für seine phänomenologische Ontologie, Ästhetik und Intersubjektivitätskonzeption*, Hamburg: Felix Meiner Verlag.

Breeur, R. (2005), *Autour de Sartre. La conscience mise à nu*, Grenoble: Éditions Jérôme Millon.

Breeur, R. (2010), 'Les passions imaginaires et la neutralisation du réel', in R. Gély and L. Van Eynde (eds), *Affectivité, imaginaire, création sociale*, 63–85, Bruxelles: Facultés Universitaires Saint-Louis.

Breeur, R. (2015), *Autour de la bêtise*, Paris: Classiques Garnier.

Breeur, R. and Burms, A. (2008), 'Persons and Relics', *Ratio (new series)* XXI (2): 134–46.

Cabestan, P. (2004a), *L'être et la conscience. Recherches sur la psychologie et l'ontophénoménologie sartriennes*, Bruxelles: Éditions OUSIA.

Cabestan, P. (2004b), 'What Is It to Move Oneself Emotionally? Emotion and Affectivity According to Jean-Paul Sartre', *Phenomenology and the Cognitive Sciences*, 3: 81–96.

Catalano, J. S. [1974] (1985), *A Commentary on Sartre's* Being and Nothingness, Chicago and London: Chicago University Press.

Cormann, G. (2012), 'Émotion et réalité chez Sartre. Remarques à propos d'une anthropologie philosophique originale', *Bulletin d'analyse phénoménologique*, 8 (1): 286–302.

Daigle, C. (2010), *Jean-Paul Sartre*, London and New York: Routledge.

Davies, O. (2012), *Magic: A Very Short Introduction*, Oxford and New York: Oxford University Press.

de Beauvoir, S. [1949] (1986), *Le deuxième sexe. Tome I. Les faits et les mythes* and *Tome II. L'expérience vécue*. Paris: Éditions Gallimard.

de Warren, N. (2010), 'The Inner Night: Towards a Phenomenology of (Dreamless) Sleep', in D. Lohmar, I. Yamaguchi (eds), *On Time – New Contributions to the Husserlian Phenomenology of Time*, 273–94, Dordrecht, Heidelberg, London and New York: Springer.

Deleuze, G. and Guattari, F. [1972] (2008), *Capitalisme et Schizophrénie: L'Anti-Œdipe*, Paris: Les Éditions de Minuit.

Deonna, J. A. and Teroni, F. (2014), 'In What Sense Are Emotions Evaluations?', in S. Roeser and C. Todd (eds), *Emotion and Value*, 15–31, Oxford: Oxford University Press.

Dickens, C. [1854] (1995), *Hard Times, for These Times*. London and New York: Penguin Books.

Didion, J. [2005] (2012), *The Year of Magical Thinking*, London: Fourth Estate.

Dinnage, R. (2000), 'Introduction', in D. P. Schreber [1903] (2000), *Memoirs of My Nervous Illness*, trans. I. Macalpine and R. A. Hunter, xi–xxiv, New York: New York Review Books.

Elpidorou, A. (2016). 'Horror, Fear, and the Sartrean Account of Emotions', *The Southern Journal of Philosophy*, 54 (2): 209–25.

Fell, J. P. [1965] (1966). *Emotion in the Thought of Sartre*. New York: Columbia University Press.

Fink, E. [1957–1975] (2016/2010), *Play as Symbol of the World and Other Writings*, trans. I. A. Moore and C. Turner, Bloomington and Indianapolis: Indiana University Press/*Spiel als Weltsymbol*, München: Verlag Karl Alber Freiburg.

Fitzgerald, F. S. [1936] (2009), 'The Crack-Up', in Edmund Wilson (ed.), *The Crack-Up: With Other Miscellaneous Pieces*, 69–84, New York: New Directions Books.

Fox, S. [1984] (1997), *The Mirror Makers: A History of American Advertising and its Creators*, Urbana and Chicago: University of Illinois Press.

Freud, S. [1905] (2010), 'Der Witz und seine Beziehung zum Unbewußten', in *Der Witz und seine Beziehung zum Unbewußten/Der Humor*, 23–249, Frankfurt am Main: Fischer Taschenbuch Verlag.

Freud, S. [1911] (2001/2012), 'Psycho-Analytic Notes on an Autobiographical Account of a Case of Paranoia (Dementia Paranoides)', in *The Standard Edition of the Complete Psychological Works of Sigmund Freud, Volume XII (1911 – 1913)*, trans. J. Strachey et al., 9–82, London: Vintage Books/'Psychoanalytische Bemerkungen über einen Autobiographisch Beschriebenen Fall von Paranoia (Dementia Paranoides)', in *Gesammelte Werke, Bd. VIII.*, 239–320, S. Fischer Verlag.

Gardner, S. (2009), *Sartre's Being and Nothingness: A Reader's Guide*, London: Continuum.

Goldie, P. (2000), *The Emotions: A Philosophical Exploration*, Oxford and New York: Clarendon Press.

Hartmann, M. (2016), 'A Comedy We Believe In: A Further Look at Sartre's Theory of Emotions', *European Journal of Philosophy*, 25 (1): 144–72.

Hatzimoysis, A. (2011). *The Philosophy of Sartre*. Durham: Acumen.

Hatzimoysis, A. (2014). 'Consistency in the Sartrean Analysis of Emotion', *Analysis*, 74 (1): 81–3.

Heidegger, M. [1927] (2012/2006), *Being and Time*, trans. J. Macquarrie and E. Robinson, Blackwell Publishing/*Sein und Zeit*, Tübingen: Max Niemeyer Verlag.

Heidegger, M. [1931–1932] (1997), *Vom Wesen der Wahrheit. Zu Platons Höhlengleichnis und Theätet*, Frankfurt am Main: Vittorio Klostermann.

Hervy, A. (2014), 'Émotion et aliénation', *Études sartriennes*, 17–18: 21–40.

Hobbes, T. [1651] (2007), *Leviathan*, Cambridge: Cambridge University Press.

Hoffman, B. (2003), *The Fine Art of Advertising*, New York: Stewart, Tabori & Chang.

Hopkins, R. (2011), 'Imagination and Affective Response', in J. Webber (ed.), *Reading Sartre. On Phenomenology and Existentialism*, 100–17, London: Routledge.

Hubert, H. and Mauss, M. (1902–1903), 'Esquisse d'une théorie générale de la magie', *L'Année sociologique*, 7: 1–146.

Hume, D. [1738–1740] (2001), *A Treatise of Human Nature*, Oxford and New York: Oxford University Press.

Hume, D. [1748] (2007), *An Enquiry concerning Human Understanding and Other Writings*. Cambridge: Cambridge University Press.

Husserl, E. [1918–1926] (1966), *Analysen zur Passiven Synthesis. Aus Vorlesungs- und Forschungsmanuskripten 1918–1926*, Den Haag: Martinus Nijhoff.

Husserl, E. [1931] (2012), *Cartesianische Meditationen. Eine Einleitung in die Phänomenologie*, Hamburg: Felix Meiner Verlag.

Jackson, K. (2013), 'Sartre's Concept of *The Look*: Hell and Other People', *Existential Analysis*, 24 (2): 238–49.

Johnston, A. (2005), *Time Driven: Metapsychology and the Splitting of Drive*, Evanston, IL: Northwestern University Press.

Laing, R. D. [1960] (2010), *The Divided Self: An Existential Study in Sanity and Madness*, London: Penguin Classics.

Lothane, Z. (2003), 'Ethical Issues in the Schreber Case', in J. Corveleyn and P. Moyaert (eds), *Psychosis: Phenomenological and Psychoanalytical Approaches*, 59–73, Leuven: Leuven University Press.

Mazis, G. A. [1983] (1997), 'A New Approach to Sartre's Theory of Emotions', in William L. McBride (ed.), *Sartre and Existentialism. Philosophy, Politics, Ethics, The Psyche, Literature, and Aesthetics. 4. Existentialist Ontology and Human Consciousness*, 117–33, New York and London: Garland Publishing, Inc.

Merleau-Ponty, M. [1945] (2014), *Phénoménologie de la perception*, Paris: Éditions Gallimard.

Miguens, S., Preyer, G. and Morando, C. B. (eds) (2016), *Pre-reflective Consciousness. Sartre and Contemporary Philosophy of Mind.* London and New York: Routledge.

Miller, A. [1980] (1997), *For Your Own Good: Hidden Cruelty in Child-Rearing and the Roots of Violence*, trans. H. and H. Hannum, London: Virago Press.

Moyaert, P. (2003), 'Body, Drive, and Affect in Schizophrenia, from the Psychoanalytic Perspective', in J. Corveleyn and P. Moyaert (eds), *Psychosis: Phenomenological and Psychoanalytical Approaches*, 43–57, Leuven: Leuven University Press.

O'Shiel, D. (2011), 'Sartre's Magical Being: An Introduction by Way of an Example', *Sartre Studies International*, 17 (2): 28–41.

O'Shiel, D. (2013), 'Drives as Original Facticity', *Sartre Studies International*, 19 (1): 1–15.

O'Shiel, D. (2015a), 'Public Egos: Constructing a Sartrean Theory of (inter)personal Relations', *Continental Philosophy Review*, 48: 273–96.

O'Shiel, D. (2015b), 'Kolnai's Disgust as Violation of Value', in M. Delville, A. Norris and V. von Hoffmann (eds), *Le Dégoût: Histoire, Langage, Politique et Esthétique d'une Émotion Plurielle*, 25–39, Liège: Presses Universitaires de Liège.

O'Shiel D., [2016] (2017), 'From Faint Mood to Strong Emotion: Merging Heidegger and Sartre?', *Philosophia*, 42: 1575–86.

Packard, V. [1957] (2007), *The Hidden Persuaders*, New York: Ig Publishing.

Pincas, S. and Loiseau, M. (2008), *A History of Advertising*, Hong Kong, Köln, London et al.: Taschen.

Ratcliffe, M. (2008), *Feelings of Being. Phenomenology, Psychiatry and the Sense of Reality*. Oxford: Oxford University Press.

Reichert, T. (2003), *The Erotic History of Advertising*, New York: Prometheus Books.

Richmond, S. (2011), 'Magic in Sartre's Early Philosophy', in J. Webber (ed.), *Reading Sartre: On Phenomenology and Existentialism*, 145–60, London: Routledge.

Richmond, S. (2014), 'Inconsistency in Sartre's Analysis of Emotion', *Analysis*, 74 (4): 612–15.

Rieger, B. (2013), *The People's Car: A Global History of the Volkswagen Beetle*, Cambridge, MA and London, England: Harvard University Press.

Sartre, J.-P. [1936] (2012/2012), *The Imagination*, trans. K. Williford and D. Rudrauf, London and New York: Routledge/*L'imagination*, Paris: Quadridge/PUF.

Sartre, J.-P. [1936, abbreviation: **TE**] (2004/2003), *The Transcendence of the Ego*, trans. S. Richmond, London and New York: Routledge/'La transcendance de l'Ego', in V. de Coorebyter (ed.), *La Transcendance de l'Ego et autres textes phénoménologiques*, 93–131, Paris: Librairie Philosophique J. VRIN.

Sartre, J.-P. [1938, abbreviations: **STE/ETE**] (2002/2009), *Sketch for a Theory of the Emotions*, trans. P. Mairet, London and New York: Routledge/*Esquisse d'une théorie des émotions*, Hermann.

Sartre, J.-P. [1938, abbreviation: **N**] (2000/2014), *Nausea*, Penguin Books/*La nausée*, Paris: Éditions Gallimard.

Sartre, J.-P. [1939–1940] (1995), *Carnets de la drôle de guerre (Septembre 1939 – Mars 1940)*, Paris: Éditions Gallimard.

Sartre, J.-P. [1940, abbreviation: **IM**] (2004/2005), *The Imaginary. A Phenomenological Psychology of the Imagination*, trans. J. Webber, London and New York: Routledge/*L'imaginaire. Psychologie phénoménologique de l'imagination*, Paris: Éditions Gallimard.

Sartre, J.-P. [1943, abbreviations: **BN/EN**] (2005/2012), *Being and Nothingness. An Essay on Phenomenological Ontology*, trans. H. E. Barnes, London: Routledge/*L'être et le néant. Essai d'ontologie phénoménologique*, Paris: Éditions Gallimard.

Sartre, J.-P. [1945] (1983), *Cahiers pour une morale*, Paris: Éditions Gallimard.

Sartre, J.-P. [1946, abbreviations: **ASJ/RQJ**] (1995/2013), *Anti-Semite and Jew*, trans. G. J. Becker, New York: Schocken Books/*Réflexions sur la question juive*, Paris: Éditions Gallimard.

Sartre, J.-P. [1948] (1985), *Qu'est-ce que c'est la littérature?*, Paris: Éditions Gallimard.

Sartre, J.-P. [1960] (1976/1985), *Critique of Dialectical Reason I. Theory of Practical Ensembles*, trans. Alan Sheridan-Smith, London: NLB/*Critique de la raison dialectique, précédé de Questions de Méthode. Tome I – Théorie des ensembles pratiques*, Paris: Éditions Gallimard.

Sartre, J.-P. [1971] (1981/2010), *The Family Idiot (Volume One). Gustave Flaubert 1821–1857*, trans. C. Cosman, Chicago and London: The University of Chicago Press/*L'idiot de la famille. Gustave Flaubert de 1821 à 1857, Tome I*. Paris: Éditions Gallimard.

Schatzman, M. (1972), 'Paranoia or Persecution: The Case of Schreber', *Salmagundi*, 19: 38–65.

Schatzman, M. (1973), *Soul Murder: Persecution in the Family*, New York: Random House

Scheler, M. [1913–1916] (2009/2007), *Formalism in Ethics and Non-Formal Ethics of Values. A New Attempt toward the Foundation of an Ethical Personalism*, trans. M. S. Frings and R. L. Funk, Evanston: Northwestern University Press/*Der Formalismus in der Ethik und die materiale Wertethik. Neuer Versuch der Grundlegung eines ethischen Personalismus*, Halle: Verlag von Max Niemeyer.

Schreber, D. P. [1903] (2000/2003), *Memoirs of My Nervous Illness*, trans. I. Macalpine and R. A. Hunter, New York: New York Review Books/*Denkwürdigkeiten eines Nervenkranken*, Berlin: Kulturverlag Kadmos

Smith, A. D. (2002), *The Problem of Perception*, Cambridge, MA and London: Harvard University Press.

Szmigin, I. and Piacentini, M. (2015), *Consumer Behaviour*, Oxford: Oxford University Press.

Tappolet, C. (2016), *Emotions, Values, and Agency*, Oxford: Oxford University Press.

Tungate, M. [2007] (2013), *Adland: A Global History of Advertising*. London, Philadelphia and New Delhi: KoganPage.

Van der Wielen, J. (2014), 'The Magic of the Other: Sartre on Our Relation with Others in Ontology and Experience', *Sartre Studies International*, 20 (2): 58–75.

Visker, R. (1999), *Truth and Singularity. Taking Foucault into Phenomenology*, Dordrecht, Boston and London: Kluwer Academic Publishers.

Visker, R. [2004] (2008), *The Inhuman Condition: Looking for Difference after Levinas and Heidegger*. Pittsburgh: Duquesne University Press.

Visker, R. (2007), 'Was Existentialism Truly a Humanism?', *Sartre Studies International*, 13 (1): 3–15.

Webber, J. (2004), 'Philosophical Introduction', in J.-P. Sartre [1940] (2007), *The Imaginary. A Phenomenological Psychology of the Imagination*, trans. J. Webber, xiii–xxvi, London and New York: Routledge.

Webber, J. [2009] (2013), *The Existentialism of Jean-Paul Sartre*, New York and London: Routledge.

Zahavi, D. (2014), *Self and Other: Exploring Subjectivity, Empathy, and Shame*, Oxford: Oxford University Press.

Zinck, A. and Newen, A. (2008), 'Classifying Emotion: A Developmental Account', *Synthese*, 161: 1–25.

# Index